RESTORING
the
PLEASURE

OTHER BOOKS BY CLIFFORD AND JOYCE PENNER

The Gift of Sex

Counseling for Sexual Disorders

Getting Your Sex Life Off to a Great Start

The Way to Love Your Wife

52 Ways to Have Fun, Fantastic Sex

Sex Facts for the Family

RESTORING
the
PLEASURE

COMPLETE STEP-BY-STEP PROGRAMS
TO HELP COUPLES OVERCOME THE
MOST COMMON SEXUAL BARRIERS

Clifford L. Penner, PhD
Joyce J. Penner, RN, MN

W Publishing Group

An Imprint of Thomas Nelson

Published in Nashville, Tennessee, by W Publishing, an imprint of Thomas Nelson.

Thomas Nelson titles may be purchased in bulk for educational, business, fundraising, or sales promotional use. For information, please e-mail SpecialMarkets@ThomasNelson.com.

Unless otherwise noted, Scripture quotations are taken from New American Standard Bible®. Copyright © 1960, 1962, 1963, 1968, 1971, 1972, 1973, 1975, 1977, 1995 by The Lockman Foundation. Used by permission. (www.Lockman.org)

Scripture quotations marked KJV are from the King James Version. Public domain.

Scripture quotations marked NIV are from the Holy Bible, New International Version®, NIV®. Copyright © 1973, 1978, 1984, 2011 by Biblica, Inc.® Used by permission of Zondervan. All rights reserved worldwide. www.zondervan.com. The 'NIV' and 'New International Version' are trademarks registered in the United States Patent and Trademark Office by Biblica, Inc.®

Any Internet addresses, phone numbers, or company or product information printed in this book are offered as a resource and are not intended in any way to be or to imply an endorsement by Thomas Nelson, nor does Thomas Nelson vouch for the existence, content, or services of these sites, phone numbers, companies, or products beyond the life of this book.

The authors grant permission to copy the pages where indicated.

ISBN 978-0-7180-7755-6 (rev. ed)

Library of Congress Cataloging-in-Publication Data

The Library of Congress has catalogued the earlier edition as follows:

Penner, Clifford.
  Restoring the pleasure : complete step-by-step programs to help couples overcome the most common sexual barriers / Clifford L. Penner, Joyce J. Penner.
     p. cm.
  Includes bibliographical references and index. ISBN 0–8499–3464–8
1. Sex instruction.   2. Sex in marriage.   I. Penner, Joyce.
II. Title.
HQ31.P4465 1993
613.9'6—dc20
                                                              93–4349
                                                              CIP

Printed in the United States of America
16 17 18 19 20   RRD   10 9 8 7 6 5 4 3 2 1

In appreciation of . . .

all the couples
who have so openly shared
their lives with us
and
our niece, Robin Buhler, for her supportive help
editing, proofing, and encouraging

The authors welcome readers' comments and responses about the information in this book, but they regret that they cannot answer letters. They will respond to e-mails and calls.

penners@passionatecommitment.com
626-449-2525 (anytime) or
626-793-5241 (8:00 a.m.–6:00 p.m. Pacific Time)

For further information regarding seminars or other speaking engagements, please go to www.passionatecommitment.com or write us at

Clifford and Joyce Penner
200 East Del Mar Blvd., Suite 126
Pasadena, CA 91105

Contents

CONTENTS

FIGURES, FORMS, TABLES, AND ASSIGNMENTS

Introduction

A Minor Change Can Make
a Major Difference

All he does is push this sex business," Maria complained with disgust. "All he's interested in is sex—sex, SEX, SEX! And kissing, that's another subject," Maria continued. "All that sloppy, yucky, passionate kissing—why is that so important?" The intensity, anger, and disgust in her voice were building.

Then, more softly and with resignation, Maria described the sexual activity that happens whenever Clarence insists. "I let him feel my back and shoulders. Then he goes to my breasts. What he sees in those ugly hunks of flesh I'll never know. All they do is get in the way. I'd like to have those things chopped off. As far as the genitals are concerned, I told him early in our marriage to skip that. I tolerate enough of his animal urges!"

Clarence's anger was equally intense and loaded with blame. "It started on our wedding night. I don't know what happened to her," he stated disgustedly. "She sure wasn't that way before we got married. She liked all that lovey-dovey stuff. Then all of a sudden, wham! Just like that, she didn't want to have sex. But I insisted! After all, I had waited a long time—until we got married. She rejects everything! She rejects any sexual suggestions. I insist, but she refuses!" He pounded his leg with his fist as he yelled.

Three weeks later, after seeing us for one hour every day for two weeks in what we call a "sexual therapy intensive," Clarence and Maria were both enjoying physical closeness. Several times a week they had soft kissing times, and twice a week they had total-body pleasuring leading to intercourse and ejaculation for Clarence. Afterward, Maria invited genital stimulation to orgasm—sometimes to several mini orgasms and other times to one intense orgasm.

Maria had never been orgasmic in twenty-nine years of marriage. What changed? Clarence. He learned to back off completely and allow Maria to gradually become comfortable with sharing her body and accepting her intense sexuality. However, even though Maria was responding intensely and they were having regular, mutually fulfilling times of sexual pleasure, Clarence still struggled to keep himself from insisting or pushing for *more* variety and *more* frequency. He still wanted to be able to "have it" whenever he wanted it. Gradually he realized that when he is able to control his tendency to demand, he gets so much more than when he pressures Maria for more.

Tony and Jill came to us after one month of marriage. Before marriage, they had enjoyed full loveplay, except that they refrained from intercourse. Both got intensely aroused to orgasm and thoroughly enjoyed their times of pleasure. Then came the low blow. On their wedding night Jill was anxious about intercourse, afraid of the pain of breaking the hymen. Tony was eager, inexperienced, and somewhat unsure of himself, so rather than comforting Jill, he tried to enter but couldn't. Jill panicked and pushed him away. They hadn't tried since.

After two months of weekly one-hour therapy sessions with us, Jill's daily use of vaginal dilators, and three sexual retraining homework assignments per week (one on teaching, one on pleasuring, and one on communication), Tony and Jill are having regular body pleasuring leading to intercourse without pain and with fulfillment for both.

Terry and Marge volunteered to be interviewed for a video series we produced even though we had never met them before the recording session. We interviewed them for one hour in a studio under stage lights and five cameras. For eight months Marge had been frustrated with the quantity of their sexual relationship. Her desire for sex was much higher than Terry's. She said she was "climbing the walls" and facing temptations outside of marriage. To prepare for the interview, Terry and Marge had been given a survey similar to the assessment form in chapter 11 (see page 121). They completed it individually, then shared their responses with each other. Marge was shocked to discover that Terry would like her to initiate sex more often. She had wanted sex more often but had waited for him to initiate it. In the two weeks before we interviewed them, Marge dramatically increased her requests to be with Terry sexually, and both were thrilled with the results!

MINOR CHANGES CAN MAKE MAJOR DIFFERENCES

If you are experiencing tension or disappointment in your sexual relationship, you are not alone. It happens to lots of couples. But there is hope! You may think it is unlikely—or even impossible—that you will be able to restore pleasure to your sex life, but we would disagree. We've seen it happen hundreds of times. Pleasure may be one minor, but significant, change away.

We hear a wide range of stories from couples who come to our sexual-enrichment seminars or telephone us for sexual consultation or come for counseling in our offices. Some, like Terry and Marge, report minor misunderstandings or difficulties. Others describe boredom and disinterest.

For them, the spark has gone. Still others, like Clarence and Maria, are in despair due to years of pain and feel unable to change their direction. We are their last-ditch effort.

What Can Make the Difference?

We help couples restore the pleasure to their sex lives by helping them improve their communication, by educating them about each other's sexual response, and by guiding them through the sexual retraining process.

Communication. Improved communication radically altered Terry and Marge's sexual relationship and eliminated the stress they were experiencing because of their differing desire levels. Marge's discovery that Terry would like her to initiate sex more frequently relieved Terry of the pressure to initiate sex to keep Marge happy. Marge's frustration was eliminated. When she experienced sexual urges, she was able to have those needs met. You may ask, "Why wouldn't they have talked about a minor detail like that sooner?" As the two of you work through the exercises in this book and share your responses with each other, you will be surprised how many little details you have assumed about each other and never thought to clarify. Those are the minor issues that can change your sex life from pain and frustration to pleasure, delight, and even ecstasy.

Sex education. Jill and Tony learned that the opening of the vagina is controlled by a muscle. That muscle can tighten up and become so rigid that entry into the vagina is not possible. For Jill, that tightening happened as a result of rigid antisexual upbringing that led to an incredible fear of something entering the vagina. Jill had to learn how to both stretch and relax that muscle before entry could happen. In addition, she had to learn a positive view of sexuality. Education was vital to Jill and Tony consummating their marriage.

As clinicians, we were surprised to find how much change could happen in couples' sexual relationships just as a result of education. In 1974 we were asked to teach a weekly class on human sexuality to sixty women for ten weeks. These women were all married, so we focused on the sexual relations in marriage. At the end of the class, the number of women who reported significant positive changes in their sexual relationships with their husbands was shocking. That is what led us to begin teaching seminars and writing books on sexual adjustment in marriage. If information can make a difference, we decided, let's make that information available!

Sexual retraining. You are probably saying, "But we don't need sex therapy," or "The chances of finding a sexual therapist near us are highly unlikely," or "We can't afford to fly to Pasadena, California, to see the two of you for two weeks like Clarence and Maria did."

That is why you have this book. We believe strongly that *self-help is effective in reversing sexual patterns* if you have the correct tools and if neither of you brings to your sexual relationship serious psychological problems that might sabotage your success in working through this book together. For example, if you have sexual abuse in your history or if you come from a chaotic, highly dysfunctional family, you will get more benefit from this book if you work through those issues first.

The process of sexual therapy is a *retraining process* in which you learn to *behave with each other* in ways that will *enhance the pleasure, reduce anxiety, and eliminate demand.* To benefit from this retraining process, you both must be committed to setting aside the time and following the detailed instructions provided here. This book will provide *communication tools* (talking exercises), *education* (sexual information), and *sexual retraining* (talking, touching, and teaching assignments). The more diligent the two of you are in walking through the steps together, the more success you will find in *restoring the pleasure* of your sexual relationship. Have fun in the adventure!

PART ONE

COMMUNICATION

The Key for the Door to Sexual Pleasure

ONE

Are You Talking About It?

We live in the era of the post-sexual revolution. Sex is so freely displayed in magazines, in movies, and on all types of electronic screens that people think sex should be easy to discuss. But for most people it's not easy at all. The sexual revolution has not necessarily made us better informed about how to function sexually either. Rather, it has just made us more comfortable in viewing sexual activity and hearing sexual terms used boldly. It also has made society more tolerant of a great range of sexual activity. But if you're like most people, being exposed to increasing sexual explicitness has not helped you as a married couple experience a comfortable, informed approach to sexuality. You may still lack the tools for sharing the inner struggles of your sexual relationship.

If this is the first time you have ever talked openly about your sexual concerns with your spouse, you may feel some initial discomfort, which can sharply raise your anxiety level and insecurity. To ease your discomfort, we will guide you through this process carefully and gradually so each step leaves you with a sense of accomplishment and gives you the courage to move on.

Jerry and Ann sat across from us in our office. They had come because Ann was not completely happy with their sexual life, but she couldn't get Jerry to talk with her about her concerns. They had come to see us upon her request. Aware of his discomfort, we eased into the topic of sex and kept the discussion more general and less explicit than usual. Even so, Jerry changed positions frequently and looked away when he answered our questions regarding their sexual activity. Even the question "How is kissing for you?" was met with a sigh of disbelief that we would ask anything so personal.

As Jerry and Ann left that session, we were concerned that even our most tactful approach had violated Jerry's sense of privacy so much that we would never see them again.

To our surprise, as we got up to the podium to teach our sexual-adjustment seminar in a church in the greater Los Angeles area the next weekend, we spotted Jerry and Ann in the audience. As we openly shared our own sexual journeys, along with much of the educational content of part 2 of this book, we could see that Jerry was becoming more comfortable. Our presentations were followed by individual writing and reflection times for each participant (as the two of you will do as you follow the step-by-step guidelines in this book). Then participants shared their thoughts on each topic with each other using the Communication Format (see page 16).

By the end of the seminar, Ann was ecstatic. Jerry had become familiar with sexual terminology, shared his inner experience of sexuality, and listened actively to Ann's feelings. They had made an about-face and were heading down the road toward sexual retraining.

They did come back to our office, but only to review with us what had happened for them when they started communicating. They were able to continue building their sexual relationship by using the tools we had given them at the seminar and our book *The Gift of Sex* (Thomas Nelson, 2003).

Many couples have found that communication is the key that opens the door to sexual pleasure. Some communicate by reading *The Gift of Sex* or

The Way to Love Your Wife out loud to each other. Others discuss our video series, *The Magic-Mystery of Sex.*

But for other couples sexual communication without step-by-step guidance is difficult, if not impossible. In the next two chapters we will give you this easy-to-follow guidance, just as we would if you were coming to our offices for sexual therapy.

TWO

Sharing Your Secrets

S o why do we have to talk about it?"

"There's too much emphasis on sex these days. What's the big deal?"

Maybe you share some of these sentiments. As Joyce's grandmother wrote to us in 1982 when she was in her mideighties, "I don't think what you're doing is necessary. Adam and Eve didn't need it. Abe and I didn't need it. So I don't agree with what you're doing, but I love you just the same."

We believe that effective communication between a husband and wife about their sexual lives and feelings is not only appropriate; it is necessary! Increased openness will not destroy the romance and mystery; it will help keep the spark alive over the decades of intimately sharing your lives together.

Throughout Scripture the sexual relationship between a husband and wife is used as the symbol of God's relationship with his people. In the New Testament, Christians are talked about as the bride of Christ. If we do not communicate with God through reading the Bible and praying, our relationship with him quickly becomes boring. Similarly, if you do not take time to communicate with each other about your sexual worlds, your sexual relationship will rapidly lose its vitality and passion.

6

We hope we've convinced you that open communication is the key to restoring and maintaining sexual pleasure. But we know that some of you may still be uncomfortable or unable to actually start to communicate openly. It's understandable that old habits and attitudes are hard to change.

"Even though our sexuality is basic to who we are as human beings, we may harbor unexpressed issues of sexuality inside ourselves. These issues can be our most private secrets. We have difficulty sharing them and revealing what we really think and feel. We lack knowledge, and feel inadequate and unsure of ourselves."[1] Thus, you need to open your inner worlds to each other gradually and safely. In this book we will provide the tools and the structure for that adventure of self-disclosure.

SHARING YOURSELF

In his book *The Transparent Self,* Sidney Jourard wrote about self-disclosure as the "portal to man's soul." To reveal oneself takes both courage and knowledge of oneself, said Jourard.[2] We can only know each other as we know ourselves and make that self-awareness known to each other. This is definitely true when it comes to sex. You must first know yourselves sexually: What do you believe, think, and feel about sex? Until you are able to sort out your own sexuality, it will be difficult to communicate openly with your spouse so that your sexual relationship can flourish. That is why we will ask you to complete each communication exercise individually, separate from each other, before you share your reflections with each other. Take plenty of time to ponder and explore your inner worlds of thoughts and feelings as you respond to the questions or statements of each exercise.

Revealing Secrets

More secrets exist in the sexual realm than in any other area of life. To open your sexual world, you must reveal some of those secrets, whether they are about fantasy, pornography, adultery, inadequacy, or desires. You may find this difficult to do because, like all of us, you have probably been taught that it is wrong to tell secrets. You may also feel intense discomfort, worrying that your public image is at stake if your spouse does not keep your secrets private. Thus, the danger of sharing your secrets is very real. Fear about your spouse's reaction is also real. Hence, because of anxiety or lack of trust, you may have difficulty sharing certain sexual secrets.

Being Vulnerable

Because sex is very private and very personal, anything that has to do with the sharing of details about your sexuality makes you feel vulnerable. It is hard enough to discuss intimate sexual issues you feel confident about; sharing sexual failures is almost impossible. What you share sexually reveals much about you beyond the sexual data. It indicates the kind of person you are, the values you believe in and live by, and your secret, inner world. So it is completely understandable that you feel hesitant to talk about sexual problems. Yet this hesitancy must be overcome if the two of you are going to get past the sexual barriers you are experiencing.

Sharing Past Hurts

One major consequence of opening your sexual world is that this may bring up past hurts such as sexual abuse, a negative body image, past sexual experience, low self-esteem, or other problems.

Childhood sexual abuse. The pain of past sexual abuse is the most obvious example of a past hurt that can affect your sex life. Estimates vary as to the percentages of people who were sexually abused as children, but it is commonly accepted that this kind of abuse does occur. For some, those memories have been so totally repressed they cannot be reported. For others, the feelings about past abuse may be so vague they have not faced them directly.

If your memories are so vivid that they haunt and plague you, reliving those instances will seem like dragging out a dead corpse, a reminder of pain. You want to be rid of the memory and to avoid talking about it, so it is frightening to discuss it openly, digging up the ugly past. Yet the very difficulty that is causing problems in your sexual relationship may be identical to the pain you experienced as a child. Getting relief from the current difficulty requires undoing those past hurts, yet the discomfort that comes with sharing those hurts will obviously nudge you toward resistance. You must gently yet persistently encourage each other to explore and share such abuse so that you can release the grief and reduce its impact on your present sexual life. You will probably need professional help with this part of the sharing process. Groups are often available in churches to work through past abuse.

Negative body image. A negative body image may be another source of past hurt that contributes to your difficulty in talking about sex. You may have struggled with a physical handicap, obesity, or an accidental or congenital deformity. Or you may be attractive by all external standards, but because you were labeled, teased, or abused as a young child, you have a negative view of your body.

Past sexual experience. Past adult sexual experience may be painful to share because it was hurtful to your own self-worth, your conscience, or your image, or because learning about the past experience may hurt your spouse. Be cautious! The value of this sharing may not be worth the possible hurt and destruction it causes. Get outside guidance to help you decide when and how much to share about your past sexual activity. If you became pregnant while single, you may have suffered the embarrassment of an obviously quick marriage, or you may feel guilt about giving up the baby for adoption or trauma from having an abortion. There may also be guilt from premarital sexual activity or self-deprecation because of long-term failure in your own sexual relationship.

Low self-esteem. Self-worth is determined in part by how you perceive yourself as a sexual being. Self-esteem, both general and sexual, will influence how freely sexual details can be shared. Your sexual self-esteem may have been hurt by something that was said to you during dating, by myths that you believed, by past experiences, by lack of knowledge, or by your relationship with each other.

Sexual issues are important, so important that they must be talked about in detail. God intended for men and women to have sexual fulfillment in marriage. The only way for you to gain this fulfillment is to share your anxieties and difficulties. In order to build positive sexual self-esteem and establish new sexual patterns, you must first understand your old patterns and perceptions. And you must be clear in describing how you each have experienced your sexual interaction.

So often when we interview spouses separately, they tell us completely different stories. One will say their kissing is great and passionate, while the other will say all they ever have are little pecks. One may report having sex as little as twice a month, while the other spouse may say it's as frequent as twice a week. Afterward, we sometimes joke that we must have mixed spouses in the waiting room. But we know that when a couple hasn't talked about sex, their views of what is actually happening can vary greatly. We predict that you will find it fascinating to compare your own responses to the Defining Your Sexual Experience form and see how each of you views what has been happening in your sexual times together. We hope this will be an exciting and rewarding adventure even if you must blast through some painful barriers and revelations as you grow together.

THREE

Hearing Each Other

So often with those we love—spouses, children, friends—we behave as though the most important part of communication is getting our point across, saying what *we* want to say. When you are frustrated with each other over a difference of opinion, what are you feeling? *If I could just say it so he or she could understand.* Many times we repeat the same words over and over with increased intensity and emotion, hoping we will finally be understood. If only we could know deeply and practice consistently the most effective skill to being heard—**active listening!**

"But that doesn't make sense," you may be saying. "How can I be heard while I am listening?" Read this carefully: *As you are able to listen to each other, reflecting what the other has shared, in a way that lets the other know that you understand what he or she thinks and feels, you will communicate a care for each other that will draw you closer. That closeness will then open the door to allow you to hear each other and understand each other's feelings.*

Please reread the previous paragraph until the concept described above sinks into your inner being. *Hearing each other is the key to effective communication, which opens the door to sexual pleasure.*

What's so difficult about communicating? Your emotions, your word choices, and your past experiences all affect how you send and receive messages. That's why one message can have different meanings for each of you. We all know the frustration of trying to communicate a simple, but important, message and not being heard accurately. That is when the natural tendency kicks in to keep repeating the same words with more intensity. When you notice that happening, STOP! Back up and follow the process visualized for you in the Communication Model on page 15 and described in more detail in the Communication Format, page 16. The Communication Format will provide the most benefit if the two of you read it out loud together now and before you share your responses to each of the Communication Focus exercises.

Communication Focus exercises will appear throughout the book. These are the tools you will use to gradually open your inner worlds of sexuality to yourself and to each other. They begin with a more general tone and gradually increase in the detail of personal data they are designed to reveal. This helps you learn effective sharing, listening, reflecting, and clarifying skills before the sharing gets too intense. These skills will be of great benefit as the intensity increases.

The Communication Focus exercises have been used with thousands of people in our "Discovering Greater Passion and Intimacy in Your Marriage" seminars and in sexual therapy in our office or by telephone. We find that the benefit of each exercise varies greatly from one couple to another, depending on your individual issues and conflicts. The more difficult the exercise, the more work will be needed in the tension-producing areas of that particular exercise.

We recommend that you decide together on a scheduled time and date to share your responses to each Communication Focus exercise. It may be difficult for you to be aware of what is going on inside yourself. You may have grown up in a home where you were not encouraged, or even allowed, to know what you thought, felt, believed, or wanted. You may have gotten the sense that it was not safe to share your real responses with your spouse. There may be such pain at the core of your being that you have chosen not to open yourself to those feelings. You may need help from a supportive friend or a mental-health professional. Or you may be ready to take the risk of opening yourself with your spouse. Proceed at your own pace.

Before you share your responses with each other, think how your words will affect your spouse. If you are afraid that what you have to say will be threatening to your spouse, soften that threat by choosing words and gestures that are nonthreatening. For example, Joyce has a habit of shaking her finger when she is upset with Cliff, but Cliff cannot hear what Joyce has to say when her finger shakes. So if Joyce can remember not to shake her finger, Cliff is much more likely to receive her intended message. Similarly, Cliff easily reflects either fatigue or intensity in a harsh tone of voice, and this tone greatly affects Joyce. She tends to blur out what Cliff is saying when he sounds irritable. If Cliff can control and soften his tone of voice, Joyce is much more likely to hear his real message.

In choosing your words, use "I" statements rather than "you" statements. Talk about what *you* think, feel, and need, not about your spouse. Use statements that begin with "I want," "I feel," "I need," "I like." Avoid commands such as "You have to . . ." Avoid labels: "You're irresponsible," or "You're uncaring." Avoid analyzing: "We have this problem because you're the kind of person who . . . ," or "You always act that way because you . . ." Most statements that begin with "you" are best eliminated in order to share in a way that will be heard.

Step 2 of the Communication Format (page 16) will help you actively listen to each other. It takes discipline to put aside your own thoughts and feelings and get "under the skin" of the other person. This is called empathy. Christ was a perfect model of empathy; he denied himself to become like us so he could truly understand. In Philippians 2, Paul challenged his Christian friends not to be self-centered and to remember what Christ did for them. He encouraged them to be of the same mind, maintaining the same love and doing nothing out of selfishness. He said they should

have this attitude in yourselves which was also in Christ Jesus, who, although He existed in the form of God, did not regard equality with

13

God a thing to be grasped, but emptied Himself, taking the form of a bond-servant, and being made in the likeness of men. Being found in appearance as a man, He humbled Himself by becoming obedient to the point of death, even death on a cross. (Phil. 2:5–8)

So do not look out for your own personal interests, but rather the interests of each other (Phil. 2:4). Pretend that you are the mirror helping your spouse see what he or she thinks, feels, or needs by reflecting back what was shared. This rephrasing without judging sends the message that you are accepting your spouse's thoughts, feelings, and needs and that you care about him or her. It does not mean you agree (and you do not need to point out that acceptance does not mean agreement) or that you have to offer a solution. What you have to offer is your understanding, care, and acceptance of what was shared.

ACTIVE LISTENING

The ♡ of human communication is active listening.

ACTIVE LISTENING includes
looking and listening carefully,

reading "body language" for feelings expressed,

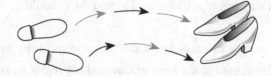

and putting yourself in another person's shoes (empathy).

As this process of sharing, reflecting, and clarifying continues back and forth, you will begin to know each other more deeply. It may require self-sacrifice. And it only happens between people who care. Hearing each other takes work, but the rewards are endless. Enjoy the challenge!

COMMUNICATION MODEL

SENDER: RECEIVER:

> STEP ONE

Listen to your inner self.

Determine what it is you think, feel, or need.

Choose carefully the words, gestures, and emotions that will accurately reflect the message you wish to send.

< STEP TWO >

Put aside your thoughts and feelings.

Listen to and observe the words, body language, and feelings of the other person.

Rephrase in your own words what you think the sender is trying to say.

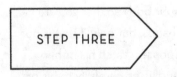

> STEP THREE

Affirm that you indeed said what you meant and that your message was received accurately.

OR

Clarify, rephrase, or add to your message.

COMMUNICATION FORMAT

(Based on the Communication Model, p. 15)

© Copyright Penner & Penner

For all communication exercises, look into each other's eyes to increase the brain chemical oxytocin, which builds trust and attachment; actively listen and share honestly and openly with no sense of judgment. There are no right or wrong answers, only your responses. The communication forms are designed to stimulate your individual thinking and your communication with each other. Do not limit yourselves to the exact response requested.

STEP 1

A. Complete each communication form individually, taking time to reflect and listen to your real feelings.
B. To determine what you think, feel, or need, write whatever comes to your mind in response to the statement or question on the form.
C. Read your responses out loud to yourself first. Then choose carefully and write the words you want to use to communicate most clearly to your spouse. Share these responses with your spouse.

STEP 2

A. While the first spouse is sharing his or her responses, your task is to put aside your thoughts and feelings about what your spouse is sharing and about your own response to the same statement or question.
B. To increase your listening ability, position your body so that you are facing your spouse. You may want to hold hands, but **only if** that is not distracting for either of you. Look at your spouse. Watch his or her expressions, feelings, and body language, and listen carefully to his or her words.
C. Put into words what you heard your spouse say and what you sensed he or she was feeling. You might try several different words to reflect your sense of what was communicated. Avoid labels, evaluations, or judgments.

STEP 3

A. The spouse who shared needs to listen carefully to the reflection of that sharing. Position yourself so you have eye contact as your spouse tries to empathize with you.

B. Either affirm that you communicated accurately and were heard correctly, or clarify, rephrase, or add to your first message. If your words and gesture did not communicate the first time, try new ones.

Communication is complete when the message receiver has been able to put the message sender's words and feelings into the receiver's own words *and* the message sender has recognized the accuracy of the feedback. When you are both clear that this process has been completed, reverse roles: the message sender will now be the receiver, and the message receiver will be the sender. Repeat steps 1, 2, and 3.

COMMUNICATION FOCUS EXERCISE 1
Getting Started
© Copyright Penner & Penner. Permission to copy is granted.

1. I am interested in opening our sexual communication because

2. I would hope that by learning more about my sexual self I will

3. Sexually, I view myself as

4. The best thing about me sexually is

5. The thing I want most to work on sexually is

Individually complete your responses to this exercise. Share these with each other using the three steps of the Communication Format (page 16). Then use the Listener's Rating Sheet (pages 19-20) to evaluate your own listening skills.

COMMUNICATION FOCUS EXERCISE 2
Listener's Rating Sheet
(For Rating Yourself)

Listener's Name _____

While I was listening, my eyes were

My eyes communicated

While I was listening, my body was

My specific movements or postures were

My body communicated

My verbal response indicated that I (check one)

___ fully understood

___ mostly understood

___ partly understood

___ mostly misunderstood

___ totally misunderstood

COMMUNICATION FOCUS EXERCISE 3
Listener's Rating Sheet
(For Rating Each Other)

If this assignment seems too high risk, skip it and go on.

Listener's Name _____

While you were listening, your eyes were

Your eyes communicated

While you were listening, your body was

Your specific movements or postures were

Your body communicated

Your verbal response indicated that you (check one)

___ fully understood

___ mostly understood

___ partly understood

___ mostly misunderstood

___ totally misunderstood

A CREDO FOR MY RELATIONSHIPS WITH OTHERS

You and I are in a relationship which I value and want to keep. Yet each of us is a separate person with his own unique needs and the right to meet those needs.

When you are having problems meeting your needs, I will try to listen with genuine acceptance in order to facilitate your finding your own solutions instead of depending on mine. I also will try to respect your right to choose your own beliefs and develop your own values, different though they may be from mine.

However, when your behavior interferes with what I must do to get my own needs met, I will openly and honestly tell you how your behavior affects me, trusting that you respect my needs and feelings enough to try to change the behavior that is unacceptable to me. Also, whenever some behavior of mine is unacceptable, I hope you will openly and honestly tell me your feelings. I will then listen and try to change my behavior.

At those times when we find that either of us cannot change his behavior to meet the other's needs, let us acknowledge that we have a conflict of needs that requires resolving. Let us then commit ourselves to resolve each such conflict without either of us resorting to the use of power or authority to try to win at the expense of the other's losing. I respect your needs, but I also must respect my own. So let us always strive to search for a solution that will be acceptable to both of us. Your needs will be met, but so will mine—neither will lose, both will win.

In this way, you can continue to develop as a person through satisfying your needs, but so can I. Thus, ours can be a healthy relationship in which each of us can strive to become what he is capable of being. And we can continue to relate to each other with mutual respect, love, and peace.

Thomas Gordon, PhD
Founder, Effectiveness Training Associates
Pasadena, California
© 1972 Thomas Gordon

PART TWO

EDUCATION

The Door to Sexual Pleasure

FOUR

The More You Know, the More You Enjoy

In today's world, it is difficult to imagine that sexual dissatisfaction is due to sexual ignorance. But it is true—sexual ignorance is extremely common.

When sexual inadequacies are due to a lack of knowledge, correcting them is relatively simple and most rewarding. In this situation, attending a seminar or reading a self-help book like this one is the ideal way to begin. Many couples who restored the pleasure to their sexual relationship as a direct result of attending our sexual-enhancement seminar, "Discovering Greater Passion and Intimacy in Your Marriage," were merely suffering from lack of knowledge. They gained the knowledge they needed through individual reflection (getting to know themselves), communication skills (getting to know each other), and the accurate sexual information presented in the seminar. In the first part of this book we shared our methods for improving self-awareness and communication. Now in part 2 we delve into the important sexual information we present in our seminars.

You may benefit from specific sexual information, depending on your particular needs. We find that education has an especially powerful impact on couples who have failed to engage in effective sexual behavior because one or both of them were religiously inhibited, physiologically uninformed, culturally misinformed, or experientially naive.

THE RELIGIOUSLY INHIBITED

Regardless of their religious orientation, the religiously inhibited falsely connect sexual pleasure with sin. Because of this false connection, the believer has difficulty enjoying sexual feelings, even though they occur within the sanctified married relationship.

Rich Buhler hosted a popular radio talk show in Los Angeles called *Talk from the Heart*. One day when we were the substitute hosts, we chatted about this phenomenon at the opening of the show. Then, for four hours, we received telephone calls from those who struggled with the dilemma of sexual pleasure and its connection with sin. Each problem had a different history, but the common denominator was the lack of sexual enjoyment in marriage. Some couples said they had been sexually active and fulfilled before they made a commitment; then their Christian mentors asked that they no longer live together and that they abstain from sex. They heard the message that sex was sin. Now that they were married, their previous "sinful," but enjoyable, sexual life seemed a far-distant past.

Other callers said they had been sexually promiscuous until they became Christians. Then they straightened up their lives, married, and expected sex to be wonderful; but they found they had no sexual desire. Still others had been raised in strict homes with strong teachings against masturbation, with rigid premarital physical boundaries, without much affection between the mother and father, and with no teaching that sex was good and of God. Usually these people felt intense sexual desire during dating, but they felt nothing once they were married.

Teaching the Bible's pro-sexual message counteracts this association of sex and sin and connects religious beliefs with sexual pleasure. We encourage you to invite God into your sexual feelings and experiences and thank him every time you have a sexual thought or feeling. When you do a genital self-exam (which will be assigned as one of the sexual retraining exercises), focus on the uniqueness of God's creative power. During your sexual experiences, verbally recognize pleasure as a gift from God. Get active in the integration of your sexuality and spirituality.

In teaching the pro-sexual message, we attempt to show how the church sometimes couches the cultural restrictions of an era in religious dogma and uses them inappropriately to control lusty passion within marriage. Too often the church has failed to differentiate between God-given, healthy sexual feelings and sexual misbehavior outside of marriage.

Some of the questions we commonly receive also reflect a confusion about spirituality and sexuality:

One man asked, "Biblically speaking, is there any sex technique that is not acceptable? What about oral sex?"

One woman wrote, "My husband and I have fun using sexy words and slang when we make love. It's exciting for us. Is there anything biblically wrong with this kind of sex play if it's just between the two of us?"

We are also asked many questions about the rightness of birth control. One person said, "Birth control is a real hindrance and a problem for us. We pray, but we cannot get clear in our minds whether to rely on God's supremacy, his trustworthiness, or to take responsibility for ourselves, knowing that his plan for the human body has been set into motion to work as it does (i.e., when a sperm meets an egg, pregnancy results). We know God does not go against his plan of creation and the technical workings of the body; but on the other hand, if he is truly in control, does he keep a sperm from meeting an egg?"

Another person asked, "Is there a sensuous, biblical, and effective method of birth control?"

Masturbation is another controversial subject. People ask, "What does the Bible say regarding masturbation? Is it right or wrong?" and "What about masturbation in marriage?"

The next chapter, "Sex Is Good and of God," provides the biblical framework for fully enjoying sexual pleasure in your marriage. *The Gift of Sex* also may provide more specific information for answering some of these questions. When the Bible is silent on an issue, we use the Pauline principle that all things are lawful but not all things are edifying, and one should not be enslaved by anything. We also suggest that you examine whether the behavior being considered will edify or distract from your relationship with each other and your relationship with God. When the activity being questioned is within the bounds of scriptural teaching, we heartily encourage you to freely enjoy each other as a married couple.

THE PHYSIOLOGICALLY UNINFORMED

Physiological information describes how our bodies function. Many times a sexual problem occurs simply because one of the partners doesn't know what's happening in his or her (or the spouse's) body during sexual activity.

For example, women who block out feelings of sexual arousal believe they are unresponsive. However, when they learn that they are experiencing nipple erections and vaginal lubrication, which are indications of arousal, they finally are able to recognize and connect with their responsiveness.

Likewise, men who ejaculate prematurely can attune themselves to oncoming ejaculation by learning to recognize warning signs. Women can help when they learn that continual, vigorous penile stimulation without rest will bring the man to ejaculation and that if they want the arousal to last longer before ejaculation, they can momentarily stop the stimulation. In addition, women must understand that, unlike a woman's orgasm, a man's ejaculation cannot be stopped once it has started. Control has to be enacted before the warning that the man is about to ejaculate. When these facts are known and acted upon they can bring major change.

Both husbands and wives also need to know the changes that take place in the woman's body during sexual activity. Stimulation and time are required for the reflex of orgasm to happen. It is common for both the man and the woman to rush through the stages of erection, entry, thrusting, and ejaculation, and then be dismayed that the woman is not responsive. Neither may know where the woman's clitoris is, its erotic potential, or that nondirect stimulation is usually most delightful for the woman. In contrast to most men, a woman can respond indefinitely, so she may desire more stimulation even after one orgasm.

Lack of understanding about the involuntary nature of erections causes difficulty for many men. Erections can come and go during extended loveplay. Anxiety about maintaining an erection often interferes with the body's normal response. Erections are involuntary responses that occur every eighty to ninety minutes while men sleep, so every erection is not a precious commodity that must be used. In fact, most are never used and no crisis or discomfort results. An erection does not require follow-through to ejaculation.

For their own orgasmic satisfaction, some women want their husbands to keep their erections, even after ejaculation. That demand is relieved when the woman learns that most men need a refractory period, in which the penis becomes flaccid, before they can be restimulated to another erection. This period can range from twenty minutes to several hours or even days after ejaculation.

Women who inhibit their orgasmic responses are helped greatly by learning two facts. First, the orgasm is an active response, so women should be active and go after what their bodies crave, rather than lie back and hope the response will happen. Second, the facial grimaces, gasping noises, and heavy breathing are involuntary, positive sexual responses. If women inhibit those responses because of self-consciousness with overtly sexual behavior, they will inhibit their orgasms as well.

We also hear questions that are unique to the virginal couple as they prepare to consummate their marriage. For example, they might ask, "Is there a mess after intercourse? If so, what do you do with it?" Anxiety is relieved by knowing that there will be secretions, which can be handled by having a box of tissues beside the bed or a hand towel or washcloth available for wiping. For women who are susceptible to cystitis, it is recommended that they urinate and rinse off their genitals before and after sexual intercourse.

Some men who are going into marriage as virgins are concerned that when they have an erection, their penis points upward or to one side. They worry that this is abnormal and that it will make intercourse difficult. It is important to know that the penis can be aimed easily in any direction and that men's penises vary greatly as to where they point when they are erect. Similarly, a few women have been concerned that their nipples look ugly when they are aroused or get cold. They think this could be disappointing to a husband and are greatly relieved to discover that nipple erection is a positive sign of sexual arousal for all women and a turn-on for men.

General and specific anatomical and physiological knowledge brings freedom, new discovery, and intensity to the sexual experience for all couples. The physiological facts discussed in chapter 7 will be most helpful both in correcting misinformation and gaining new awareness that enhances pleasure.

THE CULTURALLY MISINFORMED

Despite years of well-publicized sexual facts, our conflicted culture perpetuates several inaccurate beliefs that damage couples' sexual functioning. Even though the misinformation places demands on the husband as well as the wife, men seem to generate many of the myths. This begins when boys pick up sexual misinformation from the "cool-guy talk" in the locker room or on the sports field or from workplace jokes. These stories typically exaggerate men's prowess, and they leave the listener comparing himself and trying to measure up to the apparent norm. In contrast, girls are more likely to discover accurate sexual data because they tend to discuss sexuality in intimate relationships with other girls.

Common Myths About Masculinity and Femininity

Sometimes education is a matter of refuting prevailing sexual myths. We have addressed some of those myths on the following pages:

Myth 1. Some men's penises are not large enough to "satisfy" a woman. Dr. Barry McCarthy, author of *Male Sexual Awareness*, suggests that two out of three men think their penises are smaller than average. The fact is, even though flaccid penis size varies greatly from one man to another, erect penises are pretty much the same. When erect, most penises measure about four to six inches from the base to the tip. (See Figure 7.9, page 77.) Length is irrelevant to satisfying a woman because the erotic area of the vagina is in the outer or lower one-and-one-half to two inches. This area is controlled by the woman's PC (pubococcygeus) muscle, which controls the opening of the vagina as well as the process of urination and defecation. This area becomes engorged during sexual arousal, forming the orgasmic platform. So all a man needs to satisfy a woman is a one-and-a-half to two-inch erect penis. There is little or no contact between the penis and the area beyond the PC muscle area because the inner part of the vagina elongates and balloons out. The vagina is an organ of accommodation, and penis size has nothing to do with masculinity or sexual competence.

Myth 2. It is a man's duty to "turn on" a woman. The assumption is that when a woman has difficulty in being aroused or having an orgasm, that difficulty is the result of the man's sexual incompetence. It may be true that the couple does not engage in effective sexual stimulation for the woman, or that they have inadequate lovemaking patterns, or that they practice poor sexual techniques. But these problems reflect a mutual lack of knowledge. The woman has to become knowledgeable about herself and communicate this awareness to her husband. The man, in turn, needs to be willing to learn and participate effectively. But the project is a joint effort, not a demand on the man to provide for the woman.

Myth 3. It is the woman's duty to give the man sexual release. The false assumption behind this myth is that men need sexual release more than women. Thus, even if a woman does not experience arousal or release for herself, she still needs to satisfy him to keep him at home and happy. This demand ultimately leaves both husband and wife unfulfilled.

Myth 4. To be sexually aggressive is not ladylike. This myth can affect the sexual experience for both the husband and the wife. To blatantly admit desire by initiating sexual activity is not congruent with some women's sense of femininity. To these women, sexual aggressiveness is synonymous with maleness. Yet men like to feel that they are being pursued by their wives. Therefore, women need to feel free to be overtly sexual and learn how to initiate sexual activity.

The view that women are subtly, rather than overtly, sexual carries over into the actual sexual encounters and may be the basis for lack of orgasm. To actively enjoy oneself during sex requires an acceptance of oneself as an overtly sexual person. Instead, many women are the passive receptacles of their husbands' male aggressiveness. They accommodate rather than participate. They only apply one side of the teaching in 1 Corinthians 7, which reminds us that our bodies are each other's to enjoy. These women believe and practice the idea that their bodies are their husbands' to enjoy, but not that they are to actively take pleasure in their husbands' bodies as well. When confronted with this concept, these women often say, "But that feels so selfish," while their husbands want to scream, "Be selfish. Use me!"

Myth 5. Simultaneous orgasms or female orgasm during intercourse is the ultimate goal in a sexual experience. In fact, this belief can wreak havoc on the husband-wife relationship. The husband, his prowess at stake, believes he is inadequate because he is unable to make it happen. The wife feels like a failure because she cannot respond at the appropriate time. Both falsely believe they are falling short of sexual normalcy.

Sure, it can be fun to have mutual orgasms, and the woman may desire the sensation of orgasm with the penis in the vagina; but neither situation has anything to do with sexual competence. The fact is that most women do not have orgasms during intercourse. Only a very small percentage of couples say they have simultaneous orgasms. And even when it does occur, it is not reported as the ultimate in sexual bliss. In fact, many prefer to take turns in order to double their pleasure, enjoying each other's and then their own.

Myth 6. Elderly people are not sexual persons. It is a myth that the elderly are not sexual beings—a myth that, unfortunately, is generally accepted in our culture. For the elderly to have sexual desires is often seen by their children or by younger adults as disgusting. The fact is, we are all sexual beings from birth until death—that is the way God designed us. Elderly people do have sexual and sensual needs. Many times those needs are not being met, but this does not mean the elderly are void of feelings.

The oldest spouses we have counseled for sexual therapy were in their late eighties. They apologized for seeking help at their age. They had always had a fulfilling sexual relationship but were struggling with some changes that occurred as a natural part of aging. A few sessions later they were happily on their way.

Many people get into trouble sexually as they age because they have not been informed about the normal changes that occur with aging. For example, men's testosterone levels decrease with age and this produces some changes, but these changes do not have to negatively affect the sexual relationship. For women, changes are caused by the reduction of estrogen.

Changes that occur with aging. Some of these changes that occur in both men and women include:

Change 1. Older men will not feel the sexual urgency they had when they were younger. Their desire will be more similar to women's desire for pleasure and closeness, and the arousal and release that will follow. They can continue to enjoy sex as often as every day, but they will not feel a desperate need for it every day or even every week. The more active they continue to be sexually, the greater the need.

Change 2. A man may need direct penile stimulation to become erect. In younger years just words, thoughts, or the sight of his wife's nude body may have produced a response. Now that response comes as the result of sexual play. Some older men come to us complaining of loss of sexual desire. But when we gather the data, we discover that they have assumed that arousal and desire are synonymous rather than accept the fact that desire precedes arousal. They expect to come to the sexual experience with an erection as they may have done when they were younger.

Change 3. The man's erections may not be as firm as in earlier years. This does not mean a man has erectile dysfunction or is unable to perform sexually. Anxiety about reduced penile fullness may lead to erectile dysfunction, but the change in penile fullness itself is the result of aging.

Change 4. With age men may need longer and more intense stimulation to bring them to ejaculation. (This is usually a benefit to most women.) Older men also may not need to ejaculate with each sexual encounter. As long as they know this fact, it does not interfere with their pleasure.

Change 5. If their ovaries have not been removed, the primary changes in older women are the thinning of the vaginal walls and the lessening of vaginal lubrication. Both problems are relieved by the use of a vaginal lubricant or the use of an estrogen-replacement cream. These are not signs of decreasing sexuality; they are only physical changes that result from menopause. The ovaries continue to produce androgen hormones even after natural menopause, and these hormones keep sexual desire alive. However, if surgical menopause (a complete hysterectomy) has taken place as a result of the removal of the ovaries, women may experience a lack of sexual desire. Sometimes small amounts of androgen may be given to aid the return of a woman's sexual drive. Hormonal replacement therapy may be recommended by your physician for either natural or surgical post-menopausal symptoms.

Whether sexual myths are about masculinity, femininity, or aging, they need to be dispelled with accurate information that will free couples of all ages to function fully in their sexual lives. We trust the information in this book will bring that freedom for you. Chapter 8, which deals with sexual responsibility, will be particularly helpful in showing you what is expected during a sexual experience from an emotional and relational perspective.

THE EXPERIENTIALLY NAIVE

The experientially naive person has been raised in a social and emotional vacuum. This person's parents did not model affection and sexual expressiveness, and emotions were not easily conveyed within the family.

Intense emotions were not acceptable. The spoken or unspoken goal of the home was to keep the environment even-tempered. Because of this background, the person has had minimal or no recognition of sexual stirrings. Without this sexual awareness, there was probably no exploratory play, self-stimulation, and no bumbling, junior-high activities. Consequently, this adult may be totally ignorant about being a sexual person. Passionate kissing or touching does not come naturally. In marriage, this naivete may cause awkwardness about knowing what to do and how to get the bodies together—nothing flows naturally. It is one cause of unconsummated marriages.

Education is vital for the experientially naive person. It should include specific information about sexuality, as well as instructions for hands-on sexual encounters. Reading this book, attending a sexual-enhancement seminar such as our "Discovering Greater Passion and Intimacy in Your Marriage," and being guided through the talking, touching, and teaching exercises of sexual retraining are all positive steps toward life-changing goals. In these settings, naive individuals are like empty sponges, ready to soak up anything that is offered to help them. Change is rapid. If you are sexually naive, you will benefit specifically from the discussion of sexual curiosity in chapter 6, and you will find great help from all of the educational and retraining chapters of this book.

FIVE

Sex Is Good and of God

What is the difference between finding sexual fulfillment through a *Christian* approach and through a responsible secular approach? Technically, there is none. The same skills are used by both approaches. Despite the similarities, though, therapists who bring a biblical understanding to sexual therapy offer a unique perspective.

The primary distinction is a practical one. When you come to us for counseling with your personal sexual lives intricately intertwined with your backgrounds of religious training, we are skilled to help you sort through these interweavings. The word *religious* is intentionally used here because most of the time, when sexual freedom within marriage is inhibited for what seem to be "Christian" or "biblical" reasons, the barrier is actually caused by religious rigidity rather than specific biblical teaching. By presenting the biblical perspective of sexuality, we help you sort out the wrong ideas and affirm your sexuality as being good and of God.

The Scriptures present a high view of the human sexual dimension. In that sense, sex is similar to a family jewel or heirloom. It is a precious gift to be stored carefully and not allowed to tarnish until it is shared with a special person. However, in society today, sexuality is often treated more like a piece of junk jewelry, something given to a child at age fourteen to be worn to school and later thrown into the bottom of the bike bag.

The Bible speaks about sexuality in a highly prized way. It designates sex for marriage because it is within this commitment that the qualities of a highly held view of sexuality can be fulfilled. The Bible portrays sex as a symbol of the relationship between God and his people. It puts sex in the context of the deepest commitment one human can make to another: a lifelong commitment to honor, cherish, and be faithful to each other until death. When we accept sex and sexuality as a precious gift from the Creator, it clearly sets us apart from those who misuse it as junk.

In the book of Genesis, the Bible tells how Adam and Eve were naked and unashamed, experiencing a free, open relationship that had no barriers. Their relationship was not based on power, intimidation, social myths, or cultural control. Later, Scripture refers to Christ as the "last" or new Adam and teaches that believers are in Christ's *image* (1 Cor. 15:45–50). This makes sex without shame a viable potential for the Christian. Unfortunately, the church has let social culture dictate many negative distortions about sexuality. When we as Christian couples can rid ourselves of these limitations and live lives of freedom and openness with each other, then we, of all people, ought to be the most sexually free and fulfilled.

Whether you come from a Christian or other religious background, we hope this biblically based view will become central to your attitude in dealing with your sexual dilemma, so in this chapter we will review the principles of sexuality that are clearly presented throughout the Scriptures. These principles form the foundation for our understanding of sexuality.

OUR SEXUALITY AS A PART OF THE CREATION ORDER

Men and women are sexual beings not only by birth but also by creation, according to God's plan and design. The Bible is not an instruction book for sexual functioning, but it does give a clear picture of how highly God values humans as sexual beings and the sexual relationship in marriage. Because of this, we can affirm the physical body, including its sexuality, as being conceived in the mind of God. We are his creations, male and female, sinless before the fall. Our maleness and femaleness are part of his perfect plan.

Another reason to affirm our sexuality is that it reflects God. Maleness and femaleness are in the image of God, as stated in Genesis 1:26–27:

> Then God said, "Let Us make man in Our image, according to Our likeness; and let them rule over the fish of the sea and over the birds of the sky and over the cattle and over all the earth, and over every creeping thing that creeps on the earth." God created man in His own image, in the image of God He created him; male and female He created them.

God created us with a particular model or design that is described as the "image of God." (See also Genesis 5:1–2 and Genesis 9:6.)

What does being created male and female in the image of God mean? The animals were created male and female. They have sexuality and physical bodies that they use to procreate. Yet they were not created in the image of God. How is mankind's sexuality different? As beings in the image of God, we have the desire and capacity to be in relationship with each other and with God; animals do not. Human beings can think, communicate with God and each other, act self-consciously, and respond and interact at a relationship level.

When Kristine, our youngest child, was six years old, she seemed to have an answer for anything in the world. One time when our dog, Biff, ran off during a thunderstorm and had not returned by the next day, Joyce was beginning to explain that perhaps Biff had been lost and we would never see him again. Confidently Kristine said, "Well, I'm sure he's okay. He's probably just off mating. If I were mating, I wouldn't want Julene and Greg [her older sister and brother] to be around watching."

Obviously, at this age she had not differentiated between the human dimension that is private, conscious of self, and made in the image of God, and the lack of this dimension in animals. We doubted that Biff was "off mating" since he had been neutered. Fortunately, though, he did return the next day.

The Genesis account of creation affirms our sexuality and begins the biblical teaching that sexual intercourse in marriage is blessed by God and is for enjoyment. Many people grow up believing that sexual union is the result of man's fall into sin. Masters and Johnson, founders of the sexual counseling field, even refer to this misconception of the Adam and Eve story as though it were fact.

On the contrary, the first biblical reference to the sexual union is a teaching from God that occurs before Adam and Eve disobeyed God and fell into sin and shame. Genesis 2:24 reads, "For this reason a man shall leave his father and his mother, and be joined to his wife; and they shall become one flesh." Becoming "one flesh" refers to sexual intercourse, which was part of God's perfect plan and design for us—not the result of our disobedient, sinful human nature. In this blissful state sex was without sin and shame. The relationship between man and woman was completely open: "The man and his wife were both naked and were not ashamed" (Gen. 2:25). In the same way, Adam and Eve had a completely open relationship with God; they walked and talked with him. Sin interrupted this openness.

Sex is sin only when it is misused, when we break God's commands. God gave us rules to live by—not to punish or restrict, but for our good. God is a loving Father who wants the best for us; he knows our humanness, and he knows the power of evil. His commandments and directions for living take all of this knowledge into account. When we violate those commandments, we sin. Most often, sexual violations of biblical guidelines occur when we only look at the feelings of the moment. Fortunately, even when we have sinned, we can be forgiven.

So the underlying message is: *Sex and sexuality are of God.* Sex becomes sin only when we disobey God's guidelines for its practice.

MARRIED SEXUAL UNION SYMBOLIZES
THE GOD-MAN RELATIONSHIP

Not only is our sexuality part of God's perfect plan and design, it also is used in Scripture to symbolize how God would choose to relate to us (Gen. 3:7–22). Disobedience interrupted the openness between God and man, and between man and woman. Genesis 3:7 says, "Then the eyes of both of them were opened, and they knew that they were naked." They became ashamed and self-conscious with each other, whereas before they had been innocent and unashamed. They no longer had the perfect relationship that was in the image of God. It was lost as the result of sin.

Adam and Eve also became self-conscious in front of God, covering their genitals in shame. God accommodated them by providing permanent coverings for their genitals, thereby giving the impression that openness with genitals is symbolic of openness with God. Sin—disobeying God—brought about shame, sexual inhibition, and a break in both the sexual openness of marriage and the relationship with God.

The Hebrew word translated as "knew" in Genesis 4:1 (KJV) refers to sexual intercourse and is the same word that is used in reference to knowing God. It is also a word for the genitals. Thus, the sexual union symbolizes the relationship between God and his people.

The concept of the sexual union being an example of the way God wants to relate to his people is further developed throughout the Old Testament. Israel is sometimes referred to as God's "bride" (Isa. 49:18; Jer. 16:9), and the word *adultery* is used to describe Israel's sin of worshiping other gods (Isa. 57:3; Jer. 7:9; 23:10).

A romantic, sensual description of God's love for unfaithful Jerusalem is found in Ezekiel 16:8–19. The passage refers to bathing her, putting oint-ments on her, and clothing her; yet she becomes an adulteress who takes strangers instead of her husband. In spite of this, God's grace is gener-ous to his bride, Israel: "Yet I will remember the covenant I made with you. . . . and you will know that I am the LORD" (Ezek. 16:60–62 NIV).

The entire book of Hosea is an account of God's steadfast love and mercy in his relationship with Israel. The sexual relationship symbolizes God's longing for a relationship with his people as described in Isaiah 62:5:

> For as a young man marries a virgin,
> So your sons will marry you;
> And as the bridegroom rejoices over his bride,
> So your God will rejoice over you.

This sexual symbolism continues in the New Testament, where the church (the body of believers) is described as Christ's bride. This teaching is found most explicitly in Ephesians 5:21–22, 25 (NIV): "Submit to one another out of reverence for Christ. Wives, submit to your own husbands. . . . Husbands, love your wives, just as Christ loved the church and gave himself up for her." The passage interweaves the sexual relationship of husband and wife with the relationship of Christ and the church. In Ephesians 5:31, Paul summarized this connection by quoting Genesis 2:24, the first reference to a sexual union in the Scriptures:

> For this reason a man shall leave his father and mother and be joined to
> his wife, and the two shall become one flesh. This mystery is great; but
> I am speaking with reference to Christ and the church.

In the New Testament, the word *mystery* always refers to something that is partially revealed or is in the process of being revealed and will become clear as we move into the final age.

The sexual relationship between a husband and wife is also used in the book of the Revelation as the symbol of the relationship between Christ and the church, which is described as Christ's bride, coming for the wedding supper (Rev. 19:7–9). Again, the full meaning of this symbolism is a mystery.

While most people do not think about or experience the symbolism of Christ and the church during lovemaking, it is our belief that in this mystical union of two bodies, body and spirit have the potential to merge into one. In this intense fusion of body, emotion, and spirit with another, we experience a glimpse of the relationship that God would like to have with us—the total giving of ourselves to him. This elevates the sexual relationship to the level of a sacrament, leaving no room for recreational sex in the life of a Christian.

PRINCIPLES FROM THE OLD TESTAMENT

The Integrated Person

The Old Testament portrays human beings in a way that is central to our view of sexuality. The Hebrews always viewed the human person as an integrated whole, not as a person divided into various parts. On the other hand, the Greeks saw the physical body as something to put down and the human spirit as important to be elevated. Their dyadic, gnostic view did not have high regard for the total person.

The Old Testament's description of the human sexual experience, "they shall become one flesh" (Gen. 2:24), means more than physical union. This refers to the mystical union that encompasses the emotional, physical, and spiritual dimensions. Husband and wife join *all* of who they are with each other. This is truly the biblical view of sexual union!

Lovemaking cannot be simply a physical experience. In order to have a fulfilling relationship, the total person—intellect, body, spirit, and will—must be shared with one's partner. When we truly understand Scripture, we recognize that the physical and sexual realms are integrated parts of us. The sexual part of us cannot be isolated. In generations past, there was little understanding that the integrated, whole person included the sexual dimension. As therapists, we realize how important it is to continue teaching the "whole-person dimension" of sex to help bring greater personal fulfillment and integration, especially to the Christian world.

The Acceptance of Passion

An additional lesson from the Old Testament is that sexuality is more than a beautiful sacrament that symbolizes our relationship with God.

Sexuality also involves earthy passion and earthly goals. This is illustrated by the lives of Old Testament men and women who are named in the "Hall of Faith" in Hebrews 11. Abraham, the father of our inheritance, visited his wife's handmaiden, Hagar, who then became pregnant (Gen. 16:4). Isaac lied about his relationship to Rebekah in order to save his own life and then was found fondling her in public (Gen. 26:7–8). Jacob (Israel) produced four of the twelve sons of Israel by sleeping with his wives' maids (Gen. 30:7–12). David, who by faith conquered kingdoms, was attracted to the beautiful body of Bathsheba, the wife of Uriah, and became sexually involved with her. He then committed murder to cover up his sin. Even Rahab the harlot, who helped the Israelites conquer Jericho, was honored for her faith: "By faith the prostitute Rahab, because she welcomed the spies, was not killed with those who were disobedient" (Heb. 11:31 NIV). In fact, Rahab is listed in the genealogy of Jesus Christ in Matthew 1:5.

So the lesson is this: Human beings are accepted by God as beings with a sexual nature. He recognizes that the human sexual dimension is a very powerful element—a forceful drive. Sometimes it drives us to sin, as in the cases of some of the biblical men and women of faith. God does not condone disobedience to his standards in the expression of our sexuality, but neither does he condemn us for being intensely sexual persons. When we disobey his rules, we violate him as well as ourselves and those close to us. And we suffer the consequence of our sin. Nevertheless, his grace is available even for sexual transgressions. We can be forgiven and continue to be used by God as were the men and women of faith like David and Rahab.

Application of Old Testament Sexual Guidelines

How do the Old Testament rules guide us today? As we study the Old Testament to determine right and wrong sexual behavior, we must be careful to study the laws in their context and purpose. Among other things, the Old Testament law was structured in terms of property rights, sanitation, and behavior "in the camp."

Property rights. First, consider the issue of property rights. Women, especially in the early Old Testament period, were part of their fathers' net worth. While choice and love certainly were factors, when a man took a wife, this marriage was an exchange of property. The tenth commandment given to Moses said, "You shall not covet your neighbor's house. You shall not covet your neighbor's wife, or his male or female servant, his ox or donkey, or anything that belongs to your neighbor" (Ex. 20:17 NIV). The commandment not to "covet" was for all of a man's possessions, including his wife.

The Old Testament rules against fornication had to do with the ruining of someone's property. During some periods of Hebrew history, a blood-stained sheet on the wedding night proved to the husband that he had received a fair deal and his wife had not been previously "used." The rules were different for men. No rules in the Old Testament stated that the man must be a virgin at marriage, but once married, he was not to commit adultery.

"In camp" sanitation restrictions. Many Old Testament rules about sanitation rights and rituals pertained to bodily excretions and acceptable behavior in the camp, the area around the tabernacle that the children of Israel used for worship. Most of the rules focused on protecting the tabernacle from unclean things such as certain kinds of animals, parts of animals, people with sicknesses, and all forms of bodily excretions (whether caused by diseases or natural bodily functions, such as menstruation, nocturnal emissions, defecation, afterbirth, and other things described in detail in the Pentateuch). These rules for living must be understood in the context of that biblical teaching that defined social and religious ritual.

PRINCIPLES FROM THE NEW TESTAMENT

Mutuality

The New Testament teaches that the barriers between men and women have been broken down because of Christ's death and resurrection. This teaching is a radical departure from the Old Testament culture.

Now, men and women no longer are to live by different sexual standards; instead, the New Testament clearly teaches mutuality. This is not to suggest that men and women are sexually identical or that they play the same roles, but that because of Christ, men and women stand equally before God. This is symbolized in the sexual relationship. Gone are the days of male domination or control in the sexual realm. Christ has broken down those barriers.

Through Christ, we have the potential to reestablish the original design of creation—to be totally open and free with each other. This includes having an equal value, ability, and position before God: "There is neither Jew nor Greek, there is neither slave nor free man, there is neither male nor female; for you are all one in Christ Jesus" (Gal. 3:28).

Ephesians 2:13–22, an extremely important passage regarding this teaching, tells how Christ broke down the human barriers and made us one household of God.

It might be said that as we become new creatures in Christ, we open up the possibility for a new kind of relationship within marriage. This is the beginning of a restoration of the experience of oneness that was lost in the garden of Eden. In the same way that Christ has restored the possibility of a relationship with God, he opens the door to new and deeper relationships with each other.

The New Testament teaches that men and women have equal rights to sexual pleasure and release. Physically, emotionally, and spiritually, a woman needs sexual pleasure and release as much as a man does. Pelvic pressure builds up in a woman just as scrotal pressure builds in a man. Emotionally, the bond of connection and affirmation is probably more important for women than for men. Spiritually, the biblical message clearly communicates the same sexual needs and expectations for women as it does for men.

Both men and women have the right to expect sexual pleasure and fulfillment. Husband and wife are told in Scripture to give themselves to each other. This is a mutual command, not one that is only for wives. It is not a command we can use to demand sex of each other; the command is not given in terms of the person's desire for sex. Rather, it is a response to each other's needs:

> The husband should fulfill his marital duty to his wife, and likewise the wife to her husband. The wife does not have authority over her own body but yields it to her husband. In the same way, the husband does not have authority over his own body but yields it to his wife. Do not deprive each other except by mutual consent and for a time, so that you may devote yourselves to prayer. Then come together again so that Satan will not tempt you because of your lack of self-control. (1 Cor. 7:3–5 NIV)

Each New Testament passage that addresses the husband-wife sexual relationship either begins or ends with a command for mutuality. Not only are husbands and wives equal in God's sight, but they also have mutual rights and responsibilities.

The concept of love between husband and wife is an expected part of the marriage relationship according to New Testament teaching. Love becomes the guiding principle for sexual behavior in marriage. The husband-wife relationship is to depict the kind of love Christ lavishes on the church.

> Husbands, love your wives, just as Christ also loved the church and gave Himself up for her. . . . Husbands ought also to love their own wives as their own bodies. He who loves his wife loves himself. (Eph. 5:25, 28)

Marriage Brings Sexual Freedom

While there are many restrictions regarding extramarital sexual involvement, the Bible gives no instructions on how to enjoy sex within marriage. The Song of Solomon is the only biblical example. It is a beautiful love story of a husband and wife delighting in each other's bodies. We would encourage you to read a modern version out loud together. If we were all free to act out the Song of Solomon in our marriage, we would be experiencing total sexual pleasure.

The writer to the Hebrews said, "Marriage should be honored by all, and the marriage bed kept pure" (Heb. 13:4 NIV). Translated into today's language, this passage might read, "In this troubled world, it is terribly important that we have a very high view of marriage. And by the way, sex within marriage is not dirty." What goes on in the sexual relationship as an outgrowth of the marital covenant is indeed honorable, wholesome, and healthy. From Genesis 2:24 throughout all of Scripture, the sexual union is referred to as "becoming one flesh." Dr. Louis H. Evans Jr. has a wonderful comment on this succinctly expressed teaching on sexuality from the New Testament:

> The one flesh in marriage is not just a physical phenomenon, but a uniting of the totality of two personalities. In marriage, we are one flesh spiritually by vow, economically by sharing, logistically by adjusting time and agreeing on the disbursement of all life's resources, experientially by trudging through the dark valleys and standing victoriously on the peaks of success, and sexually by the bonding of our bodies. In [intercourse], which is the expression created uniquely for marriage, the male and female fibers intertwine in complementation, creating a living fabric that cannot be undone without serious damage to the living fibers.[1]

Because there are many different uses and meanings of the word *flesh* in the New Testament, it is vitally important that we understand these differences. The previous paragraph described one positive use of the word; now consider an example where the word *flesh* is almost synonymous with sin or evil: "But I say, walk by the Spirit, and you will not carry out the desire of the flesh" (Gal. 5:16).

The writer of Galatians then recorded that well-known list that begins with immorality (Gal. 5:19–21). Verses 22 and 23 follow with the fruits of the Spirit. Verse 24 then says, "Now those who belong to Christ Jesus have crucified the flesh with its passions and desires." This use of the word *flesh* is understood to depict man's sinful nature, which works against God to pursue its earthly wishes rather than those that are spiritually worthwhile.

Desiring a healthy, enthusiastic, and fulfilling sexual life within marriage clearly does not mean following the lusts of the flesh. Rather, this comes under the category of sharing our undefiled desires with the one to whom we have made a covenant for life. Our mission is to help you distinguish the difference between lust-driven expressions of sexuality and the God-given gift of sexuality. We can freely enjoy each other in marriage when our sexual activities are loving (not hurtful), are mutual (as good for one as for the other), build intimacy, and don't violate any biblical principles or scriptural teachings. It is then that sexuality can grow within the context of a loving marriage, one in which the desire is to find mutual fulfillment and joy that *builds each other up and glorifies God*.

SEXUAL PLEASURE—A BIBLICAL EXPECTATION

Sexual pleasure within marriage is biblically encouraged and expected. Husband and wife are always to be available to fulfill each other's sexual needs—not only at the time of the month when impregnation can occur. In this respect God created human beings to be different from the animal kingdom—animals only have sexual drives at the time of conception. To "be fruitful and multiply" is but one purpose of the sexual relationship between a husband and wife. The Bible also endorses the concept of sexual pleasure.

Earlier, we suggested you read the Song of Solomon to each other out loud. This book is a beautiful and erotic poem of a husband and wife totally enjoying each other's bodies.

> On my bed night after night I sought him
> Whom my soul loves. (3:1)

> My beloved is dazzling and ruddy. . . .
> His head is like gold. . . .

His eyes are like doves. . . .

His lips are lilies

Dripping with liquid myrrh. . . .

His legs are pillars of alabaster

Set on pedestals of pure gold. . . .

And he is wholly desirable. (5:10–16)

How beautiful are your feet in sandals. . . .

The curves of your hips are like jewels. . . .

Your belly is like a heap of wheat

Fenced about with lilies.

Your two breasts are like two fawns. . . .

Your stature is like a palm tree. . . .

I said, "I will climb the palm tree,

I will take hold of its fruit stalks."

Oh, may your breasts be like clusters of the vine. . . .

Come, my beloved, let us go out into the country. . . . (7:1–11)

This husband and wife certainly viewed each other's bodies as a source of great pleasure to enjoy. Nothing seems to be restricted!

Another romantic passage is found in Proverbs 5:18–19:

Let your fountain be blessed,

And rejoice in the wife of your youth.

As a loving hind and a graceful doe,

Let her breasts satisfy you at all times;

Be exhilarated always with her love.

Our bodies are each other's to enjoy in marriage. If we hold back for religious reasons, we fool ourselves because there is no biblical basis to do so. We are not consistent with what the Bible has to say if we take an antisexual or antipleasure view of sex in marriage.

Based on the Scriptures' high view of sex within marriage, we have a very positive message to bring to the religious world, a world that is often in deep conflict about the acceptability of enthusiastic sexuality. The world views Christian sexuality as constrictive. But the Scriptures teach a new freedom that can bring greater joy, greater release, and greater fulfillment as you learn to enjoy each other ecstatically.

SIX

Sexual Curiosity Is Natural

God designed us as sexual beings. The sexual response is controlled by our involuntary nervous systems; it begins at birth and continues throughout life. Then what is it that hinders the sexual process from flowing naturally? Why doesn't the sexual relationship just happen? Why is sex training even necessary?

Sexual developmental tasks must be mastered from infancy to adulthood. There is a yearning to intimately connect with another that begins at birth and manifests itself differently at various stages of development. When we fail to master these developmental stages, dilemmas often result that hinder the natural, God-given sexual process.

THE DEVELOPMENTAL PROCESS

Although sexual response functions automatically throughout life, our sexuality is more than an automatic, physical response. Even though it is an integral, personal part of our total beings, it is externally influenced. Sexual feelings, responses, and behaviors seem to be very easily conditioned in either a positive or a negative direction. They are subject to social and cultural conditioning that begins at birth and continues throughout life.

The stages of sexual development are charted in Figure 6.1 and described in detail in the following pages.

Figure 6.1

STAGES OF SEXUAL DEVELOPMENT

STAGE	CRITICAL LEARNING	PARENT'S ROLE	IMPACT ON SEXUAL ADJUSTMENT
Infancy	Bonding	Build attachment	Capacity for intimacy
Toddlerhood	Touching, naming, and control of genitals	Affirm genitals and feelings as God's special design; use correct names	Positive acceptance of genitals (user friendly)
Preschool	Question asking	Reinforce, reflect, review, respond, repeat	Open communication about sex
School Age	Exploring	Affirm curiosity; set boundaries; protect from abuse	Sexual awareness with boundaries and without shame
Preadolescence	Erotic feelings and bumbling discovery	Prepare for changes; protect from pornography; affirm God-given responses; systematic education	Self-acceptance and competence in relating to opposite sex
Adolescence	Decision making	Share values; guide decision making; listen	Accept feelings; control actions
Single Adulthood	Become whole; develop all forms of intimacy	Allowing growth and independence	Capacity for intimate bond with opposite sex
Married Adulthood	Giving and receiving of sexual pleasure		Sexual responsiveness and responsibility
Older Adulthood	Adapting to challenges of aging		Slow, pleasure-oriented sex

Infancy

During infancy, from birth to age one, children learn about themselves as sexual persons from their primary caretakers, usually their parents. This learning occurs through the type of *touching* and *holding* the infant is given. When a close, warm, secure, and trusting bond is formed, children master the ability to form close relationships, including the physical relationship. Thus, the capacity for sexual intimacy is developed both physically and emotionally at an early age.

Not mastering this early sexual developmental task of bonding interferes later with the desire for and the ability to have *sexual intimacy*. Adults who were adopted after the first year of life or who were reared in an institution or who were brought up by an anxious, distant, or self-centered mother (who herself was unable to radiate warmth through her touch) may not feel the need for physical intimacy.

If bonding did not take place, sexual closeness may even be frightening. A male with this background may experience sexual drive but will masturbate rather than have sexual desire for his wife. Or a man whose intimate-touch needs were not met during infancy may express his desire for his wife inappropriately. His desire may be shown in an anxious, childlike manner that repulses his wife. A woman who missed bonding may not even be aware that she has any sexual needs. Infants who have not experienced the comfort of being touched and held closely learn to survive without that intimacy.

Toddlerhood

Toddlerhood is a *genital-centered* stage of development. From one to three years of age, it is natural for children to touch their genitals and learn that this feels good. This is the time when children learn to control elimination and to talk about and name the body parts. The cultural and social conditioning that takes place during this stage will determine whether a child accepts the genitals as a natural, beautiful part of God's creation or whether he or she views the genitals, and thus sexuality, as untouchable, unmentionable, and dirty.

Touching the genitals is natural for every toddler. Just as a child pokes a finger in his or her ear, nose, or belly button, the little boy will play with his penis and the little girl will rub over her clitoris and between her labia. Both will discover the good feelings. That is how God created human beings. The rubbing or fondling, much like sucking a thumb or holding a blankie, is soothing for the toddler. It is not usually erotic.

Because body-waste elimination and sexual functioning are both connected with the genitals, how toilet training is handled will affect the way children view their genitals specifically, and their sexuality in general. If control is learned with a positive sense of mastery rather than a punitive rigidity or lax insecurity, children will gain a sense of accomplishment. If children are given an accurate understanding of "germ theory," they will learn to view their genitals as clean, rather than dirty.

The fact is, the urinary and reproductive systems (which are housed in the genitals) are clean; no disease-producing microorganisms are present. The urinary systems in both men and women and the reproductive system in men are not only clean but also sterile. The vagina is also a clean passageway. Although bacteria are present, they are part of the normal flora that actually help fight infections. So the genitals are not dirty unless they have become contaminated from the rectum during wiping. In contrast to the urinary and reproductive systems, the rectum is highly contaminated with disease-producing microorganisms, thus requiring the washing of hands after toileting. This differentiation—between the clean genitals and the dirty rectum—is important for children to acquire during the toilet training process of toddlerhood.

How the parents refer to and name the genitals communicates vividly their view of sexuality. Parents are terribly proud when toddlers can say "eyes," "ears," "elbow," or "wrist," but then often revert to names such as "pee-pee" and "poo-poo" when referring to the genitals and the process of elimination. Avoiding the accurate names for the genitals and their functions teaches children that these parts are difficult to talk about. In contrast, parents communicate to children an acceptance of sexuality when they call a penis a penis and a vagina a vagina.

When the hand is taken away and given a slap or a "no-no," the toddler playing with his or her genitals will think of them as untouchable, something to be afraid of, like the hot stove. A sense of disgust, rigidity, or "yuckiness" communicated about elimination can teach the toddler that sex is dirty (hence, "dirty" jokes). Similarly, the toddler may learn that the genitals are unmentionables as well as untouchables when real names are not given for them. This refusal to verbalize sexual words may lead to later difficulty in talking about sex with one's spouse. In contrast, when elimination is guided with praise and the genitals are named with pride, parents give their children a gift. The children then accept their genitals as a friendly part of themselves, just as some computer software is considered "user-friendly."

When toddler sexual development has been mastered, the adult later enters the marriage relationship with an integrated acceptance of his or her genitals. When this developmental task was not accomplished, the adult is likely to sense that the genitals are untouchable and unmentionable and not a part of the body to be freely shared with his or her spouse.

Preschool

A preschooler's sexual curiosity is manifested in *question-asking*. How these sexual questions are handled at this age will set the tone for adulthood comfort regarding discussions of sexuality. If positive reinforcement was received for asking questions, and if open, factual sexual data was given with a matter-of-fact attitude, a person will be better able to communicate openly about sexuality. If sex simply was not talked about, the adult may have difficulty communicating openly about sexuality within marriage.

School Age

Curiosity continues into school age with the development of a *sense of modesty*, the indication of sexual awareness. During this age, *nudity* becomes an issue. Children begin to be shy about their bodies, first with nonfamily members and then rather inconsistently within the family. One time they will run around the house nude, and the next time they will cautiously cover themselves. This begins to occur around age four or five, usually sooner for girls than boys.

At the same time, children begin to be aware of sexual differences and may be stimulated by seeing a nude body, particularly the adult body of the opposite sex. A mother may notice her son staring at her. This is a signal to begin covering up and probably stop brother-sister baths. It is not that children should be kept from ever seeing parents' bodies nude, but rather that caution should be used not to elicit their sexual attentiveness or curiosity.

Both extremes, either overexposure or extreme modesty, inhibit the development of a healthy sexual awareness. Both produce difficulty in sharing one's body openly with a spouse, or they may lead to inappropriate curiosity behaviors in adulthood, especially for men. Some men become voyeurs because they grew up with no exposure, whereas others become voyeurs because, unfortunately, they were exposed to something addicting at this critical stage of development. One man who struggled with "peeping" as an adult had happened to be walking home from school one day and innocently passed a home where two adolescent girls were changing clothes by an open window. The scene was very arousing and led to self-stimulation to ejaculation. From that time on, he struggled with peeping as a means to sexual arousal and release. So the principle is clear: if there were no violating experiences, if the privacy and need for modesty was respected, and if nudity was comfortable but not exploitative, an adult will most likely be comfortable being nude with his or her spouse and not have unhealthy sexual habits.

Exploratory play is almost inevitable for the school-age child. It may take the form of playing house, doctor, or "you show me yours, and I'll show you mine." Exploratory play is a universal, innocent expression of sexual curiosity at this age. It signals to parents the need for specific sexual education and for teaching some matter-of-fact boundaries.

When there are no external limits and sexual play continues repeatedly throughout the school age, sexual awareness is stimulated beyond the emotional readiness of the child. Likewise, a parent's violent, traumatic reaction to the child who is found in exploratory play is devastating. Negative attention given to innocent curiosity leaves a child confused because he or she connects sexuality with something seriously wrong. This makes natural sexual expression difficult in adulthood. Exploratory play—checking out each other's genitals—by children of the same age who have not been exposed to sexual experiences beyond their age level causes no harm. Boundaries are necessary, however. For example, children should be required to keep their underwear on and leave the doors open. Parents should be nearby and make their presence known. The lack of boundaries or a traumatic reaction to being found in exploratory play can cause incredible pain throughout life.

Preadolescence

Preadolescence brings awkwardness, bursts of energy, and emotional volatility. In our book *Sex Facts for the Family,* we refer to this period as the "squirrely years." Erotic feelings begin to tingle as the hormones spurt. This is the kiss-and-run stage. Bumbling and indirect interaction with persons of the opposite sex is natural. "Going out" at this age has little romantic significance. If Jill and Jimmy are going out, it means the following sequence of events probably took place: Jill called Karen to say she likes Jimmy; Karen called Bob to tell him that Jill likes Jimmy; Bob called Jimmy. It continued until Jill indirectly heard that Jimmy wanted to go out. Her response to Jimmy got to him through at least two other friends.

Not all preadolescents are allowed this *bumbling discovery* of their sexuality. Some are pushed into adolescent dating patterns, even to the point of explicit male/female sexual activity. Others are restricted from the normal preadolescent interaction because they are socially shy, immature, overprotected by parents, or experiencing health problems that inhibit their availability.

In the case of either extreme, self-acceptance and competence in relating to the opposite sex are not mastered. If a young person is pushed into sexual activity at this age, confusion is usually connected with the sexual relationships. If restricted from all boy-girl interaction, children will grow into adulthood still feeling inept when they relate physically with the opposite sex. This is truer for men than for women. The wives of inept men often refer to their husbands as "bumblers." On the other hand, inept women are more comfortable with being taught by their husbands and consequently do not seem as inadequate.

Adolescence

Adolescence is the time to *assume responsibility for sexual behaviors* and to develop patterns of responsible sexual wholesomeness. These decisions need to be consistent with biblical teachings, family values, and commitment to the relationship. When the sexual activity engaged in is in conflict with the adolescent's inner beliefs and values, anxiety is triggered at the same time that pleasurable sexual feelings are aroused; thus, anxiety and sexual pleasure are paired. The resulting adrenaline rush becomes addicting. When the adolescent becomes an adult and marries, there is no more fear of getting caught or fear of pregnancy; there is no more anxiety. Thus, there is also no pleasurable sexual arousal. The pleasurable response has developed a dependence on the adrenaline rush.

Another difficulty can arise for the adolescents who shut down all sexual feelings so they do not violate their beliefs. *Sexual feelings must be separated from sexual behaviors.* God designed sexual feelings; sexual desire is good. Nevertheless, decisions must be made regarding the behaviors that occur in response to the desire. Adolescents can learn to redirect the sexual-drive energy into self-enhancing activities (e.g., sports, music, schoolwork, etc.). Learning to affirm sexual feelings while making decisions that control sexual actions is the task of adolescence that, if mastered successfully, leads the adult to guilt-free, unrepressed sexual expression in marriage.

Hence, in order to pass through adolescence and move into a healthy single adulthood, adolescents must allow themselves to experience vital sexual feelings while making clear decisions that limit their choices of sexual actions.

When the developmental task of each stage has been mastered, one should have an integrated sense of his or her sexuality and spirituality that will act as a guide for the tasks of adult relationships.

Not mastering one of the developmental tasks can leave a person with an inadequacy in the marital sexual relationship. Fortunately, developmental gaps can be filled; the later the stage of development, the easier the healing. For example, lack of bonding in infancy is much more difficult to replace than the lack of bumbling, heterosexual interactions during preadolescence. One of the functions of the sexual retraining process is to fill developmental gaps that have caused sexual barriers.

SEVEN

Sexual Response Is Automatic

All sexual anatomy is present at birth, confirming that we have been created as sexual beings. Involuntary sexual responses are present almost from the moment a baby draws his or her first breath. A little boy has his first erection within minutes, and a little girl lubricates vaginally within hours after birth. Thus, physical responses are present at birth, too, although these responses obviously do not have the same emotion or meaning that we associate with them in adolescence or adulthood.

Education about our bodies does not need to be a boring anatomy and physiology lecture. When we teach seminars for married couples, we spend almost two of the ten hours talking about our bodies and how they work. After the seminar, many people report that the insight they gained from this presentation made a radical difference in understanding their own situations. To be a good lover, you need to have a thorough understanding of the body and how it works. Sex is much more than the coming together of various bodily parts. Even when the feelings and spirit are in the right place, unless the parts come together correctly, sex is not going to work.

The starting point, therefore, is a thorough understanding of the body parts connected with our sexuality and a thorough grasp of how those parts work.

Even though all sexual anatomy is present at birth, hormones influence the development of our sexual organs and our feelings as adolescents and adults. These hormones begin to be secreted about three years before any observable bodily changes appear. Therefore, a seven-, eight-, or nine-year-old may experience some emotional fluctuation or sensitivity triggered by these bursts of hormones.

In the woman, the sex hormones are estrogen, progesterone, and testosterone. When these hormones are first secreted, they are very irregular and remain so until the girl has been menstruating a year or more. Eventually, the hormones should develop rhythmic monthly patterns that continue, except when the woman is pregnant or breast-feeding, until she reaches menopause.

In menopause, the changes that result from the decrease in hormonal levels may affect sexual functioning. The changes that result from decreased estrogen and progesterone are mainly the thinning of the vaginal walls and a decrease in vaginal lubrication. Both are best handled by using a lubricant and by the continued exercising of the PC (pubococcygeus) or Kegel muscle. If you are a woman of menopausal age experiencing new or increased dyspareunia (pain during intercourse), a medical examination to confirm the source of these changes would certainly be indicated. If you are experiencing decrease in sexual desire, a hormonal panel to measure your free and total testosterone levels would be indicated. Hormonal replacement therapy may be recommended.

Testosterone is the primary male sex hormone, which increases in production at the onset of puberty. Testosterone reaches its peak levels of production in the man's twenties and then declines at about 1 percent per year as he ages. At least five changes occur as the result of the man's aging process and the decrease in testosterone levels:

1. There is a decrease in the frequency of urgent physical sexual desire.
2. It may take longer to get an erection and may require more direct, firm stimulation.

3. An older man may not feel the need to ejaculate with every sexual experience.
4. The force of the ejaculation lessens with age. When a man ejaculates in his twenties, it is usually with a spurt, whereas as men age, it becomes more of a dribble.
5. The erections may not be as firm as they were in youth. (For detailed information see chapter 4, pages 33–34.)

Just as the sex hormones influence the development of our sexual organs and affect our sexual functioning, they also enhance our sexual drive. This drive gives us energy not only for sexual arousal but also for getting things done in life. It is the reason adolescents are encouraged to keep very active and busy while couples are encouraged to relax enough to have some time and energy left for sexual arousal.

Arousal is an automatic, involuntary, pleasure-seeking response in our bodies that is controlled by the relaxed or passive branch of our involuntary or autonomic nervous system—the parasympathetic branch. Some of us are more aware of the feelings of arousal than others; but all normal, healthy adult bodies experience arousal on a continual basis. A woman lubricates vaginally every eighty to ninety minutes while she sleeps, just as a man gets an erection every eighty to ninety minutes while he sleeps. Throughout the day, arousal may occur for various reasons ranging from a full bladder or an erotic thought to a sexual touch or full sexual activity.

Sexual arousal may lead to a full sexual response if positive sexual stimulation is pursued. Sexual response is controlled by the active branch of the autonomic nervous system—the sympathetic branch. When we discuss the sexual response a little later in this chapter, we will detail how each of these systems works. For now, it is sufficient to say that while the response of orgasm follows arousal, the two are under opposite nervous systems' control.

Both men and women can experience sexual arousal without experiencing an orgasmic response. Also, it is possible, though less likely, for both men and women to experience orgasm without experiencing arousal.

For example, some men ejaculate without an erection or the usual sensations of arousal. While this is not the norm, it is important to understand that arousal and orgasm are two separate responses. This is what Helen Singer Kaplan, in her book *The New Sex Therapy*, refers to as the "diphasic" physiological understanding of our sexual response.

Our sexual organs and the way they function during the sexual experience—our sexual anatomy and sexual physiology—are part of an awesome and beautiful system. Physiologically, we as men and women have all been set in motion to respond in a similar way. The intricate details of this sexual response have been measured by Masters and Johnson. Without their work, we would still be in the Dark Ages regarding our understanding of the sexual response. Much of what we share in this chapter grows directly out of the findings of their landmark research.

For descriptive purposes, Masters and Johnson have categorized their measurements of the sexual response into four phases. (See Figure 7.1.) The excitement and plateau phases comprise the arousal, or parasympathetic-dominant, stage of the sexual experience while the transition into the orgasmic phase triggers the sympathetic-dominant stage. In the refractory period (also called the resolution phase) all the parts return at various rates to their prestimulated states.

Figure 7.1

SEXUAL RESPONSE PATTERNS

Adapted from Masters and Johnson, *Human Sexual Response* (Boston: Little, Brown, and Company, 1966).

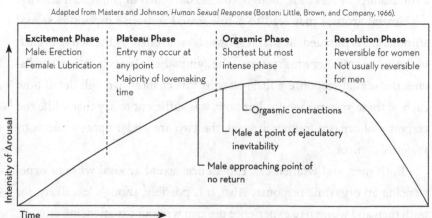

Excitement Phase	Plateau Phase	Orgasmic Phase	Resolution Phase
Male: Erection	Entry may occur at	Shortest but most	Reversible for women
Female: Lubrication	any point	intense phase	Not usually reversible
	Majority of lovemaking		for men
	time		

Orgasmic contractions

Male at point of ejaculatory inevitability

Male approaching point of no return

Intensity of Arousal

Time

These responses in the body may occur due to sexual intercourse, manual or oral stimulation, self-stimulation, necking, deep kissing, petting or loveplay, or fantasies or visual input. Sexual intercourse is not necessary for a full sexual release, nor does sexual intercourse guarantee a full sexual release. This is vital information, especially for understanding the difference between sexual feelings and sexual behavior as it relates to sexual decisions and responsibility.

THE SEXUAL ANATOMY

First, we would like you to become familiar with the male and female genitalia in their pre-aroused state so you understand the changes that occur during arousal and release.

The Female Anatomy

Ovaries. Look at Figure 7.2 on page 65. Notice the two almond-shaped organs located on either side of the uterus, below and behind the uterine tubes. These are the primary sex organs in the woman, the ovaries. Their main function is to produce the sex hormones and the ova, or eggs, for reproduction. Release of eggs from the ovaries begins in puberty and ends after menopause. All the eggs are present at birth, so they age as the woman ages. The eggs are released monthly as they mature.

In contrast, the man continually produces sperm throughout his life. Unlike women, whose reproductive capacity is limited by age, men can reproduce indefinitely. This difference may suggest one reason why it is the age of the woman rather than the age of the man that is connected with birth defects in children born to older parents; the woman's eggs have aged with her while the man's sperm have been constantly renewed.

Uterine tubes and uterus. The uterine (fallopian) tubes carry the eggs from the ovaries to the uterus, or womb, a pear-shaped organ located between the urinary bladder and the rectum. As you can see in Figure 7.3, the uterus is naturally flexed toward the front of the body. A woman may have what is called a tipped, or retroflexed, uterus, which means that it is flipped back, with the cervix falling into the vagina, and she may experience pain upon deep thrusting. Another possibility, though it is less frequent, is an anteflexed uterus that has moved too far forward; this position can make it more difficult to become pregnant and can put pressure on the urinary bladder. The ligaments that hold the uterus in place are like strong rubber bands; they can be injured during childbirth, causing intercourse to be deeply painful. If you experience pain during intercourse, a medical examination is recommended. Pain is correctable with specialized medical help.

Vagina. The vagina is the woman's most important organ for sexual functioning. It is an organ of accommodation, a muscular passageway that is very changeable in size. It can be totally collapsed when unaroused, it can accommodate any size penis during intercourse, and it can also expand to allow the birth of a baby. In Figure 7.2 you see a front view of the vagina as a passageway from the cervix of the uterus to the outside of the body through the inner labia, or lips. In Figure 7.3 you see a side view of the vagina in its collapsed, unaroused state.

The vagina is a clean passageway when it is free of infection or disease. In its natural, healthy state it is free of disease-producing microorganisms, but it does contain some friendly bacteria that help fight off infection. It is important to understand that in the genital area we have three different systems with three different conditions. The urinary tract is sterile with no microorganisms in it. The vagina is clean and contains some friendly microorganisms. The anus, part of the gastrointestinal system, is highly contaminated. This is why it is always essential for women to learn when toileting to wipe from the front to the back. This is also the reason it is important to be freshly washed for sexual play, so there is no contamination from the anus to the vagina or penis. Because of anal contamination and the added threat of transmitting AIDS and other infections, anal intercourse is not advisable from a medical perspective.

The vagina maintains its own pH (acid-base) balance to fight off infection. Because of this balance, douching is not normally recommended. What you eat can also affect this acid-base balance. Diets that are high in sugar, refined carbohydrates, antibiotics, carbonated beverages, or caffeine can negatively affect the acid-base balance and bring about vaginal irritation.

The vagina is highly sensitive to sexual stimulation. Regularly exercising the PC muscle enhances that sensitivity. For a description of recommended PC exercises, see pages 166–67. To get the PC muscle into shape, two hundred to three hundred contractions of the PC muscle per day are needed, and to keep it in shape, at least twenty-five to fifty contractions per day are necessary. The other way to maintain the sensitivity of the vagina is by regular sexual activity.

In most women lubrication automatically occurs within the first twenty to thirty seconds after sexual stimulation begins. The vagina secretes lubrication like beads of perspiration along the wall of the vagina to make the entry of the penis into the vagina a smooth and comfortable activity.

Figure 7.2

INTERNAL FEMALE GENITALIA (FRONT VIEW)

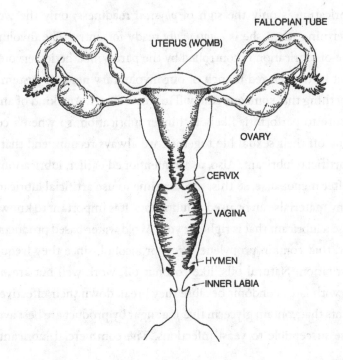

FALLOPIAN TUBE

UTERUS (WOMB)

OVARY

CERVIX

VAGINA

HYMEN

INNER LABIA

Figure 7.3

UNAROUSED INTERNAL FEMALE GENITALIA (SIDE VIEW)

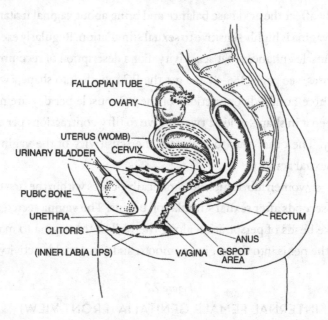

FALLOPIAN TUBE

OVARY

UTERUS (WOMB)

URINARY BLADDER — CERVIX

PUBIC BONE

URETHRA

CLITORIS

(INNER LABIA LIPS)

RECTUM

ANUS

VAGINA — G-SPOT AREA

Lubrication is only the sign of *physical* readiness; only the woman can determine when she is *emotionally* ready for entry. The involuntary response of lubrication is controlled by the parasympathetic nervous system, that is, the relaxed branch of our involuntary nervous system. It is not something that someone can will to stop or start. Any kind of anxiety or pressure to perform is likely to hinder lubrication, so when a couple is starting off their sexual life together, we always recommend that they use an artificial lubricant. Also, as we mentioned earlier, lubrication does lessen after menopause, so this, too, is a time to use artificial lubricant.

Many materials can be used as lubricants. It is important to know how to choose a lubricant that is right for you. Avoid water-based products, like K-Y Jelly, that contain propylene glycol or alcohol, since they frequently cause irritation. Natural oils, like coconut oil, work well but are not to be used with latex condoms because they break down their effectiveness. Lubricants that contain glycerin that is a sugar by-product are best avoided for those susceptible to yeast infections. The commercial lubricants we recommend at this time are Astroglide Premium Silicone Gel (latex safe, glycerin free, made from coconut oil), Astroglide Natural Liquid (condom compatible, glycerin free, made with aloe and other botanical ingredients), Slippery Stuff Gel (water-based, paraben free, glycerin free, nonirritating), Probe Silky Light and Probe Thick Rich (latex safe, nonirritating, contains glycerin—but it is vegetable not sugar), Yes Water-Based if using latex birth control, Yes Oil-Based for others. And when nothing else is available, saliva works well.

In recent years, there has been much ado about a spot or area in the upper interior of the vagina just beyond the PC muscle. This area has been called the G-spot, or Graffenburg spot, and has been found to be highly responsive to stimulation in certain women. These women report a deep orgasm that occurs when this area of the vagina is stimulated. For some of these women, there is a release of fluid connected with an orgasm brought about by G-spot stimulation. This is called a "flooding response," or female ejaculation. Some women have stopped their orgasmic response because they feel as though they are going to urinate. If this has been an issue in your relationship, talk about it, urinate before sex, protect the bed—and go for it!

Labia. Figure 7.4 shows the front view of the external female genitalia. Beginning from the outside, note the outer lips, or the labia majora, and the inner lips, or the labia minora. The top of these inner lips form the hood over the clitoris, which is a most unique bit of human anatomy. Its function is to receive and transmit sexual stimuli; no other part of the human body, male or female, has this function. Its existence certainly confirms that women have been created for sexual pleasure, not merely for procreation.

Clitoris. The structure of the clitoris has been compared to the penis. The hood—the upper juncture of the inner lips—is analogous to the foreskin of the penis as it covers the erectile tissue. The head, or glans, of the clitoris can be compared with the head of the penis. The little shaft of the clitoris that goes up under the hood could also be compared with the shaft of the penis. On the bottom end of the labia minora and majora is the perineum, which is the muscular floor between the vagina and the anus.

Figure 7.4

EXTERNAL FEMALE GENITALIA

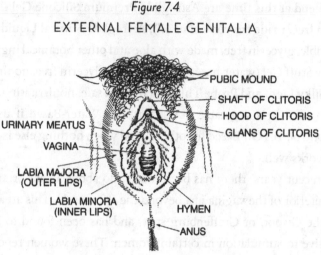

PUBIC MOUND

SHAFT OF CLITORIS

HOOD OF CLITORIS

GLANS OF CLITORIS

URINARY MEATUS

VAGINA

LABIA MAJORA
(OUTER LIPS)

LABIA MINORA
(INNER LIPS)

HYMEN

ANUS

Breasts. The breasts also play an important role in sexual stimulation. They are made up of the same structure and tissue in both the male and the female. Before puberty, the breasts are the same in both sexes. The female hormones cause the development of breasts in girls during puberty. If men were given female hormones, they could also develop breasts that could produce milk.

It is important to note that the size of a woman's breasts has nothing to do with her sexuality, sensuality, responsiveness, or sexual enjoyment. Because our culture has spread the idea that larger breasts are more sexual, some men may gain more pleasure from a woman with larger breasts, but a small-breasted woman and a large-breasted woman have equal potential for sexual intensity. Breast size certainly can make a difference in how a woman feels about herself, but large breasts do not bring any greater physical enjoyment than small breasts.

The Male Anatomy

Testes and ducts. Just as the ovaries are the primary reproductive and sex organs for the woman, so are the testes, or testicles, for the man. Look at Figure 7.5 and Figure 7.6 to see a side view of the testicles, two small glands or balls held by the scrotum. They function with the rest of the body in two ways. First, they produce the male hormone, testosterone, which is secreted into the body through the bloodstream. Second, they also produce the sperm and a portion of the seminal fluid that carries the sperm. This seminal fluid and sperm are transmitted to the penis via the vas deferens, which travels up past the bladder through the prostate gland and then on down to the base of the penis and out the end of the penis.

A word about a vasectomy is appropriate here. As the term suggests, a vasectomy is the severing of the vas, or vas deferens, so that the sperm and seminal fluid from the testes can no longer be excreted during sexual arousal and release. Instead, the sperm and seminal fluid produced by the testicles are absorbed into the body, and their production decreases.

Sometimes men are concerned that a vasectomy will diminish their masculinity, but this need not be a fear. After a vasectomy, the testicles continue to produce testosterone, which is secreted into the bloodstream, and seminal fluid continues to be reproduced by the seminal vesicles so a man will continue to ejaculate after a vasectomy. Only the sperm no longer travel outside the body.

Figure 7.5

UNAROUSED INTERNAL MALE GENITALIA

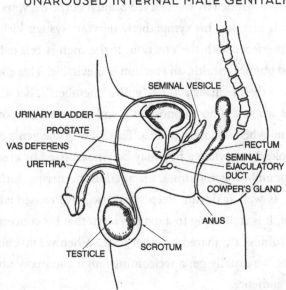

Prostate gland. The prostate gland, the donut-shaped gland around the Y-shaped juncture where the outlet from the bladder (the urinary system) meets the vas deferens (the reproductive system), can be seen in Figure 7.5. The prostate is an extremely sensitive body part that can easily give men trouble as they age. It is important for men who experience urinary urgency or a dull pain in the lower abdomen to have a medical exam for prostatitis, an inflammation of the prostate gland. Medications can often be prescribed that quickly reduce the inflammation and bring the man back to a healthy state. Taking twenty-five to thirty milligrams of the mineral zinc each day is thought to help keep the prostate gland healthy.

Penis. The penis is a truly wonderful part of the human anatomy. Unfortunately, it has often been used aggressively to inflict pain or sexual abuse. The penis has a highly negative connotation for many women because it can potentially be used as a weapon by men. However, in the context of a warm and loving relationship, the penis is a delightful part of the body that is used in sexual activity. In Figure 7.6 you can see that it is made up of erectile tissue with many venus sinuses (spaces) that rush full of blood under sexual stimulation. This rushing of blood brings about the man's erection, which is comparable to the woman's vaginal lubrication. This response is controlled by the relaxed branch of the nervous system.

If the man is anxious, his sympathetic nervous system kicks in and interrupts or interferes with the erection. If the man is relaxed, turned on, and in good physical health, an erection is inevitable. There are times that men think of their penises as their "willful member." That is, it sometimes responds when it is not supposed to, and conversely, it sometimes does not respond when it is supposed to. This view of the penis generally develops in adolescence when a boy may be embarrassed by erections at inappropriate or embarrassing times. Ejaculations occurring during necking or petting, as well as during sleep, may also have caused adolescent embarrassment. It is reassuring to a man to learn that his concerns about his penis's willfulness are shared by other men. When we talk about this in our seminars, we usually get a welcoming laugh and many nods from the men in the audience.

Figure 7.6

CIRCUMCISED EXTERNAL MALE GENITALIA (SIDE VIEW)

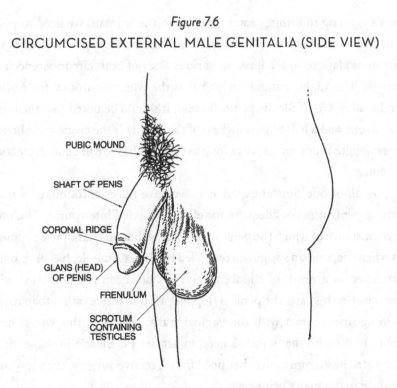

PUBIC MOUND

SHAFT OF PENIS

CORONAL RIDGE

GLANS (HEAD) OF PENIS

FRENULUM

SCROTUM CONTAINING TESTICLES

Many men are also preoccupied with the size of their penises. While occasionally a man may worry that his penis is too big and might hurt a woman, most of the time the man is concerned that his penis is too small. Usually this stems from comparisons made in locker rooms or stories and jokes heard about men with giant penises and how much pleasure they bring a woman.

In fact, the average length of the erect penis is about six inches, with a range of four and a half inches to eight inches. Often, however, men make the comparisons when the penis is flaccid. The differences from man to man in comparing flaccid penises are much greater. There is even fluctuation from time to time in each man's own penis size. The perspective of looking down on the penis from above tends to make the penis look smaller than if it were viewed from another angle, which tends to distort comparisons even further.

With regard to the whole idea that somehow the man with the larger penis is going to bring greater pleasure to the woman, we need to point out two facts: First, as we have discussed already, the vagina is an organ of accommodation, so it adjusts to various sizes of both circumference and length. The vagina extends in length as the woman's arousal intensifies, and it adapts itself for the penis. Second, it should be noted that the outer third (one and a half to two inches) of the vagina is the erotic area; hence, great length is not necessary as long as the man has a firm enough erection to enter.

In all of our clinical experience, we have never encountered a male whose penis was not adequate for effective sexual intercourse. The only circumstance in which the penis may seem as though it is not wide enough is when the woman's vagina, controlled by the PC muscle, has been over-stretched as a result of childbirth and has not been reconditioned with exercise. In this case, the penis is flopping around inside rather than maintaining firm contact with the vaginal walls. However, this would have more to do with the woman's need to get her PC muscle in shape, or in the extreme circumstance, her need for corrective surgery, than it would pertain to the man's penis size.

Sometimes there is concern on the part of the woman that the man's penis may be too large. If the concern is about circumference, the woman must understand that as she learns to relax the muscles in her vagina, she can clearly accommodate a penis of any size because the vagina is designed to expand enough to allow the birth of a baby. If the concern is about length, then she needs to understand that the vagina itself expands to make room for the penis as the uterus pulls up and out of the way. Sexual arousal helps the vagina prepare for the entrance of the penis by this expansion as well as by the lubrication that comes seconds after sexual arousal begins. The fears about a large penis that some women carry forward from childhood may be experienced as fear of penetration. These fears can seriously interfere, but they are irrational anxieties. To help move past those anxieties, a sensitive gynecological exam and the steps suggested in chapter 18 for overcoming intercourse barriers would be helpful.

THE FOUR PHASES OF THE SEXUAL RESPONSE CYCLE

Look at Figure 7.7 and Figure 7.8 (pages 74–75) showing sexual response patterns for men and women. As you read the following discussion of what happens in the man's or woman's body during each of the four phases of the sexual response, find these details on the appropriate graph. Circle any of the responses that you are aware of happening or assume are probably happening. Put a check by any of the responses that you believe are difficult for you or are not happening.

The Excitement Phase—Arousal

The excitement phase is the first stage of the physical sexual response cycle as defined by Masters and Johnson. It may occur involuntarily without any stimulation when you are relaxed or asleep. We explained earlier how the body responds in a regular way with erections for the man and vaginal lubrication for the woman, especially during sleep. During active sexual activity, the excitement phase is often preceded by sexual desire or interest, which may bring out the very first signs of arousal. Hugging, kissing, bodily touching, or genital contact provide the stimulation that cause physical changes during the excitement phase. For both the man and the woman, these changes are due to vasocongestion (blood and fluid rushing into the sexual organs).

Female excitement phase. The clitoris is most important for the woman during the excitement phase. It becomes engorged in a somewhat similar manner to the penis in that it increases in size two or three times its prestimulated length as its venus spaces rush full of blood and fluid. Although it is the most important receptor of sexual stimulation, it is vital to understand that most women prefer stimulation around the clitoris rather than directly on the glans (head). Just like most men prefer to have the shaft of the penis stroked rather than the tip rubbed.

It is also important to understand the pain/pleasure principle that operates most vividly with regard to the clitoris. Unstimulated and unaroused

Figure 7.7

SEXUAL RESPONSE PATTERN FOR MEN

Adapted from Masters and Johnson, *Human Sexual Response* (Boston: Little, Brown, and Company, 1966). © Copyright Penner & Penner.

SEXUAL RESPONSE PATTERN FOR MEN

EXCITEMENT PHASE	PLATEAU PHASE	ORGASMIC PHASE	RESOLUTION PHASE
External Genitals • Penis becomes erect as it rushes full of blood • Scrotum thickens and partially elevates	External Genitals • Penis engorges more and deepens in color • Fluid containing sperm seeps from penis • Scrotum thickens	External Genitals • Penis contracts, expelling the seminal fluid	External Genitalia • Penis becomes flaccid • Scrotum thins and drops

Internal Genitalia
• No change
	Internal Genitalia
	• Testes enlarge
	• Right testicle rises and rotates early
	• When approaching point of no return
	  - Left testicle rises and rotates
	  - Prostate contracts
	  - Seminal vesicle contracts
		Internal Genitalia
		• Seminal duct system contracts
			Internal Genitalia
			• Testes descend and return to normal size

Total Body • Nipples become erect in 60 percent of men	Total Body • Skin flushes on chest, neck, and face • Foot contracts downward (carpopedal spasm) • Heart rate increases • Pelvis thrusts • Muscles tense	Total Body • Rectal sphincter contracts • Foot spasms continue • Heart rate increases more • Blood pressure rises more • Breathing increases • Facial muscles contract • Gasping occurs	Total Body • Relief of vasocongestion and engorgement • Skin perspires • Muscles relax
Characteristics • Arousal	Characteristics • Entry may occur at any time • Ejaculatory control must be learned for extended love play	Characteristics • Shortest, but most intense phase • Internal experience	Characteristics • Tension loss • Not usually reversible (rest period required before more arousal)

Level of Sexual Arousal

Phases of the Sexual Response

Figure 7.8

SEXUAL RESPONSE PATTERN FOR WOMEN

Adapted from Masters and Johnson, *Human Sexual Response* (Boston: Little, Brown, and Company, 1966). © Copyright Penner & Penner.

SEXUAL RESPONSE PATTERN FOR WOMEN

EXCITEMENT PHASE	PLATEAU PHASE	ORGASMIC PHASE	RESOLUTION PHASE
External Genitals • Clitoris lengthens • Outer lips spread flat • Inner lips enlarge	**External Genitals** • Clitoris retracts under hood • Inner lips turn bright red and enlarge (about one minute before orgasmic response)	**External Genitals** • No noticeable change	**External Genitalia** • Clitoris returns to normal size • Inner and outer lips return to normal size and position
Internal Genitalia • Vagina lubricates (within ten to twenty seconds) • Uterus elecates	**Internal Genitalia** • Outer two-thirds of vagina expands • Outer one-third of vagina thickens and contracts, forming orgasmic platform • Uterus elevates fully	**Internal Genitalia** • Outer one-third of vagina contracts three to twelve times • Uterus contracts	**Internal Genitalia** • Cervix opens slightly and drops into seminal pool • Uterus drops back toward front of pelvis • Vagina collapses and thins
Total Body • Nipples become erect • Breasts enlarge	**Total Body** • Skin flushes over abdomen, chest, etc. • Foot contracts downward (carpopedal spasm) • Heart rate increases • Blood pressure rises • Pelvis thrusts • Muscles tense	**Total Body** • Rectal sphincter contracts • Foot spasms continue • Heart rate increases more • Blood pressure rises more • Breathing increases • Facial muscles contract • Gasping occurs	**Total Body** • Relief of vasocongestion and engorgement • Skin perspires • Muscles relax • Breasts and nipples return to prestimulated appearance
Characteristics • Arousal	**Characteristics** • Entry may occur at any time • Majority of love play	**Characteristics** • Shortest, but most intense phase • Internal experience	**Characteristics** • Tension loss • Reversible

Level of Sexual Arousal

Phases of the Sexual Response

women experience little clitoral pleasure. As the woman's arousal moves to a point where there is intense pleasure, the clitoris becomes so sensitive that she can readily experience clitoral pain, especially if the stimulation is directly on the head, is too intense, or continues too long. Many men believe that because the clitoris is the source of such great pleasure, the more and the harder they stimulate it, the better it is for the woman, yet most women report that a lighter, teasing touch is usually what satisfies the most. The intensity of the pain that can be experienced with too direct clitoral stimulation may put women on guard and stop their eagerness to pursue arousal. Both men and women need to accept the reality that the woman is the best authority on her own body, especially her own clitoris. She needs to accept the responsibility for guiding a man in clitoral touch. There is no way a man can automatically know what is going to be the most pleasurable.

In the excitement phase, the labia minora (inner lips) become engorged and extend outward while the labia majora spread flat as if the genital area is opening up to receive the penis. As the arousal builds, the woman's genitals take on a slight funnel shape in preparation for penile entry.

Internally, the uterus begins to pull up and away from the vagina; this pulls the cervix out of the way so that the penis will not strike against it during thrusting. This preparation does not occur when the woman has a tipped uterus, however. The cervix does not get out of the way of the penis in this case; so it can be struck, causing a sharp, stabbing pain during deep thrusting.

The vagina lubricates within twenty seconds of any form of stimulation, preparing the woman for entry. The inner two-thirds of the vagina lengthens and distends, allowing greater room for the penis.

The breasts also change during the initial excitement phase. Their most obvious response is that of nipple erection, as well as general engorgement that causes a slight increase in breast size. The areola, the area around the nipple, usually darkens and becomes slightly engorged, especially as the woman moves toward the plateau phase.

Male excitement phase. The penis in the man is similar to the clitoris in the woman in that it is the receiver and transmitter of sexual sensations.

Figure 7.9
AROUSED MALE GENITALIA (SIDE VIEW)

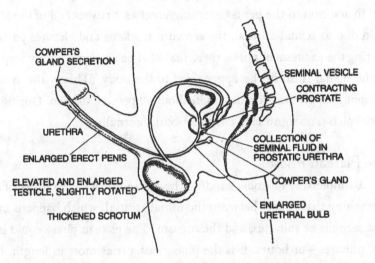

COWPER'S
GLAND SECRETION

SEMINAL VESICLE

CONTRACTING
PROSTATE

URETHRA

ENLARGED ERECT PENIS

COLLECTION OF
SEMINAL FLUID IN
PROSTATIC URETHRA

ELEVATED AND ENLARGED
TESTICLE, SLIGHTLY ROTATED

COWPER'S GLAND

THICKENED SCROTUM

ENLARGED
URETHRAL BULB

The penile response of erection is parallel to vaginal lubrication in the woman in that it is the involuntary response that is necessary to pursue intercourse. This response occurs throughout the day and night and can be brought about by sexual thoughts, indirect stimulation through general caressing, or direct stimulation on the penis itself. Whereas the woman's response is internal and less apparent, the man's response or lack of it is obvious. Because of this, the man often feels more pressure to respond. Some men are highly anxious about responding, especially when they have had difficulty with arousal or loss of erection in the past.

The penis is a highly sensitive responder. It can quickly become erect with positive physical and emotional stimulation. This erection can easily be interrupted by some negative or nonsexual stimulation such as the telephone ringing, a loud noise outside the door, a negative thought, a special concern, a harsh word, or a critical comment.

Erections can be lost and regained when relaxation and freedom exist to allow that response. During extended loveplay, this is likely to be the case; yet erections can also be maintained for extended periods of time without ejaculation. The latter is most likely to occur when the stimulation is varied and the intensity of the experience flows in waves. It is not uncommon for the erection to diminish slightly and then be regained.

In addition to the penis becoming erect as it rushes full of blood and fluid due to sexual arousal, the scrotum thickens and elevates partially. During the excitement phase, there may also be a general bodily response of the sexual flush in the upper third of the body. (This is also true for women.) Nipple erection occurs in about 60 percent of men. During this initial phase, no significant changes occur internally.

The Plateau Phase

A simple way of understanding the plateau phase is to think of it as everything that occurs between the initial arousal, which happens in the first seconds or minutes, and the orgasm. The plateau phase could last a few minutes—or hours. It is the phase that varies most in length. It all depends on how each individual responds and what the couple desires. During extended loveplay, whether it is a prelude to intercourse or simply a fully clothed enjoyment of the intense response of two people with each other, the couple will be in the plateau phase. There will be arousal, but they will not yet have reached orgasm.

The changes that occur during the plateau phase are due to the buildup of tension and increased congestion in the genitals. When a long, extended period of loveplay occurs, this buildup of intensity will usually be experienced in repeated waves of heightened arousal and then letdown. As long as there is the freedom to ride these waves, the intensity will build to the point of automatically triggering an orgasm.

When it is extended, the plateau phase changes sex into lovemaking and goal-oriented, orgasm-directed activity into extended pleasure.

Male plateau phase. Externally, the penis may become slightly more engorged and deeper in color while the glans, or head of the penis, increases in diameter. During the plateau phase, the scrotum also thickens and elevates more. (See Figure 7.9.) It should be noted that fluid containing sperm may seep from the penis during the plateau phase without ejaculation. That is why the withdrawal method of birth control—the intentional withdrawal of the penis from the vagina before ejaculation—is not a reliable method. Adolescents most often attempt to use this method, and the statistics clearly indicate how ineffective it is.

Internally during this phase, the testes enlarge 50 to 100 percent. The right testicle rises and rotates a quarter turn. Near the end of the plateau phase, some warning signs let the man know that he is approaching the point of no return. As they get near the point of orgasm, all men can sense something in their bodies that tells them they are about to ejaculate.

Three main changes take place at this point: As the scrotal sack thickens and pulls toward the body, the left testicle also rises and rotates about a quarter turn. There are contractions in the prostate gland as the seminal fluid begins to gather in that area and travel to the base of the penis. The sphincter from the bladder shuts off so that no seminal fluid will be forced by retrograde ejaculation into the bladder, nor will any urine be expelled during the orgasm. Although a man is not aware of these changes, they act as a warning that he is about to ejaculate.

It should be noted that once this process is in motion, the ejaculation is inevitable. The man is approaching ejaculatory inevitability, the point of no return. If a man struggles with premature ejaculation, he clearly must gain control prior to these physical events rather than attempt to stop the ejaculation once these warning signs have occurred.

Female plateau phase. As the sexual experience progresses, more and more is happening internally for the woman and less and less is occurring externally. This symbolizes women's more internal experience, in contrast to men's more external, performance-oriented attitude.

In the woman, there are some slight external changes. The labia minora increase in size and brighten somewhat in color a minute or two before orgasm. The Bartholin gland just inside the labia secretes one to three drops of a substance designed to enhance the possibility of pregnancy by changing the pH balance of the vagina. At the same time, the clitoral glans retracts under the clitoral hood as if to protect its heightened sensitivity from too much intense stimulation and arousal.

Internally, significant changes must occur for the woman before she is ready for her orgasmic response. (See Figure 7.10.) The uterus, which began to elevate during the excitement phase, elevates even more. The inner two-thirds of the vagina expands or balloons outward to form the area known as the seminal pool. This is the nonerotic section of the vagina where contact with the penis provides neither arousal nor much stimulation. The outer third of the vagina (one and a half to two inches) becomes intensely engorged as it forms the orgasmic platform. Some women are aware of a pleasurable vaginal-grasping response as the arousal continues through the plateau phase.

Figure 7.10

AROUSED INTERNAL FEMALE GENITALIA (SIDE VIEW)

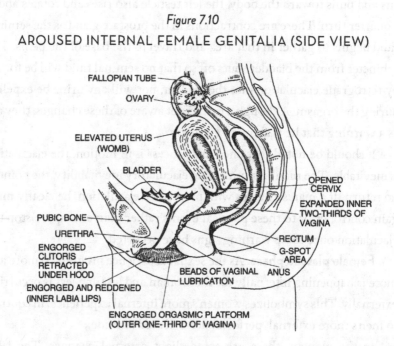

FALLOPIAN TUBE

OVARY

ELEVATED UTERUS
(WOMB)

BLADDER

OPENED
CERVIX

EXPANDED INNER
TWO-THIRDS OF
VAGINA

PUBIC BONE

URETHRA

ENGORGED
CLITORIS
RETRACTED
UNDER HOOD

ENGORGED AND REDDENED
(INNER LABIA LIPS)

RECTUM

G-SPOT
AREA

ANUS

BEADS OF VAGINAL
LUBRICATION

ENGORGED ORGASMIC PLATFORM
(OUTER ONE-THIRD OF VAGINA)

Male and Female Transition from Plateau to Orgasm

Several of the specific changes that happen for both men and women during the transition from plateau to orgasm usually go relatively unnoticed. There is the involuntary extension of the foot called the carpopedal spasm. Both the heart rate and the blood pressure increase. Involuntary pelvic thrusting occurs as arousal moves near the point of orgasm, and general muscular tension takes place with almost spastic-like contractions.

Some more obvious changes also occur. The skin flushes in the chest, neck, and face areas—almost a blushing effect due to the widespread vasocongestion. Facial grimaces are common because of the involuntary contracting of the facial muscles, as well as gasping or moaning responses that may be due in part to hyperventilation (heavy breathing), which is virtually inevitable and necessary for both men and women to reach the orgasmic phase. Women who have difficulty allowing an orgasmic response usually have difficulty allowing these intense gasping, grimacing, and breathing responses because they consider them unladylike. It should also be noted that for both men and women the transition from the plateau phase to the orgasmic phase marks a shift from parasympathetic dominance to sympathetic dominance, a switch that helps nudge the individual toward the orgasmic response.

The Orgasmic Phase

The orgasmic response is the shortest and most intense of the four phases. It is a reflex response that lasts only a few seconds. You cannot choose to respond with an orgasm like you can choose to bend your elbow, but you can control or inhibit the response from happening by stopping the natural, involuntary responses in your body that lead up to it. Or you can enhance the possibility of an orgasmic response by becoming active and going after genital stimulation—by penile thrusting for the man and by clitoral or vaginal stimulation for the woman.

As the intensity builds in the body, the tension increases to the point where the orgasmic reflex is set off. The autonomic, or involuntary, nervous system has switched control from the relaxed, receptive branch (the parasympathetic) to the active, fight-or-flight branch (the sympathetic), as already explained. Hence, the more active you are, the more your body is engaged to respond orgasmically (which is usually what the woman needs); and the quieter and more passive you are, the more your response is slowed down (which is usually what the man needs). In understanding the sexual response, it is very important to know that an orgasm is a reflex. A person who actively receives the right amount and duration of stimulation will be orgasmic.

Female orgasmic response. All the significant changes related to orgasm in women take place internally. That is why so much confusion has occurred about their orgasmic response; women regularly report that they are not sure whether or not they have had an orgasm. Men report no such doubt; they know if they have or have not.

Because the clitoris is completely retracted during the orgasmic phase, some women prefer very direct clitoral stimulation right at the point of orgasm. Internally, there are two centers of response for the woman. The uterus experiences contractions similar to those of the early stages of labor. This is why doctors may rule out orgasm if a woman is threatening to miscarry or go into early labor. When first experienced, these contractions may be felt as slightly painful; but as the woman learns to connect those contractions as part of her intense pleasure, they usually become highly enjoyable during the orgasm. The cervix of the uterus opens slightly at the end of the orgasm so it is ready to receive the sperm.

The second internal response center is in the outer third of the vagina—the orgasmic platform. It experiences contractions that are eight-tenths of a second apart, with three to five contractions in a mild orgasm and from eight to twelve contractions in a more intense orgasm. These are the contractions of the PC muscle that surrounds both the vagina (forming the orgasmic platform) and the rectal sphincter, where contractions are also experienced.

Male orgasmic response. The man's orgasm is experienced in two stages. In the first stage, the internal genitalia respond a few seconds before ejaculation, as explained in the earlier description of the plateau phase. Like the contractions of the orgasmic platform in the woman, the man's contractions of the seminal duct system, including the prostate, occur at intervals of eight-tenths of a second. Contractions also occur in the rectal sphincter as well as in the urinary bladder. These contractions move the ejaculate to the base of the penis, preparing it for stage two.

During stage two, the seminal fluid, including the sperm, is expelled. Having reached the point of ejaculatory inevitability, there is nothing that can stop the response at this juncture; it is, indeed, inevitable. The time between those initial contractions and the expulsion is the time it takes the sperm to travel through the system of the penis. The contractions at the base of the penis also occur at intervals of eight-tenths of a second. For the average healthy male, a standard ejaculation contains 3.5 to 5 cubic centimeters of ejaculate and 175 to 500 million spermatozoa.

The man's total-body responses are similar to those experienced by the woman. They include increased heart rate and elevated blood pressure, intense breathing, facial contractions with gasping responses, and foot spasms.

Orgasmic differences in men and women. Women's orgasmic responses seem to differ from one experience to another and from one woman to another. Men seem to be more similar in their orgasmic responses. This may be due to the wide range of contractions during orgasm for women (from three to twelve) and their capability for having one orgasm after another. Women have the potential to respond indefinitely with multiple or sequential orgasms. Not all women desire this or feel the need for more than one response, but they are designed with that potential. Perhaps a word should be said about the difference between a multiple and a sequential orgasm. By a multiple orgasm we mean an orgasm where a woman reaches the orgasmic level and then seems to ride that wave in what authors Alan and Donna Brauer have referred to as an "extended sexual orgasm."[1] The woman who responds with a sequential orgasm has a slight refractory period and then responds again with another orgasm.

Women have a physiologically unlimited potential for orgasms; they are limited only by their stamina and their desire. In contrast, men, except for a very small percentage, need a refractory period of at least twenty minutes—and usually several hours—before they can regain arousal, erection, and ejaculation. As a man ages, the refractory period generally increases. It also seems that the more frequently a man ejaculates, the longer it takes until he is able to ejaculate again.

The woman's orgasm can be interrupted at any point, whereas the man's cannot. Once the man has reached the point of ejaculatory inevitability, nothing can be done to stop it; the reflex is in motion. Because of this irreversibility, women have often been taught that they should not arouse a man, because once a man becomes aroused, he is no longer responsible for his own actions. This distorted teaching leads adolescents to conclude that it is a girl's responsibility to set the limits on the boy for controlling sexual activity. The fact is that men can control themselves, and they are responsible to control their own behavior, just as women are responsible for their behavior. For men, control must happen at an early phase.

Even if a man is about to ejaculate, he can still control where he does that; it does not have to happen inside a woman's vagina. Men should never be taught that their arousal excuses them from being responsible for their own actions.

If the sexual experience is the first one in a long time, a woman will tend to be slower in her response and will experience less freedom in her release, while a man will tend to be quicker in his arousal and release and experience more buildup and intensity. We believe this tendency to go in opposite directions is one more indication of the reality that we were created to be together and to experience sexual release on a regular basis.

While women experience difficulty with and pressure to have an orgasm, the active phase of the sexual response cycle, men rarely struggle with the orgasmic response. Instead they struggle to control the timing of their orgasms. Men's pressure is with difficulty getting or keeping erections, the passive phase of the sexual response cycle.

The Resolution Phase

During this final phase of the sexual response, the body reverses itself through the plateau and excitement changes to its prior, unstimulated state. Both the man and woman experience the sensation of tension loss due to the release of engorgement and the diminishing of vasocongestion. In the male, the most obvious sign of resolution is the gradual and sometimes immediate lessening of the erection. The full, firm erection will be gone immediately, but it may take some time for the penis to return to its prestimulated state.

During resolution some men experience heightened sensitivity bordering on pain on the glans of the penis. When that is the case, the man may withdraw and pull away from his wife, leaving her feeling somewhat rejected. If this is true for you, it is important that you tell your wife about this sensitivity and find a way to continue holding and affirming her without penile contact.

It is not uncommon for men to feel very relaxed and fall asleep quickly after an orgasm. This will often frustrate the woman who is coming down off her arousal more slowly and is looking for a time of intimacy through conversation and touch.

If stimulation is not continued after a woman has an orgasm, her body returns to its prestimulated, uncongested, relaxed state within a few moments. This is especially true if she has experienced a satisfying orgasm. If the woman has been aroused but not experienced release, she may feel the tension or the engorgement for an extended period of time after the sexual experience. When there has been no orgasmic release, or only partial release through a mild orgasm, the arousal dissipates slowly, often taking several hours. This can be a frustrating experience for the woman, sometimes causing involuntary crying, which then provides the release for her.

From the physiological perspective, we understand this crying as the body's way of bringing back parasympathetic-nervous-system dominance, which helps the woman relax. Unfortunately, the husband may interpret crying as a rejection or criticism of him; as a result, he may turn away, blaming himself or feeling anger toward his wife. The resolution phase can be a time of affection and intimacy, whether or not the woman has experienced an orgasm—and especially when she has not. When a couple realizes this, their resolution time can be a warm and affirming experience, despite the lack of fulfillment.

The woman's clitoris returns to its normal position in five to ten seconds and to its normal size five to ten minutes after an orgasm. It takes about the same time for the labia minora and labia majora to return to their normal size, position, and color. The uterus drops back into its unaroused position relatively quickly after orgasm. When the woman has not had orgasm, it may take longer for the uterus to reposition itself, and this may cause lower back pain. The vaginal wall collapses within five to eight minutes, while the congestion in the outer third of the vagina disappears in seconds.

In the resolution phase, you have the opportunity to confirm your intimacy regardless of the physical fulfillment that has been experienced. Some couples like to fall asleep together, whereas others like to be very active after a fulfilling sexual experience. One couple liked to get up and jog after a sexual experience. It is vitally important that you talk about your uniqueness in all four phases rather than expecting that you will fit the standard response pattern as it has been defined. To help you in understanding your body and its responses, proceed with utilizing the following pages to graph your response(s) and to compare your graph(s) with what has been described as typical for men and for women.

COMMUNICATION FOCUS EXERCISE 4
Graphing Your Sexual Response Pattern

1. You may make copies of the Graphing Your Sexual Response form on page 88. Each of you use a copy to draw one or more graph lines that represent how you respond or have responded through any form of stimulation. You may want to draw one line to represent your response to self-stimulation, one to represent manual or oral stimulation by your spouse, and one to represent intercourse. On your graph, lines may represent how you respond today and how you've responded at different times in the past.

2. On the graph(s) you drew, each of you should note any points of difficulty that occur for you repeatedly. Use the detailed graph for men (page 74) and the one for women (page 75) to identify these points. For example, if you ejaculate prematurely or if you inhibit your orgasmic response, note what is happening when the problem arises—what is happening inside of you and between the two of you.

3. Share your graphs with each other using the Communication Format beginning on page 16. Go over all the details you circled or checked on the Sexual Response Pattern (Figures 7.7 and 7.8) and the graphs you drew and problem areas you described. You may add to each other's graph any response that the other had observed that you hadn't noted.

4. Talk about what you learned about each other that was new.

GRAPHING YOUR SEXUAL RESPONSE

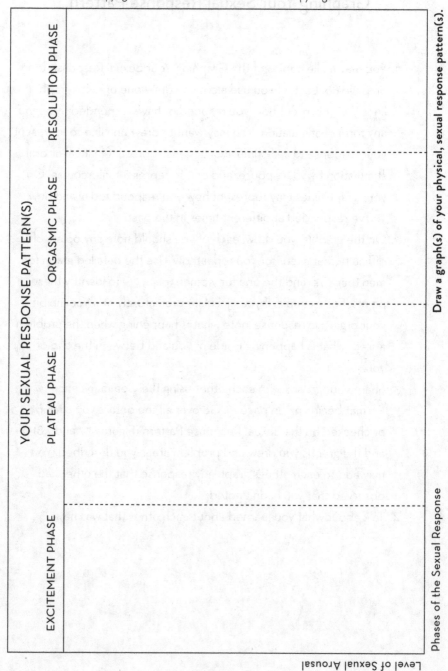

YOUR SEXUAL RESPONSE PATTERN(S)

EXCITEMENT PHASE | PLATEAU PHASE | ORGASMIC PHASE | RESOLUTION PHASE

Draw a graph(s) of your physical, sexual response pattern(s).

Phases of the Sexual Response

Level of Sexual Arousal

EIGHT

But Sex Doesn't Just Happen

S ex does not happen to us. Yes, sexual responsiveness is involuntary, but sexual behaviors are ours to choose to pursue or avoid. As it happens in the movies or media, sex is a "zap" response. Two people's eyes meet across a crowded room. Electrical connections zap between them, and before they know it, they are passionately making love. No wonder 85 percent of the time adolescents and single adults begin their sexual lives outside of marriage without any intention to do so! The passion of the moment controls them. No wonder the biggest sexual barrier facing young married couples today is less and less sex. They are waiting for the zap, rather than taking responsibility to make sex happen.

THE EMOTIONAL-RELATIONAL DIMENSIONS
OF THE SEXUAL EXPERIENCE

How do your sex lives flourish once you are married? When you can have sex with each other whenever you want to and the newness of sexual discovery is over, how can you each be responsible and committed to nurture the most intimate relationship of your lives?

In chapter 5, we showed you how the sexual relationship between a husband and wife is used throughout Scripture as a symbol of how God relates to his people. When your relationship with God was new, you probably had an eagerness to connect with him through prayer and Bible reading. And even after many years, that eagerness may be renewed from time to time, but most of us have to be disciplined and responsible to nurture our relationships with God. It doesn't just happen. Similarly, each spouse is responsible to nurture the sexual relationship in your marriage. To do that, it is helpful to understand the emotional-relational dimensions of the sexual experience and how that is similar to becoming one with God.

Sexual Desire

Sexual desire is the urge to be touched, to be close, or the urge for sexual arousal, orgasm, or intercourse. Sexual desire is God-given and innate in everyone, even though that desire is experienced differently by different people and may be totally blocked in some people.

Similarly, the Bible teaches us that mankind seeks union with God, even though sin blocks that urge for many. David expressed this in Psalm 51:1–2: "Be gracious to me, O God, according to Your lovingkindness; According to the greatness of Your compassion blot out my transgressions. Wash me thoroughly from my iniquity." Even so, God desires us. "For thus says the Lord GOD, 'Behold, I Myself will search for My sheep and seek them out'" (Ezek. 34:11).

When desire is mutual—God for man and man for God, husband for wife and wife for husband—"becoming one" is inevitable. However, God's desire for man is the only consistent, reliable ingredient in this format. We are controlled by our feelings; thus our desire for God is affected by how we feel just as our sexual desire for one another is controlled by how we feel.

Automatic and spontaneous. For some people, sexual interest has a very natural ebb and flow throughout life that may occur spontaneously and automatically. Their desire may surface somewhat regularly according to the buildup of sexual energy, or it may occur as they exercise or pamper their bodies. It may be set off by a certain expression, look, activity, or talent or by seeing or touching each other. Sexual desire may get started by something sensuous like music, the sound of ocean waves, a romantic setting, a scent, a story, or a picture.

Conditional. Others do not seem to have that automatic awareness of sexual desires, interests, or needs. They need certain conditions to make them aware of those urges. You become aware of your sexual urges when you are away from the pressures of your life—your work, your children, or social obligations.

Having special time for each other may trigger your sexual desire: a private time at home in your bedroom, a special meal together, a talk time, or a time of physical, emotional, or spiritual connection.

There may be very specific behaviors that ignite your sexual urges, actions you do yourself or behaviors you need from your spouse. You may need a hug, a kiss, help with the chores, or any action that says, "I care about you." Or you may need to take time to prepare yourself mentally by thinking about being together sexually or reading something romantic. Even reading the Song of Solomon may get you interested. When you need a specific behavior from your spouse to get yourself interested in sex, getting what you need becomes more complicated. We believe sex works best in all dimensions when each of you takes responsibility for your own needs. But when you have a need that requires the action of your spouse, you should communicate your need. Avoid the game of thinking, *If he loves me, he'll know what I need. I've told him before, so he should remember. If I have to tell him, it won't work.* If you convince yourself it won't work, it surely won't. So take responsibility to communicate clearly, openly, and consistently what is needed to activate your sexual urges.

Initiation

Acting on your sexual desire with each other is initiation. Just as initiation may begin with one of you expressing your desire for another, God has also initiated our union with him by giving us his Son, Jesus Christ, as a mediator so we can connect with him. That is, we have access into God's presence through Christ. Revelation 3:20 encourages us in this: "Behold, I stand at the door and knock; if anyone hears My voice and opens the door, I will come in to him and will dine with him, and he with Me."

Initiating sexual contact between a husband and wife may occur before any arousal or as the result of already being "turned on" or sexually excited. Initiation may be the expression of your desire to just be close and warm, or it may be intense sexual play leading to intercourse and release. It may grow mutually between the spouses, or it may come from one spouse. For example, physical contact like a hug, a kiss, or crawling into bed together may lead to mutually pursuing further sexual activity. Spending time working, playing, or just being together may spark desire that triggers mutual pursuit of sexual behavior.

More often initiation occurs when one sexually desirous spouse makes a request or suggestion to the other. This interest may be communicated in words, by reaching out physically, or more subtly. The verbal message may be a direct invitation or a more symbolic message. The physical approach works great if it is positive for both. If one spouse feels that hugs or kisses are given only to "get sex," that can lead to a feeling of being used rather than being loved. Physical initiation must be an expression of care and connection with each other without a demand from one spouse to the other. Subtle initiation can be fun if the other one catches the message. If the message is so subtle that it doesn't communicate and engage the other person, then it can be disappointing to the initiator. Preparing one's body, the setting, or a special treat for the other are all possible subtle ways to initiate sex.

Initiation flows best and causes the least amount of tension when both spouses are free to express their desires without putting pressure on the other to respond. If the other spouse does not feel open to a sexual encounter, a counteroffer is always more positive than a rejecting no. There are many other options than no. A positive response might be, "That's not where I am right now, but how about . . ." The possibilities could include a later time, a different physical activity such as pleasuring rather than intercourse, or a different focus such as pleasuring one spouse but not engaging in a total mutual experience.

Variation and open communication without demand are essential to the spontaneous ongoing expression of each spouse's desire to have physical closeness.

Pleasuring

Becoming one—totally—takes time to mesh your worlds, communicate with each other, and delight in the stimulation of each other's bodies.

Likewise, if we are to develop oneness with God, we must take time to know him and to share ourselves openly and freely with him. We need to learn to bring him into our world. That takes time for communication with him through prayer and reading the Bible. Sometimes that will happen because we feel the urge, but many times it requires discipline to schedule the time. Similarly, your physical pleasuring will last a lifetime if you schedule quality time to enjoy each other.

Meshing. Pleasuring begins with the process of getting into each other's world, bringing together your emotions, spirits, sensations, and bodies. Talking, bathing, reading, praying, or touching are all ways of connecting. Meshing will occur almost automatically when you spend time together; it takes more effort if your worlds are separate and consuming.

Communicating. Two types of communication are necessary to enjoy pleasuring: verbal and nonverbal. Talking about what you like, don't like, or would like to be different should be done apart from the actual sexual encounter. The communication skills described in chapter 3 will help you achieve this verbal interaction. Verbal messages that can be shared during sex are responses to indicate your enjoyment and positive invitations of the touch you would enjoy. Nonverbal communication lets you signal each other during sex without interrupting the flow of the pleasure. These nonverbal signals can be taught, talked about, and decided on apart from the sexual experience. Assignments included in the chapters devoted to sexual retraining will help you learn to guide each other's hands, give prearranged signals, and use body action to communicate the touch you desire.

Stimulating. Delighting in the erotic touching of each other's bodies is vital to sexual arousal and release and is an important part of pleasuring. As touching becomes stimulating, it changes from just relaxing to a more specifically arousing activity. Many times when there are barriers in the sexual relationship, touching is no longer enjoyable. Sexual anxiety has set in.

Sexual anxiety can occur because of fear of failure, demand for performance, fear of not pleasing one's spouse, or a combination of these factors. Sexual anxiety operates much like insomnia. The parasympathetic nervous system, the relaxed branch of the involuntary nervous system, must be dominant for the involuntary response of sexual arousal or sleep to occur. When a person is anxious, the sympathetic nervous system kicks in. This is the fight-or-flight mechanism that counters relaxation and getting turned on. Thus, anxiety interrupts sexual arousal. Women typically worry that they will not become aroused, that they will not have orgasm, or that they will not bring about the desired response in their husbands. Husbands' fears are similar. They fear they will be unable to get or keep an erection, that they will ejaculate too quickly, or that they will be unable to stimulate their wives effectively.

The *demand for performance* is closely tied with the fear of failure. Such a demand may come from your spouse or from yourself. It may be a demand from the man for the woman to be orgasmic, from the woman for the man to give her an orgasm, from the woman for the man to get and keep his erection or control his ejaculation, or from the man for the woman to get him erect. Demand also may come from internal expectations that you place on yourself. Even though the wife might not blame her husband for her orgasmic difficulty, he may believe he is not performing adequately if she is not orgasmic. As a result, the woman feels a need to be orgasmic so her husband will feel good about himself. The situation turns into a vicious circle.

When the need to please becomes tied up with fear of failure and demand for performance, it inhibits sexual freedom and enjoyment and keeps you from focusing on the good feelings. Consequently, the goal to please becomes counterproductive to actual pleasure. The person whose goal is to win approval by "doing well" usually feels like a failure because, ironically, trying to do well prevents doing well.

To distract yourself from sexual anxiety and focus on pleasure, we encourage you to take responsibility for your own sexual pleasure in your times together. This means:

1. You listen to your body's hunger for touch and go after that rather than expecting your spouse to figure out what you want.
2. You enjoy touching each other in ways that are pleasurable to you—you delight in each other's bodies.
3. You agree to let each other know if the other's enjoyment of your body feels negative so each can freely enjoy the experience without violating the other.

By following these suggestions, you can freely enjoy and delight in each other's bodies—this indeed is most pleasurable. This is similar to the central concept of the gospel—when we lose ourselves, we find ourselves. When we give up trying to please and totally lose ourselves to each other, the result is pleasing.

The touching-focus exercises described later in the sexual retraining chapters will distract you from sexual anxiety and retrain you to enjoy each other for the sake of pleasure. When the focus is on enjoying the stimulation rather than on producing arousal and release, there will not be a demand to respond, yet the response is likely to occur automatically.

One couple had such an extreme combination of fear of failure, performance demand, and excessive need to please that even the non-demand experiences became demands. The wife had an incredible fear of not being aroused and not enjoying the sexual experience. In response, the husband put unbelievable pressure on himself to be a good lover so that she would respond. In addition, his technical analysis—his spectatoring—of each sexual move created a feeling of demand from him for her to respond. In short, they both had a high need to please each other. So even before they started making love, they would go into spectator roles (i.e., watching and evaluating how they were doing rather than just enjoying the experience).

This situation had to be addressed in daily therapy sessions to keep tight control on all factors that might trigger the anxiety. It was important that the wife not become orgasmic too quickly because then she would feel the demand to analyze how it had happened, study the process, and try to repeat it. Whenever there is an attempt to re-create a positive sexual experience, demand ensues. Each experience must be allowed to evolve on its own. We had to try to teach the husband not to evaluate every move. For example, when the wife said she felt some sexual tingling during the self-stimulation exercises we had assigned, the husband's first response was, "Why can't she do that with me?" That kind of questioning had to be curtailed.

Being able to love each other and enjoy erotic touching without feeling the need to please, without demanding performance, and without fearing failure is vital to sexual responsiveness and to the spiritual bonding of two bodies united in holy matrimony.

Entry

Total sexual union is not necessary to enjoy total sexual fulfillment or the intimacy of bodily pleasure. When entry of the penis into the vagina *is* desired, it is best if that is initiated by the woman since it is her body that is being entered. This follows the example of our loving God, who waits for us to invite him into our lives; he never demands entry into our worlds, nor does he push himself upon us. He waits for our invitation. We all perceive a threat and experience violation when someone enters our "territory" without being invited. The man does not need to pressure himself to know when the woman is ready for entry, nor should the woman have to worry that he is going to want entry before she's ready. Ideally, she will let him know when she is ready.

Enjoying the Process

Entry of the penis into the vagina does not have to be the beginning of the end. When the focus is on pleasuring rather than climax, there can be a time of resting together and enjoying the penetration of the penis into the vagina without thrusting. There can be freedom to withdraw, reenter, and "play around," allowing the turned-on feelings to ebb and flow in intensity. There can be an abandonment of fears and inhibitions so you are free to intensify the heavy breathing, rhythmic movements, noises, and grimaces that are a natural part of sexual pleasure.

When you feel free to enjoy sex totally, the moods of your sexual experiences can vary from tenderness to passion or to fun and games. Sometimes the mood may be intensely erotic and at other times simply functional—a pleasurable way to meet your physical needs.

Letting Go

When you're not controlled or inhibited, letting go will occur somewhere in the process of lovemaking. Letting go is obvious in men, but many women struggle to let go and are confused about whether they really have. To help women understand the sensation of letting go, it helps to describe it like a pelvic sneeze. The buildup of tension in the pelvis is due to vasocongestion—blood and fluid filling the genitals—just like the nasal passages are congested before a sneeze. There is that tingling sensation both before a sneeze and before an orgasm. That is followed by the contractions in the passageways that release the tension and fullness—that's an orgasm!

Affirmation

When you allow yourselves to be vulnerable and let go sexually—to be out of control and release all of your sexual intensity with each other—there is a deep sense of warmth, satisfaction, and fulfillment.

Similarly, when we truly relinquish control and allow ourselves to be vulnerable to God and give him control, we receive deep peace and contentment.

The affirmation of shared sexual fulfillment is similar to the affirmation we experience when we have entered the presence of God, given ourselves freely, and felt oneness with him.

The closeness you feel when you have allowed yourselves to be open and vulnerable with each other sexually is a very important time of sharing. When you have not been able to let go of all the intensity that builds up during sexual arousal, you may feel tense or frustrated or disappointed. You may feel like crying. Crying is the body's natural way of releasing the tension buildup, so share the closeness of the crying. Hold each other rather than pulling away. Affirm your love, care, and commitment to each other.

NINE

Mutual Respect Is Absolutely Essential

M utual respect honors each other's sexuality as a precious gift from God. It is never ours to take from one another. Rather, our sexuality is a gift to be shared by mutual consent (within the boundaries of biblical standards). In this sense our sexuality might be compared to an inheritance.

Joyce lost both her parents within a year of each other. Over the year that followed, Joyce received some memorable items from her parents' estate. It was a joy for her to share those mementos with Cliff and the children; the sharing was a joy for all of them. However, if Cliff or the children had assumed a right to have any of the items from the inheritance, conflict, tension, and even violation might have resulted.

When respect for one's sexuality has been violated or neglected, deep emotional conflict and relational tension result. Education alone will not correct these hurts or provide the framework to sexual pleasure. It will only be the *door* to identifying your need for professional help to heal the emotional wounds of that neglect or violation. When healing has occurred, then the retraining process can lead to the fullest sexual pleasure available to you. Even then, however, the scars of those healed wounds may limit your full potential for sexual enjoyment that God intended for you.

EMOTIONAL WOUNDS

Emotional barriers and conflicts are the source of sexual dysfunction. These emotional factors keep individuals from freely abandoning themselves to the sexual experience and thus interfere with the creatively designed sexual response cycle.

Unconscious Avoidance

Many of God's sexual beings have never allowed themselves the joy of delighting in each other's bodies as did the lovers described in the Song of Solomon. They unconsciously avoid the inevitability of passionate eroticism by being obsessed with the tasks of life, pulling away from effective stimulation, or stopping sexual arousal with mundane thoughts of household chores or business contracts.

Why would some individuals exert so much energy to fight what could come so naturally and then work so hard to try to get the very result they are unconsciously avoiding?

Guilt. Whether it is authentic or inauthentic, guilt is one of the arousal stoppers. Authentic guilt occurs when individuals have engaged in or are engaging in sexual behaviors that are in conflict with the marriage relationship and Christian values. These behaviors include extramarital affairs, pornography, sexual addictions, or other illicit sexual actions. If these behaviors have not been confessed, forgiven, and brought under control, these men and women avoid sexual eroticism with their spouses.

Unfortunately, inauthentic guilt produces the same result. Even though no biblical principle or marriage commitment has been violated, the feelings of inauthentic guilt are as powerful as if there had been violation. Possible sources of this internally created guilt are previous sexual abuse and rigid antisex teaching, either religious or moral. A woman who comes for therapy to learn to be orgasmic may stop the process because she feels uncomfortable with the results. One woman who had been sexually abused by her stepfather had her first orgasm after our third session. Rather than reporting joy that she had achieved such rapid results, she said, "I never want that to happen again." She clearly stated that she did not like being that way even though she had come to therapy to be able to be orgasmic.

One young man who had never ejaculated would stop his wife when she started to intensely stimulate his penis. He had come to therapy to learn to be able to ejaculate with his wife. Stimulation of the penis was needed to bring ejaculation, but those sensations were connected with past violation and guilt for him. Many women will not allow the pleasurable process of sexual interaction. They will rush their husbands quickly to intercourse and ejaculation because the erotic sensations are associated with past abuse or past promiscuous relationships.

The most tenacious avoiders of any type of sexual interaction are Adult Children of Alcoholics (ACA), as well as men and women from emotionally tumultuous homes. As young children, they had no firm boundaries to protect their developing sexuality from emotional violation, so they internalized the need to be in control. As adults, they need order and control in all dimensions of their lives, and sex is no exception. It simply causes more havoc because the control affects their spouses. The adult child of an alcoholic typically resists sex with more vehemence than any other individual who lacks sexual desire. The confusion for the spouse is great, especially for the husband of an ACA wife. When she gives in to sexual activity and her bodily arousal finally "kicks in," she becomes intensely aroused and has an orgasm; then she immediately shuts down, does not want to be close, and may even feel badly about what just happened.

The brick wall that may have taken a month of approaching and a half hour of stimulation to carefully break down piece by piece can reconstruct itself within minutes. It is like a slapstick-comedy movie running at high speed with scenes of brick and mortar being frantically laid. The fear of being out of control is the mortar that holds the bricks together. In contrast to the speed with which the wall goes up, the scenes of tediously chiseling the mortar away and removing the bricks one by one occur in slow motion, emphasizing the painstaking process.

Anger. This is another form of unconscious avoidance. In her book *How to Make Love to the Same Person for the Rest of Your Life and Still Love It*, Dagmar O'Connor recommends that couples learn how to "make anger" as well as love. She suggests having a Ping-Pong-ball fight (throwing the balls at each other), a pillow fight in the nude, or other creative methods to release current anger with each other.[1]

But deeper anger is not that easily defused. Sometimes anger from the past is displaced on the spouse. Other times there is long-term marital tension. One of the hardest angers to undo is the resentment of having had to get married because of pregnancy. Often each spouse blames the other, and neither feels he or she chose the other—or was chosen.

When deep, unresolved anger inhibits the sexual process, Dr. Neil Warren's book *Make Anger Your Ally: Harnessing One of Your Most Powerful Emotions* is highly recommended. This book presents a most helpful program for assessing anger and then making the emotions of anger work for you, rather than using them against oneself and others.[2]

Lack of self-worth and a poor body image. These factors may also prevent intimacy with the opposite sex. These barriers may not only block sexual desire within marriage, they may actually keep someone from marrying. Women, particularly, who have not accepted themselves will sabotage the development of a marriageable relationship (e.g., by weight gain), even though they consciously want the intimacy of marriage more than anything. Others may marry, but then they inhibit the sexual experience because they do not feel worthy of their husbands' attention or cannot believe that their husbands could be attracted to them.

Whether the source of unconscious avoidance is guilt, anger, fear of being out of control, or lack of self-worth, professional counseling intervention may be necessary to resolve the inner conflicts.

Blocked Erotic Feelings (Conscious Avoidance)

Sometimes the blocking of eroticism may not be unconscious; it may be deliberate. The woman who came to us to learn to be orgasmic and was orgasmic following the third session then decided she did not want that to happen again. She changed from an unconscious avoider to a deliberate limiter of potentially arousing activities.

Both men and women choose to block erotic feelings for a number of reasons. They may not want to kiss passionately or be stimulated genitally, but most often they are not sure why. They only know that it makes them *uncomfortable.* Other times, there is a clear belief that eroticism is wrong. One devout Christian man said that he could not imagine the Song of Solomon being in the Bible. Eroticism may be avoided because of fear of emotional or physical pain. Women who have pain during intercourse may refuse to engage in other stimulating activities for fear that those activities will lead to intercourse. At times, both men and women do not allow themselves the vulnerability of intense sexual arousal with their spouses for fear of not being handled tenderly after sharing such intensity. The lack of mutual respect occurs after the sexual event.

A *physical reason* for some women to block intense arousal may be the sensation of having to urinate. A small percentage of women have a flooding response, or female ejaculation, when they are orgasmic. As these women become intensely aroused, the sensation that they are going to urinate if the stimulation is continued causes many of them to inhibit the orgasmic response. Dr. Kolodny of the Masters and Johnson Institute reported to us a number of years ago that the physician at the institute had catheterized women with this response so that their urinary bladders were empty. The women were then stimulated to an orgasmic response by their husbands. The fluid released was collected and examined. It was not urine in chemical composition or in appearance, even though it came from the urinary bladder.

A. K. Ladas, B. Whipple, and I. D. Perry discussed the phenomenon of female ejaculation in their book *The G-Spot.*[3] Women with this sensation are encouraged to read this book and discuss with their husbands the possibility of a fluid release. Then they should protect the bed and "go for it" to see what happens. Many times the result is an intense orgasm.

Conscious blocking of sexual feelings is sometimes used by Christian singles *to control sexual behavior* before marriage. Unfortunately, when the behavior is controlled by shutting out the feelings rather than through decision making about behavior and control of external circumstances, the feelings do not automatically turn on again with the words "I do."

Past Traumatic Experience

Childhood sexual molestation is the most commonly discussed past violation of mutual respect that leaves a scar on the adult's sexual wholeness. When sexual feelings are stimulated in a child or adolescent by an older person, the child is left confused. Behaviors that are designed to be pleasurable become associated with fear, guilt, and pain. If the violator is a family member, trust is betrayed and a sense of aloneness results.

Many times the abuse is not remembered, but there is a pattern that is typical of those who were abused as children. These children have a heightened awareness of sexuality that leads to active sexual expression—maybe even promiscuity—before marriage, then shuts off as the person moves toward marriage, or shortly after marriage. Once sexuality is expected or demanded, there is no interest; there may even be aversions or panic reactions to specific activities. A woman may not be able to allow her husband to touch her breasts or stimulate her genitals. Or she may be unable to look at or touch his genitals. The aversion is an indication of the abusive behavior that occurred in the past.

Witnessing explicit sexual activity during childhood can have the same effect as actually being sexually abused. This is one of the hazards of Internet pornography. Respect for the child's sexuality is neglected. Sexual awareness beyond developmental readiness is elicited and may be harmful.

Severe parental reaction to peer exploration or self-stimulation can also function as a past trauma. Such reaction violates the child's natural, developmental sexual curiosity. In the same way, when an older sibling acts out sexually and maybe even becomes pregnant, the turmoil in the home may serve as a traumatic event for the younger observer. Being determined that this will never happen to him or her, this younger child may repress sexual feelings and expressions.

Many parents do not realize that *spankings on a bare bottom,* especially after age eight or nine, will often arouse the involuntary response of erection in boys and vaginal lubrication in girls. The pairing of sexual arousal with the pain of the spanking causes conflict about sexuality similarly to abuse.

Traumatic events of adolescence and young adulthood may have violated respect for the person's sexuality. Premarital sex associated with force or guilt leaves the person with intense conflict. Date rape often is not clearly perceived by either party as rape because there may have been sex play and arousal that led to entry of the penis into the vagina. The female may have verbally resisted while her body gave mixed messages. One young woman reported that she and her date had been engaging in heavy petting when all of a sudden he shifted positions and pushed his penis into her vagina. She pushed him out just as fast as he had entered, yet ten years later, she was unable to consummate her marriage because of vaginismus (the involuntary closing of the muscle controlling the opening of the vagina).

Even a *medical examination of the genitals* of an adolescent or young adult may be traumatic. We beg physicians: when you need to genitally examine or treat a young woman, use extreme caution and extraordinary sensitivity. Many hours and thousands of dollars are spent undoing the trauma of urinary catheterizations or gynecological examinations. We have heard many horror stories. One story was told about a thirteen-year-old girl (who at the time was twenty-six years old with an eight-year unconsummated marriage) who was catheterized by a male physician who laughed at and belittled her when she reacted with fear and started crying. Another story described a nineteen-year-old woman who had difficulty relaxing for a vaginal exam. The doctor, unable to insert the speculum in her vagina, forced it in so violently that tearing and bleeding resulted—which had to be treated three weeks later by another physician. Insensitive treatment by a physician under the clout of medical necessity can be as traumatizing as rape.

The Need for Guilt and Risk

Either past trauma or rigid antisex teaching can be the stimulus that conditions a person to need guilt or risk in order to become aroused. Masturbation associated with guilt and the risk of being caught is the most common source. For this reason, we caution parents not to teach against masturbation. Anti-masturbation teaching does not stop the activity; it only connects sexual pleasure with the "hooking" adrenaline rush that accompanies the anxiety of doing something wrong. Sexual response is easily conditioned in a positive or negative direction. Adrenaline hype adds so much intensity to sexual response that even if the adrenaline comes from doing wrong, it hooks us. Then, when sex is right and of God in marriage, we cannot enjoy it. We have become dependent on the adrenaline-guilt connection.

Destructive Relationship Patterns

A destructive relationship pattern that we commonly see in our practice is the man *who insists on sex and the woman who resists.* Clarence and Maria, the couple whose story we shared in the introduction, were examples of this pattern. The problem was corrected through sexual retraining but needed our professional involvement. Self-help would have been unproductive because both saw Maria as the problem, while Clarence was the one who actually needed to change.

In this pattern, the woman comes to the marriage with sexual imma-turity or some sexual hesitation. The husband comes feeling unsure of himself in relation to women. Perhaps he lacked adequate affirmation from his mother, had little or no junior-high-level interaction with girls, or had limited dating experience. Consequently, his wife's hesitancy about sex causes him to worry about his masculinity. Her inhibitions—her inability to initiate sex, to be responsive sexually, or to have sex when he wanted to—gave him deep feelings of inadequacy.

These feelings in the husband are communicated to the wife as persistent sexual neediness. As a result, she feels that all he can think of is sex, and he is convinced that she never wants anything to do with sex, even though there is usually a flickering desire that could be kindled with love and warm wooing rather than with anxious demanding. The husband has usually read and encouraged his wife to read every book available on the subject of sex. He is usually the one who seeks our help; she may participate because of his demand. Usually she is so fed up with sex she does not want to have anything to do with a sexual therapist or with this sexual retraining process.

The husband in this pattern needs to be helped to see his power in the situation and how his neediness thwarts the very response he so desires from his wife. Her barriers may or may not need to be worked on in therapy; they may become insignificant as the husband is able to disconnect his need for sexual release from his sense of self-worth and emotional stability.

Another problem occurs when one spouse is *a second-choice mate.* For example, the wife was engaged before and her fiancé was killed, or he broke the engagement. She is now married to her second choice, and the passion just is not there.

This relationship is not emotionally destructive. In fact, it may be a very warm, caring relationship. But it is platonic, and this is sexually destructive. The emotional attachment to the previous lover has to be resolved before the sexual retraining process will be effective in building sexual attachment in the current relationship.

Another destructive relationship pattern is difficult to describe with words. Both spouses bring equal baggage into this dilemma. The one spouse, husband or wife, comes to the marriage with *limited capacity to express emotions and sexuality.* The other spouse is quite the opposite, very verbal, emotional, and sexual, yet he or she brings a serious *emotional dysfunction* that is often not obvious to either of them because the verbal one's ability to articulate the problem of the other is so dominant. Self-help sexual retraining will be impossible without first reversing this destructive pattern because the dominant one will so destructively manage the program, unconsciously sabotaging the very results he or she desires by constantly pointing out the other's inadequacies. Even a therapist may have difficulty breaking this pattern. We have had several "dropouts" because the verbal one could not accept his or her part in the difficulty and felt hurt and accused by us.

Relationship Barriers

Other relationship issues may not be as destructive or as patterned, but they clearly must be resolved before sexual pleasure can be pursued.

Emotional openness is a necessity, but it can also be a barrier. Vulnerability and self-disclosure are absolutely essential for sexual functioning. There is little possibility of sexual openness without the capacity to share one's dreams and hopes, fears, insecurities, inadequacies, strengths, and weaknesses. Emotional nakedness is a prerequisite for physical nakedness, a fact that is distorted in current culture. Very often, couples begin a relationship with sexual intimacy—that is, with sexual nakedness—without being emotionally and personally vulnerable. The sexual revolution focused on being naked with each other, but physical nakedness alone brings very shallow fulfillment. True sexuality blossoms only when it is preceded by the communication, openness, and trust that grows out of a genuinely intimate relationship.

If open communication is barely possible for the two of you, sexual retraining will be extremely difficult. If you were able to work through the communication process described in chapter 3 and are willing to share your activities, thoughts, and feelings, it may be possible for you to break through the sexual barriers with the help of effective communication. You may never have learned how to share openly. Your homes may have been functional rather than communicative. You may have chosen a partner who also does not communicate, or you may have continually sabotaged your intimacy due to lack of ability or desire to communicate.

When the ability to communicate openly has been difficult, you may need the help of a professional to open those doors of emotional sharing before sexual retraining will work for you.

On the other hand, emotional openness can also be destructive to a marriage. We are referring to the unbridled anger and venom or hurtful openness that sometimes develop either because of what each individual brought into the marriage or because of what has happened between the two in the marriage. If this destructive openness springs from deep pain or long-term frustration within the relationship, more intense work with the help of a counselor will be needed.

Don and Virginia had been in marital counseling for a year and a half when they came to us for sexual therapy. Don believed that resolving their sexual problems would help them avoid the stress in their marriage. After attempting to explore that hypothesis, we quickly discovered that the amount of distrust and anger between them made it impossible to resolve their sexual issues. The anger—even rage—and rejection between them was completely debilitating. Twenty-five years of deeply scarred hurts virtually blocked all possibility of working on the sexual issues until there was some resolution of their bitterness.

Sexual pleasure may be impossible if your relationship has evolved to the point where much of the communication is penetratingly harsh and cutting. The starting focus might need to be on resolving those emotional issues to bring you to the point of positive emotional openness and trust.

Lack of trust. Trust between the husband and wife is a natural prerequisite to sexual intimacy and is a consequence of effective communication and emotional openness. This is not merely the basic trust that one's husband or wife is sexually faithful—that is an obvious and necessary level of trust. The trust that is essential to effective sexual interaction involves believing that each spouse has the other's interests at heart.

Trust at this level deals with safety. Feeling safe with another person makes it easier to be open with him or her. Being naked with someone, whether physically or emotionally, demands a sense of confidence that says the other person will not take advantage of us if we are exposed. This kind of trust requires a safe history that allows the person to say, "I can be fully myself with this person without being hurt in response. In fact, the more I am myself, the closer we become, and the more fulfilled I feel." Mutual trust is necessary to allow sexual intimacy to evolve.

Lack of intimacy. Everything that makes a marriage run smoothly falls under the category of intimacy: communication, interests, activities, finances, spiritual connection, parenting, household management, social life, and of course, sex. In the context of a lifelong commitment, intimacy sets marriage apart from all other relationships. A marriage without intimacy is like a car that is resting on blocks in the backyard. It is a car, but it no longer serves the function for which it was designed. A marriage without intimacy is technically still a marriage, but it does not fulfill its original purpose.

Lack of respect. Although it is necessary for the man to respect his wife, it seems even more important for the husband to be worthy of the wife's respect. Respect is that sense of "looking up to" or holding the other person in high esteem and considering that person worthy. It might be lacking for either of you because of work or eating habits, drinking habits, parenting responses, backgrounds, or a great variety of other reasons.

Sometimes lack of respect may distract from sexual pleasure. The process of sexual retraining may deal with this issue. You may use the sexual assignments described in the sexual retraining chapters to understand loss of respect and to build respect for each other.

Rejection. Feeling rejected by your spouse in other areas of intimacy or commitment may make sexual response difficult. If your spouse has violated the spoken or unspoken contract, your sexual responsiveness to him or her may be difficult or even undesired.

Power struggle. The need for control interferes with sexual pleasure. The sexual relationship is designed to be physically, emotionally, and spiritually mutual. When mutuality is violated by one partner's need to be dominant, sexual pleasure will not flow.

SEXUAL VERSUS RELATIONAL ISSUES

If you are struggling sexually, your sexual barrier is either primary or secondary, depending on whether it is the main dilemma or a symptom of a troubled relationship. If the sexual difficulty is secondary to a troubled relationship, the marital problems will need to be worked on first. Then, after the marital issues are corrected, the sexual problems can be addressed.

Ana and Haig sought our help several years ago for what they defined as "Haig's sexual problem"—erectile dysfunction. After the initial interview, it was clear that even though Haig had "sown his wild oats" in the early years of their marriage, he was now a faithful husband. It was also clear that as Ana's star had risen in the corporate world, she had allowed all of her natural dominating and controlling behavior to come into her marriage. As she had become more aggressive, Haig had become more passive.

Before any work could begin on the sexual problem, they had to focus on changing their pattern of interaction. And even after their marriage improved, Haig continued to avoid sex for fear of having difficulty with an erection. At this point, sexual therapy was initiated. The marriage needed both the fuel of a working, intimate relationship and the oil of a satisfying sexual relationship.

How important is sex in a marriage? A simple answer is that, when marriage is compared with an automobile, sex is to the marriage what oil is to the combustion engine. At least a little oil is necessary to keep the engine running—without sex, one's marriage engine will eventually break down.

When the sexual dimension is flowing naturally and each spouse is fulfilled, sex is vital but encompasses only a small percentage of the relationship. The more sexual problems there are, however, the larger sex looms. By the time most couples seek help for their sexual dilemmas, those problems seem to engulf at least 80 percent of the relationship and may be the only issue one or both spouses can think or talk about. The sexual problems have grown so large they have become the couple's primary focus.

Even though the sexual dimension of your marriage needs to be taken very seriously, it must be kept in proper perspective. Sex is not everything! The oil level of the car might be just fine, but without fuel and a full complement of working parts, the car just sits there. So the other dimensions of your relationship must be in order before you begin the retraining process.

Although sexual retraining may be necessary to lubricate your marriage, at least minimal levels of positive relationship patterns, emotional openness, trust, intimacy, and enjoyment of each other are necessary to fuel the marriage.

In summary, when respect has been neglected or violated in one's developmental years, emotional wounds will be present that need to be healed before pursuing the sexual retraining process. Likewise, when respect has been neglected or violated in the marriage relationship, marital healing will be necessary in order to effectively embark on the sexual retraining process described in the next section.

PART THREE

SEXUAL RETRAINING

The Steps to Sexual Pleasure

TEN

What Is Sexual Retraining?

Sexual retraining is a systematic approach to dealing with unsatisfactory sexual experiences. Our sexual retraining process retrains you as a couple to communicate and behave with each other in a way that reduces demand, enhances pleasure, and facilitates the natural physiological sexual response.

According to Helen Singer Kaplan, "Sex therapy differs from other forms of treatment for sexual dysfunctions in two respects: first, its goals are essentially limited to the relief of the patient's sexual symptoms and second, it departs from traditional techniques by employing a combination of prescribed sexual experiences and psychotherapy."[1]

The sexual retraining process is primarily behavioral retraining consisting of sensate focus (touching) exercises, communication (talking) exercises, and teaching exercises. In the previous chapters you learned the facts about the human body and how it works, and about the sexual experience. As you progress through sexual training, you will continue to learn more about these facts and how to apply them, as well as learn more about each other. Your successful completion of the assigned behavioral exercises will determine the success of your sexual retraining. These assignments are to be completed while you are alone and relaxed as a couple. The more difficult it is for you to interact, the more precisely you need to follow the assignments. We have reworded Masters and Johnson's insights regarding the behavioral prescriptions and offer them for your consideration:

- They *alter* a previously destructive sexual system.
- They provide an opportunity for you to *learn* to make love in freer and more enjoyable ways.
- They help resolve sexual conflict by guiding you in previously avoided sexual experiences.
- They stir up unresolved conflicts and unconscious issues, which then can be resolved through effective communication or professional intervention.[2]

When deeper issues arise that require more time to resolve, be reassured that this is not a negative setback. Sexual retraining prescriptions require a capacity for intimacy and stability. You cannot hide underlying problems and still continue through the demanding interaction process. These problems are like toxic wastes that have been buried and now bubble up to the surface. If left underground, they pollute the system. It is better that they surface and be detoxified. You may need a professional helper to make that happen.

You may be saying, "But *I'm* not the one with the problem." In our practice, we treat the couple rather than the individual. Most of the time, both spouses have participated in the inadequate or destructive sexual interaction. But occasionally, we will work with one spouse more than the other. If one spouse brought dysfunction to the marriage, the other spouse may not have engaged in a way to perpetuate a disturbed system. Even in this case, most often both need to complete the shared experiences. The joint interaction is necessary to improve sexual functioning by breaking old habits and thereby bringing relief of the sexual distress. Whoever you define as the problem, the process works best when you pursue it mutually.

The goals of sexual retraining are to distract you from anxiety, remove demand, and eliminate negative or failure experiences and feelings. In addition to alleviating the negative symptoms, the process will also help you to build new patterns of sexual relating verbally and physically, build trust, develop the capacity for emotional and sexual intimacy, and acquire positive sexual attitudes.

The above goals are best met by: (1) becoming knowledgeable about your own and each other's bodies and how they function, (2) developing an awareness of and taking responsibility for your own needs and feelings, (3) learning to focus on sensations of pleasure without the demand to respond to or to please one's spouse, (4) opening effective communication within and about the sexual experience, and (5) recognizing that sex is not limited to intercourse and orgasm, but includes total enjoyment of each other's bodies, minds, and spirits.

In conclusion, sexual retraining does not train you to acquire a new skill. Instead, it aims to release your innate ability. Sexual retraining may include some development of effective techniques, but primarily, it is a process in which capacity for sexual responsiveness and enjoyment is enhanced as knowledge and self-awareness are gained, trust and intimacy are built, conflicts and barriers are broken down, and attitudes are enlightened.

The positive sexual attitudes that we hope to continue to instill during this sexual retraining process are that:

1. Sex is good and of God.
2. Sexual curiosity is natural.
3. Sexual responsiveness is automatic.
4. Sexual responsibility belongs to each person.
5. Mutual respect is essential in all sexual relationships.

ELEVEN

Assessing Your Sex Life

Your sexual data bank is loaded with emotion. Structure provides safety for expressing those emotions for both you and your spouse. Doors must be opened to allow accurate data to be revealed. On the other hand, you must be free to close doors if emotions are stirred that frighten you. Therefore, we will provide an established format to assist you in maintaining control as you open and close doors to self-disclosure.

Since this is a behavioral retraining program, exact, detailed, and explicit data are necessary. You cannot be retrained in new ways of sexual behavior unless you have an accurate picture of your present behavior. Each sexual behavior needs to be defined: how you kiss and what it is like for each of you, when entry occurs during intercourse, who initiates entry and how each of you would like that to change, and so on for all behaviors. Structured forms ensure that the two of you define and share *all* the vital information necessary to make changes in your current pattern of sexual functioning.

For example, when we began our practice as sexual therapists in the mid-1970s, we routinely asked clients about the history of their masturbatory practices. But we never asked them to describe *how* they stimulated themselves. That question became vital when we reached a roadblock with a couple who had an unconsummated marriage. The husband had masturbated to the point of ejaculation since he was twelve or thirteen years old. Since he had experienced an active masturbatory practice, we falsely assumed he could build on and transfer his ability to ejaculate to the process of consummating their marriage. However, we had missed important information—he masturbated by losing his erection and pushing his penis inside his body and rubbing it (making it almost like a clitoris), until he would ejaculate. Obviously, this procedure didn't work for intercourse with his wife. So he had to relearn arousal and release with a full, protruding penis before entry of the penis into the vagina was possible.

THE STRUCTURE

The forms that follow this section (beginning on page 121) provide the structure for assessing your sex life. You begin with the Physical History Form; take some time to complete it individually. Any of the forms used in this book may be duplicated for your personal use and convenience. You may wish to make copies so you each have a form. Or you may prefer to use an empty sheet of paper to respond to each question. When you have each completed the Physical History Form, schedule an uninterrupted block of time (one to two hours) to share and discuss your responses. It may take you less time if there are few physical issues. Use the Communication Format beginning on page 16 to effectively communicate with each other.

It may be necessary to see a physician for health issues. A urological examination is always necessary when either erectile dysfunction or inhibited ejaculation is the complaint. If genital infections are present, a medical consultation would be in order. The woman who experiences vaginal dryness or pain during intercourse, or who has not been able to consummate her marriage, needs to be examined by a pelvic floor physical therapist, a gynecologist, or perhaps a gynecological urologist who specializes in dyspareunia (sexual pain).

Hormonal studies may be warranted for a lack of sexual desire. A routine physical examination is recommended for both of you if you have not had one in the past year or two. If either of you is receiving medical treatment, your physician can help you understand how that treatment (especially medications) relates to your sexual barrier.

PHYSICAL HISTORY FORM

Age: _____ Height: _____ Weight: _____

1. HEALTH HISTORY (BIRTH TO PRESENT)

General Description	Illness and Treatments	Surgical Operations
Childhood		
Adolescence		
Adulthood		

Were you a bed wetter? Until what age? How was that handled?
(This may keep women from letting go orgasmically; it may cause men to
be anxious about letting go, which could lead to premature ejaculation
or ED.)

2. CURRENT PHYSICAL HEALTH

General Description	Illness and Treatments	Surgical Operations

Are any of these health issues affecting your sexual functioning? If you
aren't certain, determine this with your physician.

Specific Difficulties (Circle any of the following that apply to you; discuss their effects on your sex life with your spouse):

headaches	loss of appetite	depression
dizziness	bowel disturbances	anxiety
fainting spells	fatigue	fears
palpitations	insomnia	suicidal thoughts
stomach trouble	nightmares	alcoholism

Allergies and Special Diet/Food Restrictions:

List medications you are currently taking (check side effects online):

Substance Intake	No	Yes	Frequency	Amount	Type
Tobacco					
Alcohol					
Nonprescription Drugs					
Street Drugs (now or previously)					

List other illnesses or difficulties within your family of origin.

3. MENTAL HEALTH

Describe how you usually feel emotionally.

What mental health difficulties have been struggles for you?

Describe diagnoses and treatments.

4. MEDICAL TESTS

If you have been tested for any of the following, please list the results of those tests.

Thyroid function:

Hormonal levels:

Diabetes:

Cardiovascular disease:

Sexually transmitted disease:

Other:

5. REPRODUCTIVE AND SEXUAL HEALTH

Age of first orgasm/ejaculation:

Did this occur . . .

___ during sleep?

___ in response to self-stimulation (masturbation)?

___ in response to pornography?

___ during sexual play with another person?

Describe any difficulty or infection you have had or now have with your . . .

breasts

genitals

urethra, bladder, or urinary tract

rectum

(female) uterus, cervix, or vagina

(male) prostate gland

How were they treated?

Describe any medical procedure(s) that caused you discomfort as a child or adult.

List any sexually transmitted diseases (STDs) that you have had or currently have.

Genital Disease or STD	Dates of Infection	Treatments and Results

What form(s) of birth control do you use or have you used?

How did/do you respond? (Did you like it? Did it interfere?)

WOMEN
Menstrual History
Age of first period (menses):

What preparation had you received?

What was your reaction to your first period?

Are/were you regular?

Do/did you have pain?

Do/did you experience mood changes (PMS)?

Describe the effect this has/had on your sexual life.

Reproductive History

	Age	Describe	Complications
Pregnancies			
Deliveries			
Miscarriages			
Abortions			
Infertility Struggles			

BACKGROUND HISTORY

This form will gather information about what each of you brought to your sexual experience from your childhood and your past. Complete this individually, taking plenty of time to reflect on each question. Memories may keep coming to you that you can add to your initial responses. Set aside at least a two-hour block of uninterrupted time to share your responses with each other. Be sure to utilize the active listening skills of the Communication Format on page 16. If the information or hurt revealed is too big for the two of you to handle, seek professional help.

FAMILY HISTORY

Describe your family of origin.

Who lived in the household? Describe each person.

Relationship with your mother? Her attitude toward you?

Relationship with your father? His attitude toward you?

Relationship with each of your siblings?

Parents' relationship with each other?

How were you punished as a child?

What type of affection was expressed?

What was your general impression of your household?

SEXUAL DEVELOPMENT

What were your parents' attitudes toward sex?

What were the names used for genitals, urination, and defecation?

What is your first remembrance of your genitals?

Education About Sex

When were you educated about sex? By whom? What was the content of the education?

How were your sexual questions answered?

SEXUAL EXPERIMENTATION

Did you participate in exploratory play (playing doctor, house, etc.)? When? What was your reaction?

How did your peers influence your sexual experimentation (sex play, dirty jokes, pornography, etc.)?

What is your history of masturbation?

Describe your first experience: when, where, and source of stimulation.

What is your technique? What were you taught? Were there any reactions to your activity? How did you feel about it?

Describe any adolescent sexual activity.

Describe any homosexual play and/or fantasies.

Describe any compulsive habits that developed for you.

SEXUAL ABUSE

How was nudity handled in your home?

As a child, were you ever exposed to an adolescent's or adult's body in a way that made you feel uncomfortable?

Were you ever touched on your breasts or genitals by an adolescent or adult?

Were sexual or uncomfortable feelings ever stirred up in you in relation to an older person?

At what age did you first witness an explicit sexual scene in/on each of the following:

Magazines?

Movies?

Television?

Computer or other devices?

Describe any traumatic sexual experience(s).

DATING HISTORY

First date or romance?

Other dating relationships or romances?

Dating history with spouse?

SEXUAL HISTORY

Age of first sexual intercourse:

Describe the circumstances.

What was your reaction?

List negative sexual role models (men or women you believe negatively affected your development as a man or woman).

List positive sexual role models (men or women who you believe positively influenced who you are today as a man or a woman).

MARITAL HISTORY

Previous marriages (include wedding dates, length of marriages, and reasons for termination):

Current marriage (include wedding date and length of marriage):

Areas of compatibility:

Areas of tension:

Children:

RELIGIOUS HISTORY AS IT RELATES TO YOUR SEXUALITY

Home influence:

Church or group worship experience and influence:

Personal faith and beliefs:

PERSONAL DATA

What fearful or distressing experiences have you never shared?

How would you describe yourself?

How would you describe your spouse?

DEFINING YOUR SEXUAL EXPERIENCE

Completing this form is vital to the sexual retraining process and will give you a complete picture of your sexual behaviors. The structure of the form takes you through the emotional and relational experience of the sex act. Remember to use "I" statements rather than "you" statements. Again, write your responses individually and share them with each other in a two-hour uninterrupted block of time using the Communication Format on page 16.

DESIRE

What do you experience to indicate that you are sexually interested?

How would you like that to be different?

INITIATION

How do you express your desire for sexual intimacy?

Describe a typical process of initiation of sexual intercourse for you and your spouse. (Who does what and how does the other respond?)

When and where does this usually happen?

What in your process of initiation would you like to change?

PLEASURING AND STIMULATION

What does or what would help the two of you connect (bring your worlds together)?

How is kissing for you? Passionate? Full mouth?

What kind of touching is most enjoyable for you? (Describe the place, length of time, degree of pressure, etc.)

Total-body caressing?

Breast touching?

Genital stimulation?

What tends to stimulate you sexually (get you aroused—turned on)?

Any problems with getting or keeping aroused?

Do you like to talk or be talked to during sexual activity?

What inhibitions get in the way of the two of you freely enjoying the process of being together?

ENTRY

When in the process does entry occur, and who decides?

What, if anything, would you like to change about the process of entry?

LETTING GO

When does orgasm occur for you? For your spouse?

How would you like that to be different?

Describe your sensations of sexual release.

For the woman: If you do not experience release, identify when your feelings start to lessen and what is happening at that point.

For the man: If you do not feel in control of your ejaculation, describe when you ejaculate (at entry, how many minutes after entry, etc.), what triggers your ejaculation, and what forms of control you have tried.

AFFIRMING

What do you usually do and feel after intercourse?

What do you sense from your spouse?

How might you be more sensitive to each other's need for affirmation?

What sexual activities cause conflict between the two of you?

DEFINING YOUR SEXUAL BARRIER

Completing this form will give each of you time to individually sort out how you experience your dilemma. Sharing your responses with each other may clear up differences that neither of you realized. Use this structure to individually reflect on your difficulty and then listen carefully and actively clarify as you share with each other.

What particular sexual difficulty are you experiencing?

How is it affecting you?

How is it affecting your spouse?

When and how did the problem first develop?

What have you done about it (counseling, reading, self-help, etc.)?

Which one of you initiated this process to work on your dilemma?

Masturbation

___ I do   ___ It's okay before marriage

___ I don't   ___ I shouldn't

___ It's normal   ___ It's a problem for me

Sexual fantasies are . . .

___ wrong   ___ okay after marriage

___ normal   ___ a problem for me

___ okay before marriage

Lovemaking is a good experience for me. ___ Yes ___ No

Lovemaking is a good experience for my spouse. ___ Yes ___ No

We make love ___ times a month.

Woman initiates ___ percent of the time.

Man initiates ___ percent of the time.

I wish my spouse would initiate more often. ___ Yes ___ No

FOR MEN

I ejaculate prematurely (before she is or I am ready to respond)
___ percent of the time.

I have difficulty achieving or maintaining an erection ___ percent of the
time.

She is orgasmic ___ percent of the time.

She is orgasmic . . .

___ by masturbation

___ by external stimulation

___ during actual intercourse

Does she experience pain during intercourse? If so, what kind?

FOR WOMEN

I am orgasmic ___ percent of the time.

I am orgasmic...

___ by masturbation

___ during actual intercourse

Do you experience pain during intercourse? If so, what kind?

He ejaculates prematurely (before he is or I am ready) ___ percent of the time.

He has difficulty achieving or maintaining an erection ___ percent of the time.

FOR MEN AND WOMEN

I would like to enhance the sexual fulfillment of our marriage by working on the following areas (check as many as desired):

___ frequency of intercourse

___ variety within the lovemaking experience

___ increased interest for myself

___ increased interest for my partner

___ change in the pattern of initiation

___ control of ejaculation for the man

___ orgasmic responsiveness for the woman

___ ease of gaining and keeping an erection for the man

___ reducing pain for the woman

___ general pleasuring of each other's body

___ freedom of sexual activity between my partner and me

___ other:

PLAN FOR RETRAINING

1. Compare and discuss the previous three pages.
2. Determine individually and then together which is the most important area to work on. You may choose several areas. If you do, list them in order of priority. Decide this together.

GOALS FOR RETRAINING

How would your sex life be different? If sexual retraining is successful, what would your sex life be like after the retraining?

Husband's:

Wife's:

Compare your personal goals and decide on joint goals.

Compile your ideas individually, then make a joint list. Apply the effective communication skills of chapter 3 to avoid blame and defensiveness.

Now that you understand your physical histories, your background histories, your sexual experience, and your sexual barrier, we hope you have a clear picture of what the two of you have to work on to restore the pleasure of your sexual relationship. However, it may be difficult for you if the assessment process stirred up more conflict than was present before. If there are great differences in your stories, each of you needs to listen carefully to the way the other experiences your sexual relationship. Then your differences should be tactfully clarified so a common understanding can be reached. You may choose to accept the fact that you disagree.

On the next page, we have created a graph to help picture what you have learned so far and where your issues fit within that understanding. The graph shows how the physical changes in our bodies during a sexual response parallel the emotional-relational process of a sexual experience between a husband and a wife and where the problems show up when it isn't working in the way God designed us sexually. The **bold** labels on the graph describe what is happening in the body—the physical process, as you learned in chapter 7. The ***bold italic*** labels describe what happens inside and between us as sexual urges are felt and shared or acted on by decision, even when feelings may not be evident. The *italic* labels show where in the physical and emotional-relational process the issues get in the way and interrupt the natural flow of a mutually satisfying sexual experience. Each of these issues is discussed at some point in the chapters on overcoming sexual problems (chapters 13 through 19).

Figure 11.1
GRAPH DEPICTING SEXUAL RESPONSE, EXPERIENCE, AND DYSFUNCTION

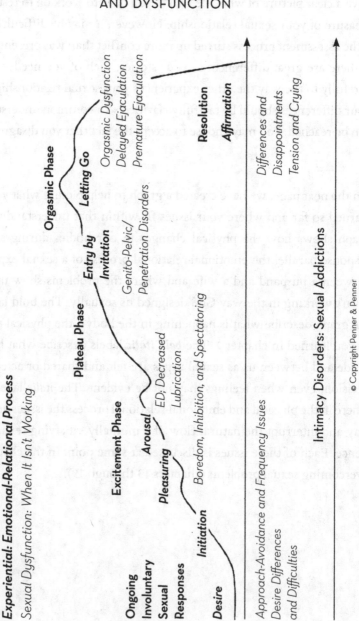

Physiology: Sexual Response Cycle
Experiential: Emotional-Relational Process
Sexual Dysfunction: When It Isn't Working

Orgasmic Phase

Letting Go
Orgasmic Dysfunction
Delayed Ejaculation
Premature Ejaculation

Plateau Phase

Entry by Invitation
Genito-Pelvic/
Penetration Disorders

Excitement Phase

Arousal
ED; Decreased
Lubrication

Pleasuring
Boredom, Inhibition, and Spectatoring

Initiation

Desire

Ongoing Involuntary Sexual Responses

Approach-Avoidance and Frequency Issues
Desire Differences
and Difficulties

Intimacy Disorders: Sexual Addictions

Resolution
Affirmation
Differences and
Disappointments
Tension and Crying

© Copyright Penner & Penner

TWELVE

Sexual Retraining

You will begin the sexual retraining process the same way, no matter what your barrier. Later, the specific format will become individualized to the particular issue you have chosen to work on and the desired goals you have identified. The prescribed sexual experiences are common to all sexual retraining.

Sexual retraining can be pursued in two ways: either in an intensive process or on a weekly basis over time. In an intensive process, you will commit ten days to two weeks to this work. You will clear your time and home from all responsibilities and focus on the prescribed exercises. Sometimes it is recommended that a couple leave home during the intensive. If you choose weekly sessions, you set aside designated times each week to complete the assignments without distraction.

The Guidelines for Sexual Retraining, which begin on page 146, define the limitations regarding sexual activities and course of actions that are an important part of the learning process. These need to be clearly adhered to in order to build trust. Notice that intercourse or attempts at intercourse are ruled out. This restriction typically brings relief from demand rather than disappointment. Specific teaching, communication, and touching experiences are assigned. These exercises follow a graduated process of learning outlined on pages 143–45, so they should be completed in order. We recommend three exercises per day for the intensive approach and three exercises per week for the weekly approach. These specific behavioral assignments, prescribed for you as a couple, are the keys to producing the necessary change.

Try to remove any hindrances by deciding every behavioral detail ahead of time. If you are following an intensive approach, plan the details of each experience before you begin. If you are using a weekly approach, select one time each week when you will plan the details of your retraining exercises for that week. Select specific times for these assignments to be completed. For example, for an intensive the first exercise might be assigned for 1:00 p.m. on Monday, the second for 4:00 p.m., the third for 7:00 p.m., and the fourth for 9:00 p.m. on Tuesday. If you are proceeding on a weekly basis, select three times per week. Assign one spouse the responsibility for choosing the setting, creating a pleasant atmosphere, and initiating the event. Alternate spouses for each exercise. The other spouse is the first active participant in the event; that is, he or she is the first one to pleasure, to share, or to teach. The responsibility is reversed for each assignment, so you take turns being the initiator and the first active participant.

Allow two to three hours for each assignment. This means you start the exercise two to three hours before you will need to stop for eating, sleeping, or any other commitment. Once you have *allowed* the time, ignore the clock; in fact, we recommend that you have no watch or clock in sight. It is not your purpose to fill the two to three hours, but rather to listen and respond from within without feeling rushed or time-oriented.

The touching exercises—the sensate focus exercises or bodily caresses—allow you to learn to enjoy each other's bodies for your own pleasure through touching and to soak in the pleasure when you are touched. Remove all demands. Express any anxious or negative feelings; stop any anxiety-provoking behavior and change to a new distracting activity. New patterns of physical relating will be established as you each develop an awareness of your own sensations and take responsibility to pursue your desires and communicate your needs, but not at the expense of the other.

The teaching exercises guide you to learn about your own and each other's bodies and about the type of touch you most enjoy.

The communication exercises serve to continue your open communication about yourselves and your sexual experience.

The later, more creative assignments, such as Pleasuring, Not Using Hands and Creative Pleasuring, help you realize the fun and enjoyment of each other's bodies, minds, and spirits without a goal-oriented focus of intercourse or orgasm. They also stretch your sensual awareness.

After completing each assignment, share with each other the details of your reactions to what happened. Emotional barriers that block further progress in the sexual retraining process may surface. The first difficulty may arise in reaction to the Body-Awareness/Mirror assignment. When you feel resistant to doing an assignment, it is important to talk about your fears and concerns. Sometimes you may need to modify the assignment to make it less threatening; sometimes the assignment may be delayed. And sometimes the anticipation of the assignment is worse than you anticipated, and the actual process is not as difficult as expected. The determination to find a way and the use of the detailed, structured directions are the keys to a happy outcome. At *all* times, we encourage you to communicate your feelings with each other.

THE SEXUAL RETRAINING PROCESS

Use the day plan if you are completing all assignments in an intensive ten-day period. Use the week plan if you are completing the assignments in a ten-week period.

FIRST DAY/WEEK
1. Guidelines for Sexual Retraining and Underlying Principles for Bodily Caressing (communication)
2. Foot and Hand Caress (touching)
3. A Sexual Assessment (communication)

SECOND DAY/WEEK
4. Facial and Head Caress (touching)

5. My Sexual Development (communication)
6. Back Caress (touching)

THIRD DAY/WEEK
7. Body Awareness/Mirror (teaching)
8. Bathe or Shower Together (no written assignment; set boundaries and reread the Guidelines for Sexual Retraining in order to make this safe for both of you)
9. Sharing Myself (communication)

FOURTH DAY/WEEK
10. Total-Body Pleasuring, Excluding Breasts and Genitals (touching)
11. Female Self-Examination (teaching); Male Self-Examination (teaching)
12. Pubococcygeus (PC)/Kegel Muscle Exercise (teaching)

FIFTH DAY/WEEK
13. Graphing Your Sexual Response (communication). Read chapter 7 out loud together; each complete your graphs on page 88; share with each other.
14. Total-Body Pleasuring, Including Breasts and Genitals Without Focus or Stimulation (touching)
15. Clinical Genital Examination (teaching/communication)

SIXTH DAY/WEEK
16. Non-demand Teaching (touching/teaching)
17. Read out loud together chapters 13 and 14 and a later chapter that fits your situation (teaching/communication)
18. Defining Your Sexual Experience and Defining Your Sexual Barrier

SEVENTH DAY/WEEK
19. Kissing (touching/teaching)
20. You and Me (communication)
21. Creative Pleasuring (touching/fun)

EIGHTH DAY/WEEK

22. Simulating Arousal Responses (teaching)
23. Vaginal Examination and Genital Affirmation (teaching)
24. Total-Body Pleasuring, Including Breast and Genital Stimulation (touching)

NINTH DAY/WEEK

25. Sharing Love (communication)
26. Pleasuring, Not Using Hands (Including Using the Penis as a Paintbrush) (touching)
27. Shared Self-Stimulation (optional)
28. Total-Body Pleasuring with Mutual Manual Stimulation (touching)

TENTH DAY/WEEK

29. Principles Learned (communication)
30. Total-Body Pleasuring with Entry (touching)
31. Read chapter 20 out loud together (teaching) and Create Your Ongoing Sexual Plan (communication)

As we said earlier, the exercises should be done in the order they are listed here. You may choose to repeat assignments; include exercises that relate specifically to your sexual barrier as instructed in a chapter that discusses that specific dilemma. References to these chapters are interspersed among the assignments.

The sexual retraining process is complete when your symptoms are relieved and your goals have been realized. When you complete all sessions, you may want to review your assessment forms and evaluate the changes you have made and the goals you have attained. If some goals have not been achieved, decide what, if anything, needs to be done. Some goals may no longer seem important. Discuss the effects of the retraining process, both positive and negative. Consider where you see yourselves now and where you would like to be. Make a follow-up plan for continued growth using Assignment 31.

Date: _____ *Time:* _____

Guidelines for Sexual Retraining

(Read out loud together and discuss.)

1. No sexual intercourse or attempts at intercourse should be made until that is assigned. (If you should go ahead before intercourse is recommended, adjust the plan by backing up and repeating the two previous touching exercises.)

2. You may repeat any previously assigned experience, but don't go ahead of what has been assigned.

3. Select one spouse to initiate each experience. (Make sure the experience happens as scheduled.) The initiator will be the first receiver, choose the location, and set the atmosphere. Be creative with the setting. Try to vary the location and the accouterments (candles, music, etc.). Select a setting that is different from that of your usual sexual experiences. Turn off the TV and all electronic devices.

4. Even though you are not likely to use the full time, allow one to three hours for each exercise. Once you have made the time available, turn clocks around and ignore the time. You may set an alarm for the maximum time you have available. There is no need to fill the time allowed.

5. Protect against interruptions by turning off the telephone and doorbell, locking all doors, and putting pets outside.

6. Even though there will be a need to push through barriers, there should be no negative experiences. Demands or anxieties should be verbalized the moment they are felt. It's better not to complete the exercise than to repeat past negative patterns and feelings. It is very important to build trust by *never* violating the boundaries of the exercise. Never allow your hands to roam beyond the body part assigned.

7. The moment you feel anxiety, demand, or uncomfortable touch, express your feelings, talk about them, and come at the experience again in another way.

8. The focus of all touching experiences will be pleasure (enjoyment, comfort, relaxation, positive sensation). As long as it is not negative, the experience has been successful. As both pleasurer and receiver, your goal is to learn how to soak in the touch (refer to Underlying Principles for Body Caressing in Assignment 1).

9. After each experience, talk about your reactions and feelings. Listen carefully and try to understand how your spouse feels without evaluating or judging his or her reaction. Each spouse's reactions are valid.

Underlying Principles for Body Caressing

(Read out loud together and discuss.)

1. **Concept of Mutuality.** First Corinthians 7:3-5 teaches that our bodies are each other's to enjoy. This mutuality works best when caressing is scheduled into our lives on a regular basis and when it is free from demand for arousal, release, or intercourse. The only expectation is that we give our bodies to each other for mutual enjoyment. Pleasure cannot be demanded from each other, but rather is given and received freely.

2. **Sexual Arousal and Responsiveness.** These involuntary processes may occur when we are relaxed and soaking in sensuous touch, but they cannot be the goal. When we try to get aroused or try to have an orgasm, our trying is likely to interfere with the natural bodily responses. That is why it is important to distract from any anxiety about responsiveness by verbalizing when we feel that demand. In all touching exercises, do not become concerned if there is or is not arousal.

3. **Body Awareness/Sensate Focus.** The purpose of the touching exercises is body awareness. They are not to be therapeutic

147

massages, but rather sensuous touches that communicate warmth. Even though our bodies are designed for pleasure, many of us have not learned to enjoy the giving and receiving of bodily touch.

4. **Receiving and Caressing.** As both pleasurer and receiver, we must take responsibility for discovering, communicating, and going after our sexual feelings and needs, but not at the other's expense. Demand is reduced when we can count on each other to share from within, rather than expecting the other to produce a response in us. We can give our bodies to each other to enjoy, but we cannot produce in each other the involuntary response of sexual arousal and release. Therefore, as

Receiver: Your only task is to soak in the touch and to redirect the pleasurer when the touch is not pleasing. Express your concern if at any time you start to wonder whether your spouse is not enjoying himself or herself.

Pleasurer: Your task is to lovingly touch your spouse in a way that feels good to you, enjoying his or her body for your pleasure. Think of radiating warmth through your fingertips (or any other part of your body) and taking in the sensation of warmth and the pulsation of your spouse's body. You might imagine that you are a blind person discovering your spouse through touch.

Trust that your spouse will redirect you if what you are doing is negative to him or her. Express your concern if at any time you become anxious rather than enjoying your spouse's body. Caress SLOWLY. Take time to mesh, relax, and discover the kind of touch that feels best to both of you.

5. **Techniques for Bodily Caressing.** Experiment with these suggestions that many couples have found helpful:

a. Touch in circles rather than straight lines.

b. Keep your hands with the contour of the other's body rather than using flat hands.

c. As the man, keep your pace behind that of your wife's in both activity and intensity. (If the man is the one who has felt rushed or left behind in past sexual experience, you may try reversing roles.)

6. **Common Interferences to Enjoyment.**

   a. **Not taking enough time to mesh, feeling rushed.** Schedule one- to three-hour blocks of time free of distractions and interruptions. Follow all the preparatory steps for each experience.

   b. **Anxiety about sexual performance or fear of failure.** If anything in a sexual retraining assignment feels like a demand that you could fail, redefine it until there is no way you can fail. For example, make sure you don't assume that pleasure means arousal; enjoy the good sensations of touch.

   c. **Discomfort with bodily pleasure.** If there is a belief that bodily pleasure is wrong, talk about that—include your spiritual mentor and the Bible. If you notice yourself pulling away from good feelings, consciously work on moving your body toward the source of touch that is producing those feelings. Talk about your internal conflict with the sensations of bodily enjoyment.

   d. **Barriers, aversions, or panic reactions.** When you come up against a brick wall, stop and talk about it and try approaching the experience differently. We work around the brick wall rather than blast through it. Sometimes, though, we encourage you to push against the brick wall to see if it might tumble.

   e. **Inability to let go and be out of control.** Reducing fears and self-consciousness requires building trust, feeling affirmed, and accepting the intensity of natural arousal responses.

Have fun! Learn to laugh and cry together as you move through the process.

SEXUAL RETRAINING ADAPTATION
FOR INHIBITED EJACULATION

Couples who are using this retraining process for inhibited ejaculation—the man has not been able to ejaculate or has difficulty allowing ejaculation in some way that he desires—should go to chapter 17, page 274, and begin the specific steps for releasing ejaculatory inhibition.

Alternate the sexual retraining assignments in this section with the steps for learning to let go in chapter 17. In other words, after completing Assignment 1, you would find a separate time to do Step 1 on page 274: Urinate with wife listening. Your next session would be Assignment 2, Foot and Hand Caress. After that you would select a separate time to practice Step 2 on page 274: Urinate with wife in room. This is the way you would alternate assignments between the sexual retraining process and the steps to ejaculatory release during intercourse.

SEXUAL RETRAINING ASSIGNMENT 2

Date: _____ *Time:* _____

Foot and Hand Caress

(Read out loud together and follow the steps. Fill in the blanks as you plan your sessions.)

STEP 1: _____ will take responsibility to initiate this experience and set the atmosphere. Choose a location in which the receiver can be seated or reclined in a comfortable, upholstered, high-backed chair or couch. The pleasurer should be positioned to be able to comfortably caress the receiver's feet and hands.

STEP 2: Bathe or shower individually. Wear comfortable clothes or robes. You may bring a pan of warm, soapy water to soak each other's feet if you both desire.

STEP 3: _____ will be the first pleasurer; _____ will be the first receiver.

STEP 4: Read Underlying Principles for Body Caressing in Assignment 1.

STEP 5: *Receiver:* Get comfortable in the chair or couch selected. Lie back and close your eyes. Breathe in deeply and exhale slowly several times, letting your body sink into the chair or couch. Soak in the gift of your spouse's touch. If your feet should feel ticklish, this is a positive sign of intense responsiveness. To relieve the ticklishness and help you receive the sensuous touch, focus on the sensations of the skin contact. You may need to direct your spouse to touch more firmly and/or move to a different part of your foot.

Pleasurer: You may or may not use a lotion. If you do, warm it in your hands first. With or without lotion, start caressing your spouse's foot. Get to know his or her foot through touch. *Slowly* explore the toes, arch, top of foot, ankle, and even the lower leg. Always maintain contact with the body part being caressed and inform your spouse before you move to the next part. Caress one foot and then the other. In the same manner, caress one hand and then the other. Enjoy all surfaces and parts of each hand and lower arm. Inform your spouse when you are finished.

STEP 6: You may want to take a rest or break before you reverse roles and repeat Step 5. _____ will be the pleasurer; _____ will be the receiver.

STEP 7: Write your reactions: What did you enjoy most? What was difficult? Discuss your written reactions with each other.

Date: _____ *Time:* _____

A Sexual Assessment

Complete the following form individually. Work privately. Respond as thoroughly and honestly as you can. Start with your most immediate, spontaneous response, then take time to reflect and write in further detail. Note that you are responding in terms of knowledge, feelings, and attitudes.

1. **Knowledge**
   a. Physiological: When it is said that our sexual response is a natural bodily function, I understand that to mean...

   b. Psychological: Every individual needs sexual fulfillment because...

   c. Biblical: The Bible teaches that sexual pleasure within the marriage relationship is...

2. **Feelings**
When I become aware of my sexual feelings, I feel...

Ten years ago my feelings about sex were...

Now when we make love, I feel...

The best feeling in a sexual experience is...

Share your responses using the Communication Format, page 16.

Attitudes (Check the column that represents your response to the statements below.)

	Agree	Disagree	Uncertain
Sex is one of the most beautiful aspects of life.	___	___	___
It is more enjoyable to give than to receive.	___	___	___
Bodily pleasure is fleshly and not of God.	___	___	___
Sexual intercourse is primarily for physical release.	___	___	___
My religious beliefs have the greatest influence on my attitudes toward sex.	___	___	___
Men and women have equal rights to sexual pleasure.	___	___	___
There are sexual activities that I would consider wrong for a married couple to practice.	___	___	___

If you agree with the above, please list:

To be satisfying, intercourse must lead to simultaneous orgasm.	___	___	___
Sexual fantasies are normal.	___	___	___
Masturbation (self-stimulation) is an acceptable means for sexual pleasuring and release.	___	___	___
The male should be the aggressor in sexual activity.	___	___	___
In general, women do not enjoy sex as much as men.	___	___	___
Men should be allowed more freedom in sexual behavior than women.	___	___	___
The quality of a sexual relationship is more than just the physical release.	___	___	___

Hold your papers side by side to compare and discuss your responses.

Date: _____ Time: _____

Facial and Head Caress

(Read out loud together and follow the steps. Fill in the blanks as you plan your sessions.)

STEP 1: _____ will take responsibility to initiate this experience and set the environment, making certain to provide comfort for both of you.

STEP 2: Bathe or shower individually. Have hair clean, dry, and away from the face. Man should be cleanly shaven.

STEP 3: _____ will be the first pleasurer, and _____ will be the first receiver.

STEP 4: Together, reread Assignment 1, Underlying Principles for Body Caressing.

STEP 5: *Receiver:* (a) Position yourself comfortably on a bed or couch, with or without a pillow, with your head near the unobstructed edge of the bed or couch. (b) Let yourself relax with eyes closed. Breathe in deeply and exhale slowly a few times, letting your body sink into the bed or couch.

Pleasurer: (a) Sit in a comfortable chair, positioned so that you have easy access to your partner's face. (b) You may or may not use a facial lotion or cream. Close your eyes and focus on the sensation of the touch as you explore your partner's face. Caress and explore as if you are a blind person getting to know your spouse through touch. Find eyebrows, eyes, all aspects of the nose, cheeks, forehead, chin, lips. Gently, sensuously, and lovingly enjoy the warmth of your partner's face. You might avoid using a full hand; some people feel smothered and prefer their faces be touched with fingertips. Check with your spouse. Inform your partner when you finish.

STEP 6: You may want to take a rest or break before you reverse roles and repeat Step 5. _____ will be the second pleasurer, and _____ will be the second receiver.

STEP 7: Write your reactions here. What did you enjoy most? What was difficult? Discuss your written reactions with each other.

SEXUAL RETRAINING ASSIGNMENT 5

Date: _____ Time: _____

My Sexual Development

Go to pages 125-30, and review or share for the first time your responses to the Background History form.

SEXUAL RETRAINING ASSIGNMENT 6

Date: _____ *Time:* _____

Back Caress

(Read out loud together and follow the steps. Fill in the blanks as you plan your sessions.)

STEP 1: _____ will take responsibility to initiate this experience and set the atmosphere, making certain the temperature of the room is comfortable and there is privacy.

STEP 2: Bathe or shower individually. If possible, you will be nude for this experience. If nudity is too difficult, use the minimal covering to provide the safety needed.

STEP 3: _____ will be the first pleasurer; _____ will be the first receiver.

STEP 4: Together, reread Assignment 1, Underlying Principles for Body Caressing, page 147.

STEP 5: *Receiver:* Get comfortable lying front down on the bed or location chosen. Focus on the enjoyment, relaxation, and gift of your spouse's touch.

> *Pleasurer:* Position yourself so that you can comfortably enjoy your spouse's back. Start by putting your hands flat on his or her back and just feeling the pulsation and warmth of the other's skin. Move your hands over his or her back at a slow, sensuous rhythm that comes from inside you. If you want to add lotion, inform your spouse and warm the lotion in your hands before you apply it to his or her back. Do not violate the boundaries and move your hands farther than your spouse's back.

STEP 6: You may want to take a rest before you reverse roles or even schedule another time and repeat Step 5. _____ will be the pleasurer, and _____ will be the receiver.

STEP 7: Write your reaction here or on the back. Give your feelings and what you learned about yourself. Discuss your written reactions with each other.

SEXUAL RETRAINING ASSIGNMENT 7

Date: _____ *Time:* _____

Body-Awareness/Mirror Exercise

(Read out loud together and follow the steps. Fill in the blanks when you plan your sessions.)

SPOUSE 1: Stand in front of a full-length mirror in the nude. Describe your body as honestly as you can to your partner. Start with general feelings about your body as you see it. Then talk about each specific body part, starting with your hair and working down. Talk about how it feels and looks, ways you wish you were different, what you feel particularly good about. If this is impossible for one of you to do—talk about it! Then modify the exercise so it can work for you (examples: wearing a thin garment, dimming the lights, etc.).

SPOUSE 2: Only listen and observe. Listen both to the words and the feelings of your partner as he or she talks. Do not interrupt! When your partner is finished, provide feedback to him or her about what you have sensed and heard.

SPOUSE 1: Clarify or expand on what your partner has heard from you.

SPOUSE 2: Fill in any positive messages that you can give that will build up him or her.

SPOUSE 1: When you feel you have been understood accurately, reverse this procedure. You will now be the quiet observer and listener while your partner describes his or her body.

   The first time:

      Spouse 1 will be _____. Spouse 2 will be _____.

   The second time:

      Spouse 1 will be _____. Spouse 2 will be _____.

Write your reactions to this experience. What did you learn about yourself? Your spouse? Share your written reactions with each other.

SEXUAL RETRAINING ASSIGNMENT 8

Date: _____ *Time:* _____

Bathe or Shower Together

Talk about each of your comfort and discomfort with this activity. Decide how best to proceed so that both of you are comfortable with the plan. This requires going with the most conservative spouse.

SEXUAL RETRAINING ASSIGNMENT 9

Date: _____ Time: _____

Sharing Myself

Complete the following statements individually. There are no right or wrong responses, only those that come to mind. Share your responses at the designated time and date using the Communication Format (page 16) as your guide.

1. Usually I am the kind of person who...

2. When things aren't going well, I...

3. I want to become the kind of person who...

4. I like such things as...

5. Ten years from now, I...

6. My best attribute is...

7. My greatest weakness is...

8. In conflict situations between people, I usually...

9. I usually react to negative criticism by . . .

10. I prefer to be with people who . . .

11. Right now I'm feeling . . .

12. I'm hoping that . . .

13. If I could just . . .

Date: _____ Time: _____

Total-Body Pleasuring, Excluding Breasts and Genitals

(Read out loud together and follow the steps. Fill in the blanks as you plan your daily or weekly sessions.)

STEP 1: _____ will take responsibility to initiate this experience and set the atmosphere. The room temperature should be set so both of you will be comfortable without clothes or covers. Prepare a room that is softly lit and has a relaxed, uncluttered environment.

STEP 2: Bathe or shower together. You may wash each other's nonsexual body parts.

STEP 3: _____ will be the first pleasurer, and _____ will be the first receiver.

STEP 4: Read Assignment 1, Underlying Principles for Body Caressing. Discuss the current instructions. As more of the body is included in the pleasuring, it is important to remember that sexual arousal is an involuntary response and not the goal or purpose of this experience. Do not become concerned if there is or is not arousal; the purpose of this experience is body awareness.

STEP 5: *Receiver:* Lie on abdomen in a comfortable position.

Pleasurer: Place your hands on your spouse's back. With your eyes closed, focus on the sensations of your spouse's body: warmth, pulsation, vibrations, and so forth. Begin to move over his or her entire back with sensuous touch, radiating your warmth and care. Proceed in the same manner to neck, arms, and legs. Inform your spouse when you are ready for him or her to turn over.

Receiver: Turn onto your back. Before receiving the caressing of the front of your body, you might have fun drawing the boundaries on your skin with lipstick or a washable pen.

Pleasurer: Sitting with your spouse's head faceup in your lap (with your genitals covered), proceed with a facial caress. Then continue down his or her neck, shoulders, arms, and hands. Move to the side of your spouse to enjoy his or her abdomen, legs, and feet. Do not touch breasts or genitals. It is important that you not violate those boundaries, marked or unmarked.

STEP 6: You may want to rest or take a break before you reverse roles and repeat Step 5. _____ will be the pleasurer; _____ will be the receiver. Couples often find with the more involved caressing assignments, it is best to complete the assignment at two different times: one day/evening, he is the receiver and she the pleasurer; another day/evening, she is the receiver and he the pleasurer.

STEP 7: Write your reactions. Were there uncomfortable movements? What anxieties or demands slipped through your minds? What was most relaxing? Most pleasurable? Discuss your written reactions with each other.

Date: _____ Time: _____

Female Self-Examination

STEP 1: Have a diagram of the female external genitalia (see Figure 7.4, page 68). Have a hand mirror and extension lamp or spotlight.

STEP 2: Shower or bathe leisurely in order to relax.

STEP 3: Assume a comfortable position with legs spread apart, light focused on genitals, diagram within view, and hand mirror between legs so you can see your genitals clearly. Look at how your outer labia come together. Then spread the outer labia and identify the inner labia. Find the clitoris and note how the labia form a hood over the clitoris. See if you can feel the shaft of the clitoris, almost like a hidden, small penis up behind the tip of the clitoris. Touch the tip or glans of the clitoris and then the areas around it, and identify what kind of touch feels good and where.

Identify the urinary meatus, the vaginal opening, and any other points of interest. Think about what genital stimulation your partner has given you or you have given yourself in the past that has felt good, what you would like more of, what touching has been negative, and how stimulation of your genitals might be enhanced. Thank God for his creation of each of these intricate parts. Thank him for any good feelings associated with your genitals. Pray for healing from any pain or scars connected with them.

This is a clinical learning experience, not for the purpose of arousal. However, if arousal should occur, it is okay.

SEXUAL RETRAINING ASSIGNMENT 11 FOR MEN

Date: _____ *Time:* _____

Male Self-Examination

STEP 1: Have a diagram of the male external genitalia (see Figure 7.6, page 71).

STEP 2: Shower.

STEP 3: In a private, well-lit room, with the diagram of male genitals in view, identify all the specific parts of the penis and testes. Note the coronal ridge and the frenulum, or "seam" on the backside of the penis. Think about the kind of touch and stimulation you have enjoyed, either when you have stimulated yourself or when your spouse has stimulated you. Imagine other kinds of touch and stimulation you might try. Think about how you might teach your spouse what you would enjoy without placing demands on her.

Thank God for the specialness of your genitals and all the positive feelings they have given you. Pray for healing of any pain associated with them.

This is a clinical experience, not for the purpose of arousal. However, if arousal should occur, it is okay.

Date: _____ Time: _____

Pubococcygeus (PC) Muscle Exercise (Kegel Exercises)

STEP 1: Identify the sensation of tightening and relaxing this muscle. While sitting on the toilet to urinate, spread your legs apart. Start urination. Then stop urination for three seconds. Repeat this several times before you are finished emptying your bladder. Some women have difficulty stopping urination. Those women need to work on tightening the PC muscle. Other women need to work on the voluntary relaxing of the PC muscle. If you can do both easily, you only need to tighten and relax the PC muscle twenty-five times per day to keep it in good condition. For those who need to improve the voluntary control of their PC muscles, proceed with the steps below.

STEP 2: Do ten to twenty repetitions of this exercise one to four times per day: Gradually tighten the PC muscle tighter and tighter to the count of four. Then hold the muscle as tight as you can while you again count to four. Now gradually relax the muscle, letting go of the tension a little at a time as you count to four.

STEP 3: Do ten to twenty repetitions of this exercise one to four times per day: Start to tighten your vagina by thinking of bringing your labia (lips) closer together, like closing an elevator door. Imagine that your vagina is an elevator. You start to tighten at the ground floor. Bring the muscles up from floor to floor, tightening and holding at each floor. Keep your breathing even and relaxed. Do not hold your breath. Go to the fifth floor. Then go down, relaxing the tension of the muscle one floor at a time. When you get to the bottom, bear down as though you are opening the elevator door (the vagina) and letting something out.

STEP 4: Do ten to twenty repetitions of this exercise one to four times per day: rapidly tighten and relax the PC muscle at the opening of the vagina in a flickering or fluttering movement.

These exercises will improve genital sensation and responsiveness.

SEXUAL RETRAINING ASSIGNMENT 13

Date: _____ Time: _____

Graphing Your Sexual Response

Read out loud together and discuss chapter 7.

At the end of chapter 7, page 88, each draw your response graph(s) following the directions on page 87. Share your graphs as directed in step 3 on page 87.

SEXUAL RETRAINING ASSIGNMENT 14

Date: _____ *Time:* _____

Total-Body Pleasuring, Including Breasts and Genitals Without Purposeful Stimulation

(Read out loud together and follow the steps. Fill in the blanks as you plan your daily or weekly sessions.)

STEP 1: ____ will take responsibility to initiate the experience and set the atmosphere with attention to temperature, privacy, and mood.

STEP 2: Bathe or shower together. You may wash each other's body totally.

STEP 3: ____ will be the first pleasurer; ____ will be the first receiver.

STEP 4: Read Assignment 1, Underlying Principles for Body Caressing. Discuss the current instructions. Continue to remember that sexual arousal is an involuntary response and not the goal of this experience. *Do not become concerned if there is or is not arousal. The purpose of the experience is body awareness.*

STEP 5: *Receiver:* Lie on your abdomen in a comfortable position.

Pleasurer: Place your hands on your spouse's back and proceed to pleasure, taking in the warmth and sensations of your spouse's back, buttocks (cheeks only; not into the crack), arms, and legs. Take time to enjoy each part as you have in previous pleasuring exercises. Inform your spouse when you are ready for him or her to turn over.

Receiver: Turn onto your back. Positively redirect your spouse if anything he or she does is negative or demanding.

Pleasurer: Sitting with your spouse's head—faceup—in your lap (with your genitals covered), proceed with a facial caress. Then continue down his or her neck, shoulders, chest, arms, and hands. Do not focus or linger on the breasts. Just pass over them as you have every other part of the body. Move to the side of your spouse (or between his or her legs) to caress his or her abdomen, legs, and feet. Include the genitals only in a general passing over them briefly. Inform your spouse when you are finished. *Do not* pursue specific stimulation.

STEP 6: You may want to rest or take a break before you reverse roles and repeat Step 5. ____ will be the pleasurer; ____ will be the receiver. Couples often find with the more involved caressing assignments, it is best to complete the assignment at two different times: one day/evening, he is the receiver and she the pleasurer; another day/ evening, she is the receiver and he the pleasurer.

STEP 7: Write your reactions. Particularly attend to any demands that are arising and any enjoyment that is flowing. Discuss your written reactions with each other.

Date: _____ Time: _____

Clinical Genital Examination

(Read out loud together and discuss any fears or needs for safety. Then follow the steps.)

STEP 1: Have diagrams of the male genitalia and the female external genitalia (see Figures 7.4, page 68, and 7.6, page 71). Have a hand mirror and adequate lighting available.

STEP 2: Shower or bathe together; lather up each other's bodies and enjoy the pleasure and relaxation of touching each other in that process, not for the purpose of arousal.

STEP 3: In a private, well-lit room, with the diagram of male genitalia, the husband identifies all the specific parts of the penis and testes. If it is comfortable for both, the husband may invite the wife to join in the exploration by touching various parts as they are identified. Wife, only participate to the extent that it is comfortable for you. Particularly note the coronal ridge and the frenulum, or seam, on the backside of the penis. After exploring the various parts of the genitals, talk about what kind of touch feels good, any stimulation of the genitals your partner has given you in the past that you would like more of, and any stimulation or handling of the genitals that has been unpleasant for you. Wife, talk about ways you enjoy pleasuring his genitals and any feelings of discomfort you have with the male genitals.

STEP 4: Wife assumes comfortable position with legs spread apart, light on genitals, diagram within view, and hand mirror between legs so you can see the genitals clearly. Identify for your husband how your outer labia come together. Then you spread the outer labia and identify the inner labia. Find and show him the clitoris and how the labia form a hood over the clitoris. Identify for him the shaft of the clitoris, almost like a hidden, small penis up behind the tip of the clitoris. Touch the tip, or glans, of the clitoris and then the areas around it, and talk with your husband about what kind of touch feels good and where. If it is comfortable for both, invite your husband to join in exploration and touching as is comfortable.

Identify the urinary meatus, vaginal opening, and any other points of interest. Talk about what genital stimulation your partner has given you in the past that has felt good, what you would like more of, what touching has been negative, and how stimulation of your genitals might be enhanced. Husband, talk about ways you enjoy pleasuring her genitals and any feelings of discomfort you have with the female genitalia. When genital touching has not been comfortable for a woman, many times it has been too direct. Experiment with putting a flat hand over the pons and the pointer and middle fingers along the labia.

STEP 5: You may write your reactions and then talk about what this has felt like for each of you, what was comfortable or uncomfortable, and what you learned about yourselves and each other.

This is a clinical, learning experience, not for the purpose of arousal. If arousal should occur, it is okay. But do not focus on it; ignore it or enjoy it without pursuing it.

Date: _____ Time: _____

Non-demand Teaching

(Fill in the blanks as you plan your daily or weekly sessions.)

STEP 1: _____ will take responsibility to initiate this experience and set the atmosphere. Pillows against the headboard of the bed usually work best. Design this for teaching, rather than romance. Guiding each other's hands can be awkward. As you follow the instructions in Step 4, start with guiding, and use that as much as possible, but also use verbal guidance; have the spouse try to follow the verbal guidance if the hand guiding doesn't work for you.

STEP 2: Read these instructions together, and clarify with each other what each of you understands you are to do. Then follow the steps.

STEP 3: Bathe or shower together in a way that brings relaxation and enjoyment of each other's bodies, not touching for the purpose of stimulation or arousal.

STEP 4: Wife should start the actual experience by sitting in front of husband in the non-demand position shown at the top of Figure 12.1, page 173). Then she places her hands over his hands and uses his hands to caress her face, breasts, abdomen, and genitals. The purpose of the exercise is for the one guiding the hands to discover what kind of touch he or she really likes. For the one being guided, the job is to let his or her hand muscles be relaxed and limp and attend to the kind of touch that he or she is being directed to give. He or she can learn what the spouse really likes. This is a particularly good time for both to do a lot of experimenting and communicating about the kind of genital touch that brings pleasure. This is not likely to be an exciting or arousing experience, but a much more clinical and teaching kind of time. If arousal should occur, however, enjoy it.

When the husband guides the wife's hands to discover and teach the touch he enjoys on the upper front of his body, he may need to slide down and use a modified version of the upper illustration of the non-demand positions shown in Figure 12.1. For example, he may slide his head, faceup, into his wife's lap. When the husband is guiding the wife in pleasuring his lower body, especially the genitals, we would encourage the use of the positions shown in the lower illustration in Figure 12.1.

STEP 5: You may write your reaction first and then talk together about what you learned in this experience as well as anything else that you have always enjoyed or has always been painful or difficult for you.

Figure 12. 1

NON-DEMAND POSITIONS

SEXUAL RETRAINING ASSIGNMENT 17

Date: _____ *Time:* _____

Select and Read Your Chapter

First read chapters 13 and 14 out loud together and discuss. Then together select the chapter (15 through 19) that deals with the sexual barrier you have chosen to work on.

- Chapter 15, Overcoming Problems of Sexual Desire
- Chapter 16, Overcoming Problems of Sexual Arousal
- Chapter 17, Overcoming Problems of Sexual Release
- Chapter 18, Overcoming Intercourse Barriers
- Chapter 19, Controlling Sexual Addictions

Then read that chapter out loud to each other and plan how you will include the suggestions and assignments into the rest of your retraining process.

SEXUAL RETRAINING ASSIGNMENT 18

Date: _____ *Time:* _____

Defining Your Sexual Experience and Defining Your Sexual Barrier

Go to the assessment chapter and, if you have not already done so, complete those two forms, pages 131–38. Share with each other as directed on those assignments.

Date: _____ *Time:* _____

Kissing

(Fill in the blanks as you plan your sessions.)

STEP 1: _____ will take responsibility to see that the experience happens. Prepare a comfortable setting with low lights and soft music.

STEP 2: Brush teeth, use dental floss, and gargle.

STEP 3: Read and discuss these instructions.

STEP 4: Sitting on the couch, fully clothed, each of you describe to the other how you like to kiss and to be kissed. Use positive descriptions rather than listing what you don't like. Reflect back to each other what you understand from the other. The spouse who is the most hesitant or reserved kisser would be the best spouse to start in Step 5.

STEP 5: _____, use your lips to experiment with kissing your spouse's lips. Pucker your lips and gently peck across your spouse's lips and cheeks from one side to the other, from top to bottom lip. Take time to nibble on your spouse's lips, taking the upper or lower lip between your lips. _____, follow his or her lead. Be passive, but responsive. Be careful, as the follower, not to take over or get ahead of the leader.

STEP 6: Reverse roles. _____, follow Step 5 to discover how you like to kiss. _____, follow his or her lead. Be passive, but responsive.

STEP 7: Take turns leading in experimenting with the use of your lips and tongue to find ways that you both enjoy: pecking, nibbling, licking, sucking, and in any other way interacting with each other's lips and tongues. Keep it soft and experimental. If kissing has been an issue for either of you, stop here; continue to practice daily the steps up to Step 8 with the hesitant one leading and the other *never* being aggressive or taking over. When this daily practice becomes comfortable, repeat this assignment and move on through Step 8 to the extent that it is okay for both.

STEP 8: Allow the involvement with each other's mouths to become mutual, simultaneous enjoyment, if that is comfortable for both of you. Take turns inserting your tongue in and out of each other's mouths. If one of you becomes too intense or forceful for the other, gently remind the intense one that you'd like to keep it soft, safe, and experimental.

STEP 9: Talk about the experience. What felt especially good? What barriers did you encounter? How would you like to enhance your kissing?

Date: _____ Time: _____

You and Me

(Complete each of these statements, then share your responses with each other using the Communication Format, page 16.)

1. My first impression of you was . . .

2. What I like about you is . . .

3. My general image of you is . . .

4. What puzzles me about you is . . .

5. I am imagining that you . . .

6. I think you see me as . . .

SEXUAL RETRAINING ASSIGNMENT 21

Date: _____ *Time:* _____

Creative Pleasuring

(Fill in the blanks as you plan your daily or weekly sessions.)

STEP 1: _____ will take responsibility to see that the experience happens and will set up the environment for your time together.

STEP 2: Together, read these instructions and Assignment 1, Underlying Principles for Body Caressing. Tell each other what each of you understands the current assignment to be. Then proceed with the steps.

STEP 3: Bathe or shower together in a way that brings relaxation and enjoyment of each other's bodies.

STEP 4: Each of you should bring to the experience three or more items to use to pleasure your partner. Think of things that would feel pleasing and sensuous against the skin. Choose items of varying texture—maybe one soft and silky, another firm, another with soft bristles, another fuzzy. Let these be a surprise for each other.

STEP 5: _____, start the actual pleasuring by having your partner lie on his or her abdomen and gently stroking his or her back with the first item you chose for this event. Then do the same with each of the other objects. Together choose one object to continue pleasuring his or her entire body. When you feel finished, reverse roles and _____, do the same thing with the items you chose for pleasuring _____'s body. Stop when you have thoroughly enjoyed your partner's total body.

STEP 6: Write your reactions. Talk about the experience. What did you enjoy? What would you have liked more of? What other kind of object could you imagine enjoying? What did you learn?

SEXUAL RETRAINING ASSIGNMENT 22

Date: _____ *Time:* _____

Simulating Arousal Responses

(Fill in the blanks as you plan your daily or weekly sessions. Assign the lead to whoever is the least inhibited or the best actor. Read aloud together and follow the steps. Keep the directions near you and read the next step after you finish practicing the previous one. If it becomes too difficult for one of you, stop, talk about it, affirm each other, and try again another time.)

This experience is to help reduce self-consciousness and inhibition of the automatic responses of sexual arousal. It can become humorous, even hilarious.

STEP 1: _____, select a setting that is peaceful, free of distractions, and as soundproof as possible. You may need to set up a sound barrier, like music playing at the wall or door that might carry your noises. This assignment should be done in daylight or with the lights on.

STEP 2: Lie side by side on the bed or on a comfortable surface, fully clothed.

STEP 3: Take yourselves through relaxation: First, together take in ten deep breaths slowly through your nostrils, hold, then breathe out through your mouths. _____, lead in the deep, relaxed breathing. Picture yourselves in a beautiful, sunny, private garden. As you let out the air through your mouths, feel the tension in your bodies relax.

STEP 4: Keeping in the same relaxed mode, _____, lead in taking five to ten deep breaths slowly in through the nose, then hold them and breathe out through your mouth with a sighing sound. Go to the next step when you feel natural and comfortable.

STEP 5: _____, lead in the next five to ten breaths. This time as you breathe in, imagine the breath warming the inside of your body, all the way to your genitals. As you let it out, imagine the breath coming from your genitals, through your body, up your windpipe, past your vocal cords. Let out a relaxed, rattling noise while you say, "Ah." Vary the pitch of the "Ah" with each exhalation.

Continue until you feel natural and comfortable with the noises and breathing.

STEP 6: Talk about your experience. Take a break, if you wish. Then, take off your clothes and proceed with the next steps.

STEP 7: Lie side by side on your backs without clothes on, with the lights on or in daylight. Imagine yourselves on a warm, sunny, private beach, totally secluded. _____, lead in taking three to five deep breaths, holding them, then relaxing into the "warm sand" as you breathe out.

STEP 8: Now, imagine that you are doing your favorite sexual activity (each can picture something different). Breathe in and out slowly and loudly with the rattling "Ah" sound. _____, lead in five to ten of these.

STEP 9: Let the sexual activity progress in your minds as you proceed with the noisy, loose breathing. This time speed the breathing slightly, making certain it continues to be deep and noisy. Tense the muscles in your body so that your foot extends outward, your facial muscles grimace, and you thrust with your pelvis. Imagine your body flushing as it does when you blush. If you have never experienced these natural arousal responses, simulate what your spouse is doing.

STEP 10: Repeat Steps 7–9 in the nude with _____ lying on his back and _____ sitting on top of him in the typical woman-on-top position. Do not insert the penis into the vagina.

STEP 11: Repeat Steps 7–9 in the nude with _____ lying on her back and _____ on top of her in the most comfortable male-on-top position. If this is uncomfortable, turn on your sides, face-to-face. Do not insert the penis into the vagina.

STEP 12: Switch to the position that is most comfortable to both; continue to build the breathing, sounds, and movements to intensify the simulation of the release of the orgasm. If you have never experienced an orgasm, imitate your spouse's acting out of what he or she usually does during an orgasm.

STEP 13: Rest together and hold each other closely.

STEP 14: Write and talk about your reactions to each step.

Date: _____ *Time:* _____

Vaginal Examination and Genital Affirmation

(Read out loud together and follow the steps. Fill in the blanks as you plan your sessions.)

STEP 1: Shower or bathe together, enjoying each other's bodies as you do, but not for the purpose of arousal. Scrub fingernails with a brush.

STEP 2: Caress each other's bodies with lotion or oil as desired.

STEP 3: Have fun choosing friendly pet names for your genitals. Begin a commitment to pat and affirm each other's genitals daily. This can become a part of your bedtime routine, waking-up time, or any other time that the two of you select.

STEP 4: With closely trimmed nails and the wife's invitation, husband gently insert finger in wife's vagina to the second knuckle. Then gently press on the wall of the vagina. If you think of the opening of the vagina as a clock, start at the twelve o'clock position and then slowly move around the wall of the vagina, pressing or stroking at every hour. (See figure on page 183.) Try varying degrees of pressure and types of touch. The wife should provide feedback about what sensations she notes. Particularly be aware of any points of pain or pleasure.

After completing this exploration, the wife tightens her PC muscle when the husband's finger is in her vagina. Talk about how that feels to each of you. Now, with the husband's finger in the vagina and the PC muscle tightened, insert your finger just beyond the inner ridge of the PC muscle. This is the G-spot area (refer to the diagram of aroused internal female genitalia in Figure 7.10, page 80). Explore that area with various degrees of pressure—stroking, massaging, and tapping. Wife, note and talk about the sensations you have in response to your husband's exploration.

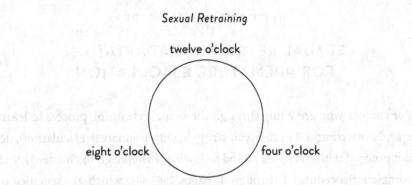

twelve o'clock

eight o'clock   four o'clock

Opening of vagina with four, eight, and twelve o'clock positions identified

STEP 5: Write and talk about the experience: what felt good, what you learned, what was uncomfortable. You may want to spend some time just holding and affirming each other.

SEXUAL RETRAINING ADAPTATION
FOR PREMATURE EJACULATION

For couples who are going through the sexual retraining process to learn ejaculatory control (because you struggle with premature ejaculation), do not proceed with Exercises 24 and following; instead, go to chapter 17 and complete Procedures 1 through 4 (pages 258–64), which are specifically designed for learning ejaculatory control.

When you feel you are in control of when you ejaculate, return to this process and complete Exercises 24 and following, incorporating the squeeze technique in your touching exercises.

Date: _____ *Time:* _____

Total-Body Pleasuring, Including Breast and Genital Stimulation

(Fill in the blanks as you plan your sessions.)

STEP 1: _____ will take responsibility to initiate the experience and set the atmosphere with attention to temperature, privacy, and mood.

STEP 2: Bathe or shower together. You may wash each other totally.

STEP 3: _____ will be the first pleasurer. _____ will be the first receiver.

STEP 4: Read Assignment 1, Underlying Principles for Body Caressing. Read and discuss the current instructions. Even though stimulation is added to this exercise, arousal should neither be expected nor stopped. Sexual arousal is an involuntary response. Do not become concerned if there is or is not arousal. Enjoy whatever happens.

STEP 5: *Receiver:* Lie on your abdomen in a comfortable position.

Pleasurer: Place your hands on your spouse's back. Enjoy pleasuring the back of your spouse's body in any way that is positive to you, giving and receiving warmth through your hands. Rely on your spouse to redirect you if anything you do becomes negative or demanding. Inform your spouse when you are ready for him or her to turn over.

Receiver: Turn onto your back. Soak in the pleasure.

Pleasurer: Sitting with your spouse's head, faceup, in your lap (if that is comfortable for both of you) proceed with a facial caress. Then continue down his or her neck, shoulders, chest, arms, and hands. Enjoy stimulating his or her breasts for your pleasure, not for the result it produces. Incorporate the knowledge you gained from the non-demand teaching as to the type of touch your spouse enjoys. Move to the side or between the legs of your spouse to pleasure his or her abdomen, legs, and genitals. Again, enjoy stimulating his or her genitals for your pleasure, incorporating what you have learned about the type of stimulation your spouse prefers. Never touch in a way that is negative to your spouse. Encourage your spouse to redirect you immediately if any touching, especially of his or her genitals, is not comfortable or becomes negative. Inform your spouse when you are finished.

STEP 6: You may want to rest or take a break before you reverse roles and repeat Step 5, but you are free to continue. _____ will be the pleasurer. _____ will be the receiver. Couples often find with the more involved caressing assignments, it is best to complete the assignment at two different times: one day/evening, he is the receiver and she the pleasurer; another day/evening, she is the receiver and he the pleasurer.

STEP 7: Discuss the experience. Write your reactions.

Date: _____ *Time:* _____

Sharing Love

Complete the following statements as candidly and honestly as you can, then share your responses with each other using the Communication Format, page 16.

1. When I love you, I show it by . . .

2. I know you love me when you . . .

3. I know you are reaching out to me when you . . .

4. When you reach out to me, I feel . . .

5. When I am turned on, I . . .

6. I know you are turned on when you . . .

7. You turn me on when you . . .

8. I feel sexual pleasure when . . .

9. When you stimulate me physically, I feel . . .

10. Our sexual relationship makes me feel . . .

Date: _____ Time: _____

Pleasuring, Not Using Hands (Including Using the Penis as a Paintbrush)

(Fill in the blanks as you plan your sessions.)

STEP 1: _____ will take responsibility to see that the experience happens and to set up the environment for your time together. The atmosphere should allow for playfulness and creativity.

STEP 2: Together, read these instructions and the Underlying Principles for Body Caressing. Tell each other what each of you understands the assignment to be.

STEP 3: Bathe or shower together in a way that brings relaxation and enjoyment of each other's bodies.

STEP 4: _____, start the actual pleasuring by following Assignment 1, Underlying Principles for Body Caressing, except this time you may use any part of your body except your hands. Make it an experimental and fun time of discovering what parts of your body you really enjoy using to touch _____. You might use your hair, nose, eyes, tongue, ears, forearms, breasts, genitals, feet, or whatever. Try many body parts.

When you have thoroughly enjoyed your spouse's total body, reverse roles. _____ will use various parts of his or her body to pleasure _____. Each of you use your hands to hold the penis, whether erect or flaccid, to stroke over the wife's clitoris, labia, and vaginal opening, but not with entry into the vagina. Stop when you feel you have thoroughly enjoyed your spouse's total body. Some attempts at using body parts may feel awkward. That is expected and not to be seen as negative.

STEP 5: Write your reactions. Talk about the experience. What felt particularly good? What did you discover about yourself? About your spouse? What barriers were there for you? What got in the way of maximum enjoyment?

SEXUAL RETRAINING ASSIGNMENT 27

Date: _____ Time: _____

Shared Self-Stimulation

This is an optional assignment described on page 251. Some couples have found it to be a helpful step for the woman who is able to be orgasmic through self-stimulation but not with her husband. Read about it together, and decide if it is fitting for you as a couple.

SEXUAL RETRAINING ASSIGNMENT 28

Date: _____ Time: _____

Total-Body Pleasuring with Mutual Manual Stimulation

(Fill in the blanks as you plan your sessions.)

STEP 1: _____ will take responsibility to initiate the experience and set the atmosphere. You might want to vary from your past locations or choose one of the favorites you have already enjoyed.

STEP 2: Bathe or shower together. Enjoy each other in any way that is pleasurable for both of you.

STEP 3: Review Assignment 1, Underlying Principles for Body Caressing, with each other. Remind each other of the guidelines that the two of you have found to be important in order to reduce demand and enhance freedom.

STEP 4: _____, begin by pleasuring the back of _____'s body. Proceed just as you did with Assignment 6, Back Caress. Reverse roles. _____, pleasure the back of _____'s body. Spend some time taking turns leading each other in kissing while embracing each other's nude body. Take time to nibble, suck, lick, and thrust tongues. Proceed to mutually enjoy each other's bodies with any form of touch that has been positive so far. Do not have entry of the penis into the vagina. Spend some time manually stimulating each other's genitals. If it's more comfortable to take turns, that's fine. Use any part of your body to enjoy any part of your spouse's body. Have fun and vary the intensity.

STEP 5: Write your reactions. Talk about what you liked best, where you still felt inhibited, what you would like more of, and what you would not like unless you ask for it.

SEXUAL RETRAINING ASSIGNMENT 29

Date: _____ *Time:* _____

Principles Learned

STEP 1: Each of you write down the principles you have learned during this sexual retraining process that would best enhance your sexual life.

STEP 2: Share your ideas with each other, taking turns being the sharer and the active listener. Refer to the Communication Format, page 16.

STEP 3: Work together with both of your lists of principles to develop one joint list. Number the principles in order of priority.

SEXUAL RETRAINING ADJUSTMENT
FOR ERECTILE DYSFUNCTION

If you are going through this process to overcome problems with getting or keeping erections, you will need to modify Exercise 30, Total-Body Pleasuring with Entry, page 194. Omit the last sentence of Step 4. Do *not* enter all the way. In fact, the first time you do this exercise, only poke the penis barely into the opening of the vagina.

Repeat this exercise many times on different occasions (varying the total-body pleasuring each time). Each subsequent time, poke the penis into the vagina a quarter-inch farther. If at any point this triggers loss of erection, anxiety, or spectatoring, STOP! Just relax and enjoy the pleasure of each other's bodies, and DO *NOT* poke into the vagina any more during that experience. The next experience or two should not include penile-vaginal contact. Go back to the previous pleasuring exercises that were enjoyable for you and distracting from your focus on getting or keeping your erection.

When you feel secure, try Exercise 30 again, starting with poking into the vagina a quarter-inch. Continue as instructed above, unless you need to backtrack to build security. Once full entry has occurred, use the instructions on page 236 of chapter 16 for continuing this assignment.

SEXUAL RETRAINING ASSIGNMENT 30

Date: _____ Time: _____

Total-Body Pleasuring with Entry

(Fill in the blanks as you plan your sessions.)

STEP 1: _____ will take responsibility to initiate the experience and set
the atmosphere. It will be important for this exercise to not only
provide for mood, temperature, and privacy, but also birth control,
if needed.

STEP 2: Bathe or shower together. Enjoy each other's bodies in any way
that is positive for both of you.

STEP 3: Review Assignment 1, Underlying Principles for Body Caressing,
with each other. Talk about your feelings of being able to proceed
to intercourse. Adjust for any concerns or demands that might
arise.

STEP 4: _____ will begin by giving _____ a facial, hand, and foot caress.
Then spend some time mutually hugging, kissing, and enjoying the
pleasure of each other's bodies in any way that is positive for both
of you. Include breast and genital stimulation and using the penis
as a paintbrush to stimulate _____'s genitals. She may invite the
husband to do some poking of the penis into the vagina by adding
a lubricant to the penis and between the labia, separating them as
she does. With the woman in the top position, poke in a little at a
time. Enter all the way when that is comfortable for both of you.

STEP 5: Rest together quietly without thrusting. Enjoy the closeness of
each other's bodies. Kiss and pleasure as you desire. Then begin
gentle thrusting. The woman should control the thrusting. Stop
to rest every few minutes. Move around in any way you desire.
When it is desirable for both, allow the intensity of the thrusting
to build. Continue as long as that is pleasurable for both of you.
If there is release for either or both of you, that is fine, but it is
not necessary. Ejaculation and orgasm are reflex responses to the
intense buildup of sexual arousal. When your body is ready for

that and you can allow it, it will happen. That is not an expectation of this exercise.

STEP 6: Write your reaction. Talk about the experience from start to finish. What was most positive? What got in the way? Was there any pain, anxiety, demand?

Date: _____ Time: _____

Creating Your Ongoing Sexual Plan

STEP 1: Read chapter 20 out loud together and discuss.

STEP 2: Using the list of principles you have prioritized and what you have learned in chapter 20, individually write out a plan for your sexual relationship that would ensure that these principles will be followed.

STEP 3: Share your plans with each other using the Communication Format, page 16.

STEP 4: Work together, combining ideas from both plans, to make a joint plan that represents all of your desires for your ongoing sexual relationship. Be realistic. If, before you started this process, you had been having sexual times several times a year, don't now expect to have them more than once a week. If it was difficult for you to schedule times to do these assignments, assume you will be able to be together about as often or less frequently than you were able to do the assignments. Evaluate your habits and lifestyle; do make changes, but not so extreme that you will be frustrated and fail.

Be very specific. Define the different types of sexual experiences you would like to have, how preparation and initiation will happen, when and where the experiences will happen, how you will handle rescheduling if a scheduled time has to be canceled, how you will decide who will be the initiator for each scheduled time, and how you will plan for scheduled and spontaneous opportunities.

THIRTEEN

Overcoming Barriers

The general retraining process described in chapter 12 includes the basic steps to sexual pleasure. This process should be adapted to address the particular difficulty you are experiencing. Most sexual barriers can be grouped into the following categories:

1. Problems due to couple dissatisfaction
2. Problems of desire
3. Problems with arousal
4. Problems with release
5. Problems with intercourse
6. Sexual addictions

The first category has to do with relationship issues. These are shown in italic on the graph on page 140 under both "Approach-Avoidance and Frequency Issues" and "Boredom, Inhibition, and Spectatoring," which interfere with the "Pleasuring" process, identified in bold italic, and with the physical phases of "Excitement" and "Plateau," identified in bold. The last category refers to sexual behaviors that have control over you. Categories 2 through 5 are technically considered sexual dysfunctions.

The earlier in the cycle the dysfunction occurs, the more difficult it is to relieve the symptom. The later in the sexual experience the problem occurs, the simpler it is to treat. For example, problems of desire often require more psychotherapy, whereas problems with release are usually remedied with the sexual retraining exercises we have provided.

You will need to coordinate the sexual retraining process described in chapter 12 with the specific suggestions for overcoming your sexual barrier found in the chapter that addresses that specific issue. Assignments in chapter 12 guide you to those specific sections as needed. Similarly, the steps in the chapters that follow will refer you back to the sexual retraining process when appropriate.

We hope the general retraining and the specific barrier retraining described in these chapters will lead you smoothly to the fulfillment you so desire. These exercises have brought success to hundreds of couples; we are confident they can work for you too.

FOURTEEN

Overcoming Couple Dissatisfaction

Chronic conflicts between a husband and a wife can slowly deteriorate their sexual fulfillment in the same way the friction of feet walking up a carpeted stairway wears the center of that carpet over time. One footstep alone will not cause noticeable effect, but long-term repetitions will destroy the carpet. Similarly, conflicts about the frequency of sexual activity, initiation, boredom, or inhibition do not show their wearing effects immediately. In fact, the difference you experience may not even seem significant at first; but eventually, your sexual life can be destroyed by what would seem to be minor wear and tear.

FREQUENCY

When spouses differ on the frequency of their desire for sexual contact, conflict is likely to result. With time, the perception of their differences becomes exaggerated. If he desires sex once a day and she is happy with it once a week, eventually he begins to believe she would only want sex once a month and she is convinced he would like it three times a day.

When you completed your assessment form and were asked how frequently each of you would like to be together sexually, you were probably shocked by the other's response. In these chapters, we will share some examples of couples we have worked with. Each couple's story begins after a large, heart-shaped symbol pierced with an arrow. The treatment for that couple's problem follows an Rx symbol.

For example, Earl came to the assessment session with the complaint that Marianne never wanted to be together sexually. Marianne said she never had a chance to experience her own need for sex because Earl always initiated it before she had a chance to feel that need. When Earl was asked how often he would like to be with Marianne sexually, he said two to three times a week would make him happy. When he was asked what he thought Marianne's desire was, he said he suspected she would not care if they went two or three weeks without any sexual contact.

When the same questions were asked of Marianne, she said she would like sex once or twice a week and thought Earl would like it every day—or even twice a day.

Clarifying for Earl and Marianne that their desire for sexual frequency was not that far apart allowed them to negotiate a compromise. Earl realized that three times a week would probably be ideal for him. Marianne thought that once a week was more realistic for her. So they compromised and worked out a plan to be together twice a week.

They decided to schedule their experiences so that they would have quality time together. In this way, Earl was relieved of his concern that he might not be able to have sex as often as he needed, and Marianne could give herself more fully to their encounters because she knew sex was not expected every night. (We also see couples where it is the woman who is frustrated because of her desire for more frequent contact and the man feels pressured.)

Rx *Resolution* of a frequency problem is not always this simple. Some differences are much more extreme. In these cases, negotiation and compromise take more work. Other times, the extreme difference may indicate a deeper issue, such as lack of sexual desire. In this situation, the sexual dysfunction needs to be addressed by referring to chapter 15.

In recent times, lack of frequency has become more of a joint concern, instead of a conflict—neither spouse is satisfied with the couple's frequency of sexual experiences. These are referred to as *low-sex/no-sex marriages*. Both may have full-time jobs and a toddler who is in day care all day. When they come home from work, they share the responsibility of caring for their child, preparing dinner, and tending to household duties. By the time they have finished all this, they need to get to sleep. Weekends are their only social and church times, so there is little or no time left for the two of them.

Scheduling is the only answer to a lifestyle that does not leave room for the husband-wife sexual relationship. When the scheduling solution is suggested, one of the spouses will usually contest it by saying, "But how can you schedule sex? You can't schedule when you're going to feel turned on."

To some extent that concern is true. You cannot schedule yourselves to be turned on. But the scheduled block of time is saved and prepared for so that life's demands do not snatch those moments away. The time is freed of distractions, as in the sexual retraining process, and designed for communicating and touching in the privacy of your bedroom. This allows sexual interest, arousal, release, or intercourse to develop if that is desired by both of you; but the expectation or demand for anything more than physical and emotional connection during this time must be deliberately removed.

When a couple is satisfied with the quality and frequency of their sexual experiences, scheduling times to be physical is not necessary. But many couples find that planned times that can be anticipated and prepared for actually enhance the delight they enjoy together sexually.

INITIATION

Initiation stress usually manifests itself as an *approach-avoidance pattern*—one pursues and the other avoids. This pattern may have started already in dating. More often, it is the man who has pursued and the woman has set the boundaries, but not always.

We have observed that there is a difference in frequency of sex when the man is the pursuer than when the woman is more eager. When the man wants sex more than the woman, they tend to have it more. When the woman wants sex more often than the man, she may complain of their lack of frequency, but their frequency does not increase. In some situations, the husband would be happy to respond as frequently as she desires if she would initiate sex. So, by her taking responsibility to express her sexual desire, the problem is often relieved, but not always. Even when the woman approaches, the couple's frequency is not as likely to increase if his desire is lower than hers.

On the other hand, sometimes what happens over time is that both spouses begin to experience their conflict as a frequency issue, similar to Earl and Marianne's. Because the wife does not show her interest in being together sexually, the husband begins to believe she has no interest in him sexually. His insecurity is triggered by her apparent lack of interest, so he anxiously begins to initiate sex more often than he would want it if he were feeling sure of himself in relation to her. She feels pressured by his initiation, so she begins to avoid him or pull away sexually. The more he approaches, the more consistent is her avoidance. The more frequent her avoidance, the more anxious is his approach. It becomes a negative spiral.

Sometimes the approach-avoidance cycle is not just a discomfort with overt sexuality, but is triggered by a difference in desire for frequency. When one spouse is always wanting sex, the other feels pressured, so he or she starts to avoid it; then the one with higher desire increases the frequency of approaching, working on averages. For example, if it is the husband who has the higher desire, he may believe if he initiates eight times, he's likely to get his wife involved once. She believes he wants it eight times, so she feels all he ever wants is sex. Then she begins the avoidance behavior.

One spouse may avoid sex because it is a negative experience. If a man ejaculates prematurely or loses his erection, he will want to avoid the failure experience. His wife may increase her approach in response to his pulling away.

Sometimes one person is exhausted. The idea of sex might be great, but he or she does not have the energy to initiate the activity. When that fatigue is ongoing, the other spouse may begin to experience the lack of initiation as avoidance and then pursue initiation of sexual activity more vigorously.

The approach-avoidance initiation pattern must be reversed by a simple problem-solving experience. The format we recommend is outlined here.

R̲x̲ Problem Solving for Initiation Problems

STEP 1: Each of you write how you experience your initiation process. What do you do and what do you feel in the process of sexual initiation?

STEP 2: During a prescheduled two- to three-hour block of time:

A. Read each other's descriptions of your initiation process.

B. Provide feedback about how you understand the other's description.

C. Clarify and expand on what you wrote.

D. Agree on the need for a change.

E. Make a plan for that change. One suggestion for a plan is:

  1. Set aside a designated period of time, perhaps one to two weeks. During this time:

    a. The usual initiator is to make no hints at sexual activity but is to be loving and warm.

    b. The usual avoider is responsible for initiating one sexual event of his or her choice.

  2. At the prescheduled ending of the designated time period:

    a. Each of you talk about your feelings that occurred during the experimental week(s).

    b. Talk about what actually happened sexually.

    c. Make a follow-up plan for the next week or two. Revise the previous plan to accommodate any difficulties that occurred.

The need to revise the previous plan may become evident at the follow-up talk if the sexually hesitant spouse shares that he or she tried to initiate sex but the other did not respond. Soon the initiator discovers the other spouse was not even aware of the initiation; the sexual subtleness then becomes evident. The plan needs to include a clear understanding of how the usual avoider will initiate on future attempts.

BOREDOM

Boredom with the sexual relationship usually sets in after a few years of the typical American lovemaking experience. The scenario goes like this: The couple is in bed. The eleven o'clock news is on the television. He has the remote control. She is half asleep. The news is over. He flicks off the television, rolls over, flops his arm over her breasts, and begins fondling her. She stirs and gets involved to some extent. He gets an erection. She may or may not get aroused. They have intercourse. He ejaculates. She may or may not respond orgasmically. Five or seven minutes later, it is over. They could both write the script. Their sexual experiences are totally predictable and primarily functional.

℞ The *solution* is again to schedule time for quality sex. When boredom is a problem, not only does the time need to be planned, so does the activity. Take turns creating the setting. The exercises described in chapter 12 will guide you in expanding your sexual repertoire. Activities like the Pleasuring, Not Using Hands and the Creative Pleasuring assignments will be particularly stretching in helping you learn how to be experimental and creative in bed.

INHIBITIONS

The friction of inhibitions may cause wear and tear on a couple's sexual relationship fairly quickly. The inhibited one feels tenaciously bound by the inhibitions, while the other's frustration intensifies quickly because of the way the inhibitions control and limit their relationship. Inhibitions can be religious or personal.

Religious inhibitions are just that; they are not biblical or Christian. You may have been raised with rigid antisexual teaching in your home or church. Now, in marriage, it is difficult to freely give your body to your spouse, or it is difficult to enjoy your spouse's body. You may carry a mental list of "shoulds" and "should nots" into each sexual experience. If this is your situation, it will be very difficult for you to connect godliness with intense sexual freedom. As one man wrote to us, "Your book is convincing ministers in my denomination that sex is to be enjoyed. Sexual enjoyment *is of the flesh.* Husbands and wives are only to fulfill their duty to one another and produce children."

If such beliefs are deeply ingrained in you, you may not be open to change. For those of you who want to integrate your spirituality and sexuality, we encourage you to actively invite God into your sexual activity. Review chapter 5, then the biblical passages teaching about sex in marriage. Read parts of the Song of Solomon in a modern version as part of your preparation for lovemaking. Thank God every time you have a sexual feeling. Actively ask God to be present and bless you as you enjoy your sexual times together.

As sexual therapists, you may see us as being spiritually suspect. If this is the case, we encourage you to seek the help of a sexually affirming spiritual mentor: your minister, minister's wife, priest, Bible-study leader, or other religious authority. We hope that person will help you connect your sexuality with your spirituality and give you permission to thoroughly enjoy your sexual relationship in marriage.

Personal inhibitions may have been triggered by a past trauma, situation, or teaching that caused you to think of certain parts of your body or secretions or activities as aversive. Some men are repulsed by a woman's genitals or vaginal secretions. Often these men do not like messes or spills. For example, Alvin did not want to touch Susan's vagina; he said it made him feel "yucky." The Clinical Genital Exam (Assignment

15) had to be assigned several times and done in small increments. He tried to look the first time, touch the second time, and actually stroke the third time. You may need to make adjustments in the assignment this same way.

Alvin was never allowed to be messy as a young child. Even now when his mother feeds Alvin's baby daughter, she constantly wipes the baby's mouth and hands and makes sure there will be no mess.

Women who were sexually abused may have difficulty or be unable to engage in the sexual activity that was forced upon them as children. Some of these women cannot look at or touch their husbands' penises. Others cannot allow their husbands to fondle them.

When inhibitions restrict the sexual experience, freedom from that bondage is desired. Often, inhibited clients have tried desperately to engage in the desired activity, but to no avail. They have learned the hard way that there is no way they can suddenly jump from where they are to where they want to be sexually. Freedom from inhibitions can be achieved, but it requires time, patience, and practice. We have used the following procedure to help many couples overcome this barrier.

℞ *Treatment for sexual inhibition is behavioral.* If you struggle with a sexual inhibition, start by defining that inhibition. Write your inhibition on the left of a sheet of paper. On the right of the paper, write the behavior that would indicate freedom from this inhibition. Next, fill in the many tiny steps you could take to get from inhibition to sexual freedom. Each step is a "just-noticeable difference" from the previous step. An example is shown in Table 14.1.

Whether the relationship issue affecting the sexual experience is dissatisfaction with frequency, stressful initiation patterns, boredom, or more difficult inhibition, the symptom must be dealt with behaviorally. The relationship patterns must be changed if the symptoms are to be relieved and mutual satisfaction enjoyed.

Table 14.1

STEPS FROM INHIBITION TO FREEDOM

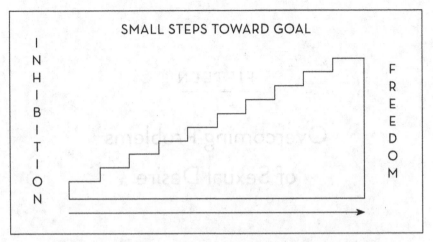

Example: A woman who has difficulty touching or enjoying her husband's penis might fill in the steps from the lowest to the highest as follows:

- Touch penis over undershorts and pants for five seconds.

- Touch penis over undershorts and pants for ten, twenty, and then thirty seconds.

- Touch penis directly for five, ten, twenty, and then thirty seconds.

- Give penis a friendly name.

- Thank God daily for your husband's penis.

- Daily, pat and claim your husband's penis as your "friend"—may start over clothes and increase contact until directly touching penis comfortably.

- Stroke and fiddle with your husband's penis on a daily basis.

- Mentally picture his penis being a warm, comforting, pleasant gift from God.

- Continue to affirm, enjoy, and stroke your husband's penis in longer and longer periods of time until ejaculation occurs.

- Freedom from inhibitions is evident when you are able to manually enjoy your husband's penis for your pleasure without negative feelings.

FIFTEEN

Overcoming Problems
of Sexual Desire

nhibited sexual desire (also referred to as Hypoactive Sexual Desire Disorder—HSDD—when it causes personal and interpersonal distress) means your natural urge to be physically close, to be touched, to be aroused, and to have release is in some way blocked so that you are not sexually drawn to your spouse.

Some people with inhibited sexual desire are not aware of any sexual feelings at all, not even a flickering. It would not be a problem for them if they never had sex. Others masturbate but have no desire for the intimacy of sex with their spouses. Still others only feel sexual desire for someone they cannot have or someone who is destructive for them. And then there are those who feel sexual urges for their spouses, but only when there is no possibility of acting on those urges.

The sexual drive can be totally blocked or it can be misdirected. Many times there is a barrier that keeps sexual energy from being expressed or experienced in the marriage relationship.

Although we are all born with a sex drive, about 40 percent of sexual therapy clients report disorders of sexual desire (as reported from the clinical practice of Helen Singer Kaplan and as we have found in our own practice). Men, as well as women, experience loss of desire. Problems of desire are usually deeper, more resistant problems than the dilemmas of arousal or orgasm.

All of us want to have sex by desire. We trust that as you work through this chapter, you will gradually regain, or gain for the first time, desire for sex with your spouse. However, sometimes that is not possible due to physical or other issues. We encourage you to never have sex out of duty or demand, but you can pursue a mutually satisfying sexual relationship by decision: decide when, where, and what would make it the best for you that is possible given your situation.

FEMALE DESIRE PROBLEMS

Desire barriers for women may be secondary to some other difficulty, or they may be the primary issue.

Secondary to Dissatisfying Experiences

When the sexual experience itself is in some way dissatisfying, over the years women will lose their desire to be with their husbands sexually.

Relationship issues. If not resolved, the sexual relationship issues discussed in the last chapter eventually lead to lack of sexual interest. More general relationship problems can also spill over and keep a woman from sexually desiring her husband. If she feels uncared for, she may believe the only interest her husband has in her is sex. He comes home from work, turns on the television, sits quietly at dinner, and watches television after dinner. Then at bedtime, he becomes friendly—and her anger sizzles. When relationship issues have resulted in loss of sexual desire, marital counseling may be necessary. The retraining process can help resolve these issues, but the underlying stress in the relationship must be resolved before desire can be restored.

Unsatisfactory sexual response. The loss of sexual desire may be due to a lack of sexual responsiveness. If a woman has difficulty becoming aroused or having an orgasm, with time the couple's initial excitement of being together will lessen.

It was 9:00 a.m. Friday and clearly felt like the end of the week. A mixture of anticipation and fatigue swept over us as we began a three-hour evaluation. The fatigue lessened, though, as we became intrigued with unraveling another couple's problem.

Tim and Nancy were a striking Southern California couple. They were tanned, well-dressed, jeweled, confident, and beautiful people. They had been sexually active for the six months before they were married. That activity continued into the marriage with excitement and more freedom. Nancy reported wanting sex as much as Tim. Initially, they were together four to five times a week.

Although Tim was usually the aggressor and more active in the sexual experience than Nancy, she would become very turned on—so aroused that she would beg for entry. But after entry, her arousal seemed to get stuck while, within a few minutes, Tim would ejaculate.

At first, this was no big deal; but the frustration that Nancy experienced after entry began to intensify as the situation was repeated. Tim was working long hours, so he would fall asleep shortly after intercourse. Nancy, on the other hand, would lie there wide awake, feeling all stirred up, and not knowing what to do with her buildup of energy and emotions.

After three years, she noted that more and more often, they were having sex because Tim wanted it; very seldom was she getting aroused. Even when she did get aroused, it was not the intense arousal that had left her awake and frustrated earlier in their marriage. Now, more than four years later, Nancy was complaining of total lack of sexual desire. As far as she was aware, she had never experienced orgasm in response to any form of stimulation.

Nancy's lack of sexual desire was diagnosed as secondary to inhibited sexual release. The graph of her sexual response from the beginning of their sexual intercourse experiences to now would be gradually declining until it was a flat line. It took longer for her to get aroused, her arousal was less intense, and eventually she did not let herself get aroused at all.

By now, even the flicker of positive anticipation of sexual activity had left. Now she was having sex with Tim once a week out of duty, obligation, and guilt for not desiring him. The graphs of her sexual response from the time of their initial sexual activity until the time of the evaluation would look like the graph in Figure 15.1.

Figure 15.1

DIMINISHING SEXUAL RESPONSE IN UNFULFILLED WOMEN

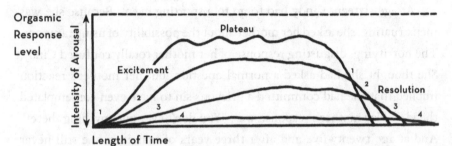

R℟ The *solution* to loss of sexual desire due to lack of response is to pursue the sexual retraining process provided in chapter 12, incorporating the specific suggestions from chapter 17 on becoming orgasmic.

Lack of Desire Due to Internal Sexual Conflict

For women (and some men), sexual desire may be inhibited due to sexual conflict, the inability to accept their sexuality, or their feelings about the sexual experience. When women or men experience conflict about being sexual, it may be because of rigid antisexual teaching, past sexual trauma, or ambivalence about being out of control and vulnerable.

Rigid antisexual teaching. Adults who were raised in restrictive homes that were rigidly antisexual and strongly religious struggle to freely express themselves sexually within their married relationship. They tend to be intensely sexual when that is not condoned by the standards they have been taught but cannot enjoy sex when it is good and of God. Spirituality and sexuality were deeply ingrained as being in conflict with each other. Relief from this conflict is possible.

One of the most extreme examples of antisexual input was reported by Cindy, a beautiful young woman who, after three years, had not consummated her marriage. She had been raised in a warm, safe, but very strict Catholic home and school. In their home, they were not allowed to shower with the lights on or to ever be in the nude in a lighted room, lest they see themselves. They were directly taught to never use their hands to touch or wash their genitals, but to always use a washcloth. Menstruation was handled with a "hush-hush" attitude and limited interaction.

At age sixteen, Cindy had to go to a sporting event. Because she was menstruating, she asked her mother about the possibility of using tampons. The horrifying, disgusting response of her mother totally confused Cindy. She thought she had asked a normal question, but her mother's reaction implied that she had committed a grievous sin to have even contemplated the idea. Her mother's response was, "You don't ever put anything there!" And at age twenty-five and after three years of marriage, she still never had. Nor had she given herself permission to be a sexual person with sexual desire and enjoyment of sexual pleasure. Attending our seminar was her first immersion into positive biblical attitudes about sexuality.

When rigid antisexual teaching is associated with religion, the conflict is relieved by following the same steps presented in chapter 4 for reducing religious inhibitions. You need to be given permission to enjoy your sexuality and receive sexual pleasure. Deliberate, positive input regarding sexuality is necessary to counteract the lifelong subtle—or not so subtle—teaching that being sexual is to be avoided at all cost.

Sexual trauma. Many who come to us for sexual therapy have had at least one sexual experience that left them feeling confused, guilty, or traumatized. They usually blame themselves for these events and, thus, they feel badly about themselves sexually. They do not feel worthy of receiving sexual pleasure and have incredible conflict when they experience sexual feelings. Whether the event was something as violating as molestation or incest, or even if it was less traumatizing like having guilt about masturbating or fantasizing, sexual feelings have been paired with wrongdoing, fear, pain, or guilt, and it is very difficult to disconnect those feelings.

Usually the traumatic sexual event(s) will have been kept secret. Some victims grow up to believe that something terrible will happen to them if they tell. Others come to believe the nasty images of themselves they have created in their minds as a result of the traumatic event. In the case of abuse, the abuser may have warned the little girl not to tell and made threats about what would happen if she told anyone.

One woman said her rapist (who raped her when she was ten) had told her she would be put in a mental institution if she told because no one would believe her. They would know she was crazy, he had said; he was a strong leader in her church.

Another woman had gone to her mother at age six to try to tell her what the father was doing to her. The mother never even let her finish; instead, the girl was reprimanded for thinking up such outrageous ideas. It is easy to understand why women with such experiences would have difficulty enjoying their sexuality and their sexual relationship in marriage.

Guilt and shame are carried into adult life. The event may have been as innocent as discovering Dad's *Playboy* magazines and becoming aroused. Children feel responsible, not realizing they are innocent victims. They often believe they elicited or encouraged the abuse or the exposure. Some little girls let the abuse happen because it was the only way they got Dad's love and affection. Yet they grow up with the heavy burden of shame, and they feel different from everyone else. They know that they have an awareness that other children their age do not have.

Girls who have experienced traumatic or negative emotions associated with sexuality may be withdrawn and shy, with low self-esteem, or they may become tough, act out aggressively, and become sexually promiscuous. In adult life, these women may have sexual phobias or aversions that make them tenaciously resistant to being sexual. Their panic reaction or avoidance may be to sex in general or to the specific sexual activities that were associated with the traumatic event. Some women who were molested as children do not want to have anything to do with sex with their husbands. Others who were forced to stimulate a man cannot look at or touch their husbands' penises, but can enjoy all other sexual activity.

The woman who was fondled by her abuser may be able to freely enjoy her husband's body, but never allow him to touch her. Yet these same women may need to fantasize the content of the trauma to become aroused and have an orgasm. This is the epitome of the conflict; the very activity that caused pain is necessary for the response. No wonder they do not desire sex and fight sexual response even though they want it.

There are women who lack sexual desire and display many of the symptoms of having been sexually traumatized, yet have no recollection of any such experiences. Either they were too young to remember, they blocked out the event to protect themselves against the inner pain, or they experienced other trauma that produced the same conflict about sexuality as abuse.

℞ *Undoing* the sexual conflict caused by a sexual experience that elicited confusion, guilt, or trauma requires more than just sexual retraining. Joining a group for victims of past abuse will be very helpful. The traumatic experience must be treated in several phases. It must be grieved and released; the sexual self must be developed (developmental tasks may need to be mastered); the guilt, shame, and trauma must be disconnected from the sexual experiences in marriage; then positive sexual feelings must be paired with safe sexual experiences through the sexual retraining process. We will offer suggestions for each of these phases in the following discussion.

Phase 1: Grieving and Releasing the Traumatic Experiences. To free themselves of the lasting effects of the sexually traumatic event, women need to *talk* about the abuse. The details of what happened must be shared on numerous occasions. *Writing down* the memories is also essential. Researchers have found that writing and talking about traumatic events can help reduce adjustment problems caused by the trauma.[1] Many women keep a journal or notebook in which they write any thoughts, feelings, dreams, or flashbacks. Writing helps you face the reality of what happened and helps you transfer the experience out of yourself onto the paper. Then you put it on the shelf. Ellen Bass and Laura Davis's book *The Courage to*

Heal[2] guides the reader through the healing process with written exercises. We differ with their acceptance of lesbianism as a possible solution to the problem. Yet their book is the best resource we know for describing this process.

In addition to talking and writing, *professional help* is often needed. Women's *sexual-abuse groups* help the abused woman find support and begin to realize that she is not alone in her pain. If you have symptoms of past abuse but no memory of it, being part of a group and hearing other women share their pain may trigger your memory. Reading about abuse can also open your awareness. Susan Forward and Craig Buck's book *Betrayal of Innocence*[3] has been the catalyst for a number of women to draw out their painful memories. We use this book as a diagnostic tool. If a woman has the symptoms of abuse but no recollection, reading *Betrayal of Innocence* will usually evoke intensely painful feelings, and quite often depression. This reaction does not seem to happen in women without an abusive past, even though the book is sad to read.

Phase 2: Developing the Sexual Self. Your sexual, and possibly your emotional, development may have been arrested when the abuse began or the traumatic event occurred. *Psychotherapy* is usually necessary to aid you in defining how you see yourself sexually. It helps you develop your sexual self-esteem so that one day you will be able to say, "Yes, I am a sexual person and I'm proud of it!" The stages of sexual development depicted in Table 6.1 on page 52 may be helpful in identifying the developmental tasks you need to master.

Phase 3: Disconnecting Shame, Guilt, and Trauma from the Sexual Experiences in Marriage. To disconnect the negative feelings from sex in marriage, you have to go through a process of *letting go of the pain.* You have to recognize that what happened to you was not your fault. You were a victim in those circumstances. Even if you were cute and "sexy," even if you did get aroused when you found your dad's magazines, you did not intentionally choose that event. The adults in your world should have protected you and should not have broken the trust and taken away your innocence.

You need to face the hurt, hate, and revenge for what happened. You need to relinquish the pain and *begin to forgive* the adults in your world for violating you and not protecting you. But the process of forgiveness takes time and hard work. It is not a quick solution. Lewis Smedes's book *Forgive and Forget: Healing the Hurts We Don't Deserve*[4] is excellent to help with that process.

The possibility of *confronting your abuser* or your mother (for not protecting you) is usually raised. This issue must be considered most carefully to protect you from another abusive event. We encourage you to gather as much data as possible about the current interaction patterns of the person to be confronted and then to prepare yourself for all possible responses or lack of response. Some victims can let go after they confront, even if there was no response or a non-caring, hurtful response. Others are devastated if they do not receive a response that promotes healing.

Phase 4: Pairing Positive Sexual Feelings with Safe Sexual Experiences. In the final phase we help you work on your sexual relationship with your husband. He must be a part of this *sexual retraining process*. You must be able to trust your husband to keep to the boundaries of the assigned experiences and respect any request from you during the experience.

You must learn to verbalize or give your husband a *prearranged signal* when you have flashbacks of the abuse. Behaviors that cause phobia or aversive reactions are strictly avoided to begin with and then gradually desensitized during the process of retraining. This process of desensitization is the same as was described in chapter 14 for reducing personal inhibitions. Complete all the sexual retraining assignments in chapter 12, unless a recommended experience feels violating. In all touching exercises, you are encouraged to keep actively involved. You are to focus on the fact that you are involved with your husband, that sex is good and of God, and that it feels good to touch and to be touched. It will help to keep your mind actively engaged in positive pictures of the two of you enjoying yourselves.

The goal is that, with the release of the past trauma, the growth of more positive sexual self-esteem, and the disconnection of the negative feelings from the husband-wife sexual encounters, the process of sexual retraining will safely and gradually lead you to learn to delight in your sexual connection with your husband. This process often takes a long time.

Sexual ambivalence. Another source of sexual conflict is ambivalence about being sexual. Even though women experiencing conflict can be very sexually responsive, they relentlessly resist being sexual. This is not a passive lack of interest in sexual activity; it is a persistent avoidance of sex. These women's sexual response graphs look like the graph in Figure 15.2, below.

These women usually come from alcoholic and dysfunctional homes. They struggle with control issues—and to them, being sexually responsive is to be out of control. Their homes were out of control, so they *know* how to let go sexually; but they stubbornly fight it. The woman who lacks sexual desire because of ambivalence is an enigma to her husband. It is confusing to him to try to understand why she would resist when she is so responsive once she "gives in" and her arousal takes over.

R͜x First, the sexually ambivalent person, more often the woman, needs to be able to *decide to be sexual.* This takes time and a trusting, loving relationship. This is very much like a conversion experience. You have been going one direction—fighting being sexual—and now you must go the opposite direction, *deciding* to be sexual, even though you may not feel desire.

Second, your pattern of passively controlling your sexual relationship through resistance must change to one of actively taking control of

Figure 15.2

RESPONSE GRAPH FOR THE SEXUALLY AMBIVALENT SPOUSE

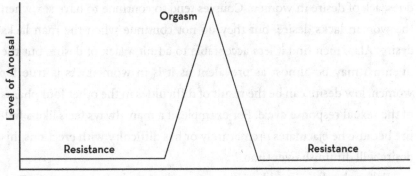

the sexual relationship by planning times to be together sexually. You need *active control*. You have had passive control, but not by decision and not to promote sex. You keep the control, but you do so by deciding to be sexual.

Third, you will have to *schedule* and *initiate* the sexual encounters you have planned, or plan them with your spouse as directed in the sexual retraining process described in chapter 12. It is most difficult to schedule sex without the feeling of desire. You may want so badly to wait until you "feel" like having sex, but our experience suggests that it will be a long time until you initiate sex out of desire. Instead, we recommend that you set aside time on your calendars to be with your spouse at least twice a week—the more often the better.

The fourth task is for the *spouse to assume a passive role*. He no longer initiates or pursues; he allows her to take charge. This may feel wonderful to the spouse of the sexually resistant person because sexual initiation has been completely his burden. These tasks along with the *sexual retraining process* will help you reduce sexual conflict and enhance your sexual relationship. In addition, you may benefit greatly from participating in an ACA (Adult Children of Alcoholics) group.

MALE DESIRE PROBLEMS

Inhibited sexual desire in men can cause more havoc in a marriage than does lack of desire in women. Couples tend to continue to have sex when the woman lacks desire, but they do not continue when the man lacks desire. Also, men find it less acceptable to admit a lack of desire, but the dilemma may be almost as prevalent as it is in women. As is true for women, low desire can be the result of difficulties in the other four phases of the sexual response cycle. For example, if a man always feels like a failure because he ejaculates prematurely or has difficulty with erections, his desire will diminish over time.

When the desire problem is not secondary to performance failure, it is often due to the husband's being sexually naive, overly entrepreneurial and goal-oriented, emotionally and sexually blocked, or homosexually oriented.

The Sexually Naive Male

The sexually naive male may lack desire because of feelings of inadequacy and underdeveloped emotional expression. Perhaps he never mastered the developmental tasks of the preadolescent years (see Stages of Sexual Development, Table 6.1). He was probably raised in an overprotective home or a home where emotional intensity and expression were not allowed. He may even have missed the usual childhood expressions of sexual curiosity such as exploratory play. His dating experience before marriage was probably limited. Thus, he entered marriage still feeling physically awkward with a woman. He may not even know how to kiss passionately. One man put it so aptly. He said, "I feel like a junior-higher in an adult body. When I'm trying to make love to my wife, I just don't know what I'm doing. Nothing flows. When I try to caress her, I jab her with my elbow. Sex just feels overwhelming to me."

℞ The sexually naive male is extremely responsive to *education about sex* (see part 2 of this book) and to the *sexual retraining process*. He is like an empty sponge ready to soak up any information or guided experience that is offered. Education can make a major difference. If he has a loving, cooperative wife, the process flows easily.

The sexual retraining presented in chapter 12 is ideal for training you to be a sexual adult. Start from the beginning and learn to touch; then complete the teaching and talking exercises. The process can usually be followed as we have designed it with few changes. Full, confident sexual functioning is only a few weeks away. Once you have confidence and pleasure, desire will surface rapidly.

The Entrepreneurial Male

The entrepreneurial or overly goal-oriented male has done a great job of courting his wife, who is usually an attractive, competent, and sensual woman. He has provided a beautiful home, maybe a child or two, and a well-managed life. His wife does not have to work, so she has time to pamper herself, take tennis lessons, and so forth. She may even have a housekeeper. In other words, she has plenty of time and space to feel her sexual urges.

One of the entrepreneurial male's goals was to establish an ideal family and home. Now that he has accomplished that, he is on to other goals. These may be building better and bigger companies, developing shopping malls, starting and building churches, or whatever happens to be his interest. He is the type who sees the potential in a project, works it well, turns it over to be run by someone else, and then moves on to the next project—very much like he has done sexually with his wife.

Ellen had prepared a gourmet dinner for Jim (having just finished a French cooking class), had the children in bed, and was waiting in a candlelit room. Jim said he would be home between 8:30 and 9:00 p.m. The clock struck 10:00, and he was still not home. At 10:30 p.m., Ellen got a call from Jim, who said he had just finished negotiating a big business deal and he would be home in about twenty minutes.

This was not a surprise to Ellen. This same, disappointing call had come many times in their eight years of marriage. She had been looking forward to a sexual time together; it had been getting longer and longer between their times of physical closeness. A lonely pang rang through her well-prepared body. But then she remembered the thought that had kept her from complaining: *He has given me so much. I have a great life.* And she went to stretch out on the couch to enjoy the novel she was reading.

Unfortunately, Ellen is clearly being set up for an affair. All her needs are being met—except her sexual and intimacy cravings. Just as he does with all his other projects, the entrepreneurial male prepares his wife to be taken over and managed by someone else. He is goal-oriented. He sees the big possibilities. He cannot be bothered by such trivial details as sexual needs, not his own, nor hers.

R The entrepreneurial male *can* make changes, but the *changes* have to fit his approach to life. If you fit this pattern, you must, by decision, make your wife and your sexual relationship one of your priorities; she has to be scheduled in. Even then you may miss scheduled times because of business pressure. A matter-of-fact approach works best: If you miss your scheduled time, what are the consequences? Maybe you make up the time before you leave for work the next morning, or give her double time the next evening, or take her away for a day. Don't try to *buy* her something for the time missed. Lost intimacy *must* be replaced with intimacy, not gifts.

Some entrepreneurial men have actually chosen to give up their marriages rather than make these seemingly minor adjustments in their lifestyles. Others are very eager to find a system that works for both them and their wives. Some find they can only allow their sexual-drive energy to surface when they can get away somewhere with their wives or families. Fortunately, they can afford to get away on a regular basis and that makes both of them happy. The solution to the entrepreneurial male's lack of sexual desire is primarily one of problem solving, priority setting, and time management. Scheduling is absolutely necessary. Your wife needs to be an appointment on your datebook.

Emotional-Sexual Blocks

Deeper and more emotionally based barriers that cause lack of sexual desire in men present a more difficult challenge. In fact, psychotherapy will be needed for these more tenacious issues. Positive sexual anticipation may be blocked for a man because of lack of bonding in infancy, sexual trauma, rigid antisexual teaching, or a controlling, male-depreciating mother.

Lack of bonding in infancy. The capacity for intimacy is learned during the first year of life. Basic trust develops from the maternal-infant bond.[5] During this critical learning period, the ingredient is acquired that prepares us to be able to be transparent with both our feelings and our sexual desires, to bond affectionately with our spouses, to be able to mutually give and receive pleasure from each other's bodies, and to responsibly and deeply care for each other. This is intimacy.

The *fear of intimacy* occurs in both men and women. Thus, many of the issues related to men's avoidance of sex because of fear of intimacy can also apply to women. In our practice, it has been easier to isolate the intimacy or lack-of-bonding factor for men than for women, possibly because women also display the other issues of sexual conflict. Another reason may be that more mothers have difficulty bonding with infant sons than they do with daughters because of their own fears of sexual feelings that arouse them when they are close to their baby boys.

Men who have been raised with an intimacy deficit (have not had their needs for closeness met early in childhood) are often as resistant to behaving sexually with their spouses as are women who were raised in alcoholic-type homes. They have sexual drive, but they have no capacity for closeness and warmth with a woman. They may even verbally express their desire for what they unconsciously avoid or sabotage by their inappropriate behavior. They may roll away in bed when they notice they are aroused; they may watch television or be distracted in other ways to avoid connecting; they may pick a fight; or they may approach in a way that they have been told many times will be a turnoff rather than a turn-on to their wives.

Many of these men have compulsive masturbatory habits that may be boyish in nature or be connected with a fetish. In this way they are anxiously and guiltily meeting their sexual-drive needs while avoiding the intimacy of a sexual relationship.

James was adopted from institutional care after his first birthday. His adoptive home was adoring, but somewhat lacking in physical and emotional warmth and closeness. As an adult, James was verbally the one desiring more sex. Yet, when we assigned sensate focus/touching exercises, he refused to do them because he said his wife was "just doing them out of obligation."

Later that day he would approach his wife, Ann, in their old pattern that was sure to be a disaster for both of them. He would often have an attack of rage before they were to go away by themselves for a romantic weekend. She was labeled as the one with lack of sexual desire; yet his behaviors indicated that, even though he had the sexual drive, he had incredible fear and avoidance of being sexually intimate with Ann.

Sexual trauma. Sexual trauma produces the same phobic reactions to sex in men as it does in women. The abuse also leaves men with negative feelings about themselves as sexual persons and with uncomfortable feelings—shame, guilt, humiliation, and so on. Thus, the man who experienced childhood sexual abuse or incest usually suffers from low sexual self-esteem. The same guidelines described earlier in this chapter for helping women recover from past sexual abuse should also be used by men who were abused.

Rigid antisexual teaching. Men may have aversive feelings toward sex with their wives as a result of rigid antisexual teaching or a very tight, moral, restrictive upbringing. If your hand was slapped when you discovered your genitals in toddlerhood, if you were punished for exploratory play, or if natural, curious bumbling with the opposite sex was prohibited during junior-high years, you are likely to feel restrictive and anxious about sex. If you also were strictly taught not to masturbate or faced a violent reaction when you were caught masturbating, you probably connect anxiety and guilt with being sexual.

Controlling, male-depreciating mother. If a boy grew up in a home with a mother who totally usurped any of his sense of power and independence as he was developing, he will be very hesitant to allow himself to be open and vulnerable with a woman. Having sex with his wife may elicit an overwhelming sense of panic at being swallowed up or controlled. In addition to being dominant and controlling, if the mother ridiculed his father, the boy's role model, the boy will now grow into manhood feeling very unsure of himself and inadequate as a man. He will have low sexual self-esteem. Fear of being vulnerable with a woman and a sense of sexual inadequacy are clearly components that lead to insufficient sexual desire.

R̶x̶ Men with emotional-sexual blocks will usually require a skilled, creative therapist who can adapt the sexual retraining process to the level of intimacy the man can experience without feeling anxiety or aversion. They will need a combination of *sexual retraining exercises, desensitization,* and *psychotherapy.* The sexual retraining assignments described in chapter 12 may demand too much intimacy and trigger avoidance behavior, but they are worth a try. Even less-anxiety-provoking assignments may be needed. Kaplan said she "employed such tasks as lying near each other, first clothed, then unclothed, for several weeks, until this behavior becomes comfortable, before proceeding to more intimate behavior."⁶ We have assigned taking daily walks together and holding hands, patting and affirming each other's genitals every night at bedtime, or hugging and kissing every morning for ten to fifteen seconds. The Guidelines for Sexual Retraining (Sexual Retraining Assignment 1 in chapter 12) must be adhered to rigidly so that demand experiences are stopped and negative feelings are verbalized.

The man must be desensitized to aversive sexual behaviors using the process described in the treatment of personal inhibitions in chapter 14. It is helpful if the husband defines the small steps he must take to move from his point of resistance to sexual freedom. He might also write out or verbally picture the physical contacts or events that would be positive or possible for him.

When negative feelings are triggered by doing the sexual retraining assignments, or when the assignments are in some way avoided or sabotaged, the process should be interrupted and psychotherapy enlisted to gain insight into the elements that are blocking your desire. To gain this insight, it is recommended that you talk with your wife about the negative feelings and write about them or talk about them with your therapist. You and your wife should talk through each experience in detail, noting exactly what was enjoyable or free of negative feelings, and noting when the negative reaction occurred and what that felt like. Writing about dreams can also help you gain insight into your unconscious reasons for the resistance.

Again, the goal is to relieve the symptoms of avoidance, help you gain a positive connection with your sexual feelings, and accept yourself as a competent sexual person.

Craig's mother was a distant, cold, high-society lady who had no capacity to radiate a warm, loving touch. She clearly let everyone in the family know that she was in charge and superior to her husband in almost every way. He was almost pathetic or disgusting in her eyes. Craig was raised with all the social skills; he was a dapper young man with high moral standards.

Before his marriage to Erin, he was appropriately physical with her.

Erin did not sense his difficulty with sexual intimacy until their wedding night, when they were to have their first sexual intercourse. Craig kept avoiding. He wanted to go for a walk. When they got to their beautiful honeymoon suite, he turned on the television. He ordered a snack to be brought to the room. His negative anticipation of sexually bonding with his wife became very apparent.

When they did have sexual intercourse, it was a quick, genital act. He had no capacity to be passionate or intensely enjoy his wife's body. He resisted almost all future attempts that Erin made to engage him sexually. Sex only seemed to happen on rare occasions if she caught him off guard when he was partially asleep. Later, to her fury, Erin discovered that Craig had a masturbatory fetish that he practiced at least daily. His sexual need was high, but his desire for his wife was absent because of his never having experienced the warmth of a giving mother. He also held a low view of men (and thus of himself) in relation to women, and he had an unconscious fear of losing himself to a woman. In his view, women controlled and dominated men and put them down.

When assigning Craig and Erin sexual retraining exercises, we had to anticipate his sabotage. The exercises had to be modified to start building intimacy gradually. Walking around the block holding hands was successful, and other exercises of controlled intimacy went fairly well. The first real avoidance came with the facial caress. Even after talking through the experience in the session and anticipating his resistance, he still could not proceed when they were home alone together. Craig had limited ability to express his feelings. All he could say was, "I just can't do it."

We, the therapists, started to express his feelings for him with the help of his wife. We talked about his discomfort with touching a woman's face, the body part most connected with personhood. As he heard his feelings of awkwardness and anxiousness expressed, he could identify them. He even began to expand on the feelings as they were expressed for him. We spent some time talking about the images of his mother and how Erin was different from that image. The retraining process for Craig and Erin was slow. Appointments were often missed, and assignments were not completed. In each step of the process, we took time to gain insight into Craig's resistance. At the same time, we had to empower Craig to actively participate in the retraining decisions and in the experiences with Erin. To some extent, Craig will always have to consciously decide to have sexual times with Erin, but those times are now relieved of the helpless, anxious, inadequate feelings of avoidance that plagued every sexual encounter before they came for retraining.

THE HOMOSEXUALLY ORIENTED SPOUSE

Homosexual orientation will make it difficult for a spouse to positively anticipate sex with a heterosexual spouse, just as it would be difficult for a heterosexual spouse to picture himself positively with a same-gender spouse. A person may have always felt that he was more attracted to the same sex than the opposite sex, but never acted upon that attraction. He may have married to be socially and morally acceptable, and he may have been able to function sexually in that marriage, but only by decision or felt necessity, not by desire.

Some couples who have come to us for sexual therapy when one lacks desire due to same-gender attraction, have made the decision that they both wish to find sexual satisfaction in their heterosexual marriage. Occasionally, a couple has come and the one spouse never revealed that he or she is attracted to the same sex. If you are that person in a heterosexual marriage, we encourage you to be open with your spouse. Get nonjudgmental counsel that will help you and your spouse sort out your situation.

℞ Problems of desire in a heterosexual marriage due to homosexual orientation usually respond to the sexual retraining process if the spouse is determined to stay in the marriage and has chosen to have a heterosexual relationship, by choice, not by coercion. The sexual retraining is effective in helping him gradually connect his sexual feelings with one woman, his wife. It will not elicit sexual responsiveness toward women in general nor change his sexual attraction.

OTHER FACTORS THAT REDUCE DESIRE

Both men and women experience lack of sexual desire at some time in their married lives. External circumstances can distract from the sexual-drive energy they feel for each other. *Relationship stresses* can raise a barrier between the spouses' physical anticipation of each other. *Physiological factors* can interfere. Illness may drain most of your erotic energy but leave you still needing touching and closeness.

Alcohol is a depressant; in small quantities, it can reduce anxiety and increase availability, but any more than a little usually takes away sexual-drive energy. *Drugs*, both street and prescription, can interfere with the autonomic nervous system that regulates the sexual response cycle. In her book, *Disorders of Sexual Desire*, Kaplan has an extensive chart showing many types of drugs and their effect on the sexual response cycle.[7] *Hormonal changes* can also affect sexual desire. Oral contraceptives with high progestin and low testosterone activity (e.g., Demulen, Yaz, Desogen, Mircette) are likely to have this effect. Removal of a woman's ovaries removes her primary source of testosterone production. Low testosterone is often the reason for loss of desire in men. Other *emotional stresses*, such as depression or anxiety, will also lower sexual drive.

Whatever the cause of the loss of sexual desire, and whether the woman or the man experiences the struggle, the most effective approach is multifaceted. The goal is to reduce the symptoms and regain new, positive mental expectations of sexual encounters with one's spouse. Psychotherapy, problem solving, priority setting, scheduling, sexual talking, teaching and touching exercises, desensitization, and pro-sexual teaching are all a part of the retraining process. Desire barriers are often more tenacious and more difficult to break through than other sexual barriers. Thus, you may need professional help.

SIXTEEN

Overcoming Problems of Sexual Arousal

Sexual desire in marriage usually leads to sexual activities that stimulate sexual excitement or arousal. Failure of the natural, involuntary bodily response of sexual excitement is usually due to anxiety, although physical and medical causes should be ruled out before assuming an emotional basis.

PROBLEMS OF AROUSAL FOR WOMEN

Lack of Feelings of Arousal

Inhibited sexual excitement for women, once negatively labeled *frigidity*, is usually experiential, not actual. In other words, the woman's body is responding with vaginal lubrication, nipple erection, and initial engorgement, but she does not feel aroused. Her emotions are not connected with her involuntary bodily responses.

These women who lack the feelings of arousal are mentally disconnecting themselves from their bodies. They have not allowed themselves to be sexual persons or to enjoy the giving and receiving of sexual pleasure.

They see sex as a duty they perform to keep their husbands happy and to keep themselves from feeling guilty. They do not visualize themselves in positive sexual activities, nor do they view themselves as having sexual feelings. Usually they devote most of their energy and fill their minds with the tasks of life: their children, their household chores, their jobs, and their social lives.

Even in the actual sexual experience, they will be physically passive and mentally focused on everything but the sexual touching they are receiving. One woman reported that she would count the drops of the water dripping in the shower, trying to focus her mind on anything but sex.

This difficulty with feeling aroused is similar to the sexual conflict that causes lack of sexual desire in women (see chapter 15). Something has happened in these women's pasts that makes it difficult for them to positively associate sexuality with themselves. They have a low sexual self-esteem and certainly a blocked awareness of their sexuality. They are not receptive to sexual stimulation nor the arousal it produces.

R̶x̶ The first task for women who lack feelings of arousal—even though their bodies are responding—is to shift to a *positive mental sexual attitude*, visualizing themselves as sexual beings. The second task is to *encourage positive bodily sensations* while *eliminating negative feelings* associated with sexual touching. By developing a positive sexual mental set, you can learn to enjoy, rather than block out, the feelings of your bodily responses.

You can best accomplish these tasks by (1) giving yourself permission to be a sexual person and to enjoy sexual feelings, (2) connecting sexual feelings with your bodily responses, (3) removing demands and the need to please, and (4) actively listening to your body and vigorously going after sexual pleasure.

The first task is the most difficult. The mental images must change first, then the emotions; the pleasure follows. The reasons for the negative sexual images may have to be explored in psychotherapy before they can be replaced with positive pictures. The programming of positive mental images works best if it is deliberate. Sometimes it is helpful to picture yourself with your spouse in a past positive situation. If you have never experienced positive sexual feelings under any circumstances, you may need to read examples like the Song of Solomon or watch educational videos of positive sexual encounters or imagine what would be positive for you.

Giving yourself permission to be and to feel sexual is an important part of the mental change. You need to make an active decision that you are a sexual person and believe that this is good and of God. Write yourself a note inside your calendar, reminding yourself that you are a sexual person. Stick up verses from the Song of Solomon on the refrigerator door. Look in the mirror and thank God for creating you as a sexual person. These are little ways of reprogramming your mental images and giving yourself permission to be sexual.

The sexual retraining outlined in chapter 12 is the best process for taking on the second task, encouraging positive sexual feelings and eliminating negative ones. Assignment 1, Guidelines for Sexual Retraining, must be followed precisely to remove all performance and response demands.

The touching exercises of the sexual retraining process help you develop the ability to receive and give pleasure for the sake of pleasure. If you feel resistant to proceeding through the process, write about and talk about those feelings. When reporting their reactions to the assignments, women with lack of sexual feeling have pointed out that they felt nothing during the exercises. In these situations, we define neutral as positive; if there was no negative feeling, then it was positive.

We have developed a one-to-ten rating system. Number one is no negative sensation, number two is comfortable, number three is warm, number four is relaxing, and so on. Thus you do not have to say that an experience was positive, but you can rate the experiences with this numbering system that has very low expectations. You likely experience nipple erection and vaginal lubrication, even though you have no feelings associated with these responses. Because of this, numbers nine and ten on the positive-rating system are labeled as nipple erection and vaginal lubrication. Hence, whatever level of functioning is possible, the focus is on the positive aspects of the giving and receiving of pleasure.

Learning to enjoy bodily responses begins with learning to know your body. The female self-exam (Assignment 11 in chapter 12) is vital. Education (part 2) is also important. Reading *The Gift of Sex* aloud with your husband may be an additional help. Graphing your sexual response, as explained in chapter 7, will teach you what to expect and confirm to you that what is happening in your body is sexual. We encourage you and your husband to note bodily responses and affirm them: "I am (You are) aroused!" "Your nipples are erect!" "I am lubricating!"

You can change sex from being an ordeal that you perform to please your husband to a pleasurable experience in which you feel (and enjoy) the sensations of arousal.

Lack of Vaginal Lubrication and Engorgement

Emotions can interfere with the actual physical response of arousal for women just as they do in men. The lack of vasocongestion in women is the same as the inability to get or keep an erection for men. In women, this actual lack of physical arousal is rare, probably because women tend to be more passive sexually and arousal is a passive, parasympathetic nervous system response. Anxiety can, however, interrupt or prevent arousal for women. The sympathetic nervous system becomes dominant because of the anxiety and interferes with the involuntary nervous system responses.

Most women who lack arousal also do not have release. Nevertheless, there are some women who report being orgasmic but do not experience vaginal lubrication or nipple erection. The reflex of orgasm happens without all the enjoyable buildup. This could be compared to some men who learn to ejaculate without an erection. The treatment for this would be much like treating erectile dysfunction in men, which will be discussed later in this chapter.

The most common reason for lack of physical arousal in women is lack of stimulation. This is usually due to sexual naiveté on the part of both the man and the woman. The couple is not kissing passionately, stimulating breasts, or fondling genitals. In fact, they are not engaging in much love-play at all. They have intercourse when he has an erection, and that is the extent of their sexual involvement. Other times, there may be loveplay, but there is no knowledge of or experimentation with effective stimulation of the woman.

℞ The guidelines and exercises in the *sexual retraining process* in chapter 12 can reverse this dilemma. Assignment 16, Non-demand Teaching, and Assignment 15, Clinical Genital Examination, are most helpful to counteract the naiveté and begin expanding awareness and learning effective techniques of sexual enjoyment. As mentioned earlier (in chapter 4), lack of vaginal lubrication may also be due to a decrease in estrogen during and after menopause. Artificial lubricants are helpful in these cases, and hormonal replacement therapy may be necessary.

PROBLEMS OF AROUSAL FOR MEN

An erection is the most significant response of arousal for men; therefore, difficulty with excitement for men manifests itself physically as erectile dysfunction.

Erectile Dysfunction

Erectile dysfunction refers to a man's difficulty in achieving or maintaining an erection. Difficulty with erection can occur at various times during the sexual experience. Some men gain no erection at all. The usual kind of stimulation occurs, but the penis remains flaccid. For others, an erection may occur in response to physical enjoyment, but it is lost as the loveplay continues. When a man does not have the knowledge that it is normal to lose and regain erections during longer times of sexual enjoyment, the lessening of his erection may trigger anxiety, and the anxiety may interfere with the parasympathetic response of erection.

For others, the erection may be adequately maintained up to the point of entry. When entry is contemplated or attempted, it is as if the penis gets afraid that it is not going to do its job, so the erection dissipates. For some men, the erection can be maintained beyond the point of entry, but it is lost after thrusting inside the vagina.

When we wrote *Restoring the Pleasure* in 1993, the belief was that ED was primarily caused by anxiety. However, since that time, research has shown that 85 percent of the time ED is due to physiological issues. Thus, the first step to diagnosing and treating ED is to see a male sexual dysfunction specialist.

It will be helpful to use the graphing exercise described in chapter 7 to determine (1) when in the process the loss of erection occurs, (2) what activity is happening at that point in the loveplay, and (3) what mental thoughts and feelings are associated with that event.

All men of all ages experience erectile difficulty at some time. The occasional inability to get or maintain an erection need not be an issue of concern; that is normal. Just because people may occasionally have a sleepless night does not mean they have insomnia. Similarly, the occasional loss of an erection does not mean a man has erectile dysfunction.

Causes of Erectile Dysfunction

The causes for erectile dysfunction are complex because erections involve many body systems: the nervous system, the cardiovascular system, cellular reactions, and chemicals released by muscular reactions. Today, ED is most often thought of as a symptom of an underlying physical condition or a side effect of medication. Because of the complexity of the physical factors, a man with ED needs to be diagnosed by a male sexual dysfunction specialist (an Internet search may be necessary to find one).

The diagnostic process needs to include tumescence evaluation (a measuring of penis reaction during sleep) at a sleep center. In addition, cardiac and vascular medical evaluations are often warranted because erectile dysfunction may be an early sign of cardiac or vascular impairment. An erection is a vascular response. During sexual excitement, the penis must be continually pumped full of blood, with a pressure greater than is flowing out of the penis. Diabetes, circulatory problems, and endocrine hormonal problems can interfere.

All medications should be studied to determine whether ED is a side effect. Antihypertensives, beta blockers, and alcohol are drugs to be suspected.

When the cause is emotional, the erection is interrupted at the moment the man becomes anxious or begins evaluating the state of his erection. The anxiety pattern has a definable sequence. The pattern begins with an experience in which the man does not respond with an erection as usual or he loses it during the process and does not regain it. This initial incident may be totally coincidental, or due to such things as fatigue or alcohol or drug use. Or the loss of erection may occur in response to his wife if she is critical, negative, or unresponsive, or if she in some way sets off feelings of anxious inadequacy. Guilt can also cause an initial difficulty with erection. Authentic guilt about an affair may cause the husband to have difficulty in the affair or with his wife after the affair. Inauthentic guilt about being sexual in some way with his wife may also affect his erectile response. Other emotions, including anger, depression, or anxiety about external factors, such as finances, can keep a man from focusing on the sexual pleasure and interfere with his arousal response.

Once anxiety about the erectile difficulty has occurred, it tends to perpetuate itself. This is true even if the reason for the original difficulty is removed. The man may no longer be fatigued, depressed, angry, or under the influence of alcohol. Yet he continues to feel anxious about his erection. It is this anxiety caused by anticipation of failure that perpetuates the problem.

The anxiety increases with each failure. As the anxiety increases, a preoccupation develops. The man becomes a spectator. He constantly monitors the state of his penis, almost like reading an ongoing computer printout. This may lead to frequent initiation of sex in an attempt to prove himself, or it may lead to loss of interest in sex because of fear of failure.

The stress may be so intense that he mentally dissociates his penis from his body as it loses all feelings, almost becoming numb, or anesthetized. General despair and depression often follow. Erectile dysfunction severely attacks a man's self-esteem. It often makes him feel that he has lost his manhood.

The woman will also be affected. She may become anxious and stop any form of effective penile stimulation, thus perpetuating the difficulty with erection. Many women become angry when their husbands have difficulty with erections; this creates more performance demands and decreases the possibility of reversing the problem. Some women feel badly about themselves, unrealistically believing that if they were more attractive or more sexual, this problem would not be happening. Feelings of rejection are also very common for the wife of the man who is struggling with erectile difficulties.

Besides this anxiety pattern that started with loss of erection due to an external event or pressure or medical reasons, the following long-term difficulties may wear on the man and lead to ED:

1. Premature ejaculation may lead a man to attempt to distract himself from sexual pleasure and sensations so he will not ejaculate so quickly. Unfortunately, it is impossible to mentally and emotionally stop one response without affecting the other. The man with premature ejaculation starts watching his response and trying to mentally control it. This spectatoring then interrupts the natural erectile response.

2. Being dominated or made to feel inadequate may eventually lead to the inability to get or keep an erection. This may begin with a dominant parent and then be perpetuated by a dominant wife.

3. Any long-term negative emotions connected with sexuality or the sexual act can eventually lead to difficulty with erection. Rigid religious upbringing may cause a man to become uncomfortable and anxious when he is doing anything sexual. Fear of rejection may grow out of a long-term negative relationship. If his wife has gradually lost respect for him or constantly is in conflict with him, ED could result from fear of rejection.

Whatever the original source of the erectile dysfunction—whether physical or emotional—the anxiety pattern described usually keeps it going.

℞ Erectile difficulties are *reversible*! The medical issues need to be treated and the sexual retraining process pursued. As you proceed through the sexual retraining process, the following behaviors are necessary: (1) distract from anxiety, (2) express performance anxiety, (3) focus on sexual pleasure without making demands of yourself, (4) encourage your wife's enjoyment of your body for her pleasure, (5) no ejaculation without an erection, (6) allow erections to come and go, (7) use the penis as a paintbrush, (8) poke the penis into the vagina, (9) enjoy times of quiet vagina, and (10) thrusting.

The reversal process starts with *open communication*. A time of talking, confessing, crying, and forgiving may be necessary to begin to diminish the hurts and disappointments.

This communication is crucial to relieve the self-doubts, blame, anger, resentment, and frustration that have grown in both of you as the erectile dysfunction has interfered with your sexual pleasure.

Distraction from anxiety. Distraction from the anxiety for getting or keeping an erection begins by ruling out intercourse or attempts at intercourse. This limitation is the most powerful anxiety reducer for the man.

Almost as powerful is accepting the fact that the touching exercises are not expected to produce arousal. In fact, if an erection occurs during the pleasuring times, no attempt should be made to pursue that response. Rather, the sensations are to be enjoyed, allowing them to come and go. The ability to enjoy the increased and decreased engorgement of your penis will eventually give you erectile security.

Expressing performance anxiety or spectatoring during sexual play. As soon as you begin to focus on your response or feel yourself slipping into the spectator role, inform your wife that you are feeling anxious, self-conscious, or evaluative about your penile response. Verbalizing interrupts the spectatoring. Expressing anxiety is difficult for most men, yet it is crucial to regaining erections. The talking, which is a left-brain function, brings the feelings from the right brain, where you have little control over them, to the verbal left brain. Therefore, expressing your concerns about your erections moves your anxious thoughts to the left brain, where they are in your control.

Many men are concerned that telling their wives about their worries will only make both of them feel more discouraged and frustrated. There is a tendency to want to ignore the thoughts and feelings with the hope that they will go away and will not negatively affect the response. However, if the anxiety is not expressed (switched from the right brain to the left brain), it will become more overpowering. This is true with any fear. When a speaker finds his hands are shaking, his saying, "I guess I am anxious about speaking to you today. My shaky hands are certainly giving me away," will usually relieve the anxiety and stop the shaking. Thus, interrupting the anxiety by expressing it is absolutely necessary.

After you identify and express your performance anxiety, you should change the focus of your sexual touching away from the penis or away from the activity that stimulated the anxiety and enjoy non-demand pleasuring. Usually it is necessary to switch the focus from the wife's pleasuring you to you pleasuring your wife. Being active distracts you from spectatoring. Enjoying her body takes you out of the spotlight, where you feel the demand to respond.

Focus on pleasure. The change of focus from preoccupation with the state of your penis to skin-to-skin contact and the fun of enjoying each other's bodies can only happen as all demands to attain and keep erections diminish and disappear.

To switch the focus off the erection (or the loss of it) and onto the enjoyment of pleasure, follow the steps of the *sexual retraining process*. Naming each other's genitals and claiming them as your friends are very important steps. From that point on, pat and affirm each other's genitals every night before you go to sleep or at the time of day that is best for you. This will reduce your anxiety and your perceived demand for response that you have connected with your wife's touching of your penis. The patting and affirming is positive touch without any expectations. We call it "fiddling." The touching exercises may be repeated several times; slow down the process in order to securely establish the patterns of experiencing the pleasure of each other's bodies without demand for response.

Enjoyment of your body by your wife. Your wife will need to be taught to pleasure your body, not for the response she can produce, but rather for the pleasure it brings her. This is the purpose of the sexual retraining touching exercises. The more freely she can totally relax and delight in your body and allow you to delight in hers, the more likely the natural response of erection will begin to occur. It is comparable to the biblical concept of losing your life to gain it. When both of you stop trying to produce an erection—when you let go and enjoy yourselves—an erection is the most likely outcome.

When the sexual retraining progresses to include direct penile stimulation, this step must be handled most carefully. Your wife is of critical importance. She must learn to practice keeping the penis hungry for more touch rather than touching too long and thereby communicating a demand for response. It is great if she can be playful with your penis, talking to it, naming it, and enjoying it, as well as learning to stimulate it in a way that is most pleasurable for you. She needs to be taught to build up the intensity of the stimulation and then move away from the penis to enjoying other parts of your body. She needs to keep you off guard so you do not know what to expect and, therefore, cannot anticipate demands.

No ejaculation without erection. In all of the penile stimulation, there must not be an ejaculation without an erection. That is a firm and fast rule. Some men who struggle with erectile dysfunction have learned to attain the release they want without making their penises do their part of the work. We call it the "lazy penis syndrome." You will never interrupt your erectile barrier if you allow yourself to ejaculate without an erection.

Allowing erections to come and go. As the pleasuring experiences continue along the prescribed guidelines, erections will come and go. They may be short-lived at first. But every response should be enjoyed without any pressure for more and without attempts to figure out what "made it work." Attempts to determine the reason for penile response create a demand pattern that must be broken. As you learn to enjoy your penile responses without the demand to keep them or reproduce them, you will gain confidence in your ability to attain, lose, and regain erections. You begin to rediscover that you *can* experience erections. If there is a dip in arousal that causes your penis to become flaccid, you will start to have the security that it will respond again. You will learn to interrupt any anxious or demanding thoughts as soon as they appear without allowing them to interfere with your pleasuring times.

Paintbrushing. Before any attempts at entry are made, the penis and the vagina must become reacquainted. They need to be gently and gradually reintroduced to each other as friends, not as feared objects. To help your penis become familiar with the vagina without performance anxiety, both of you use the penis, whether flaccid or erect, as a paintbrush across the clitoris and the opening of the vagina (refer to Sexual Retraining Assignment 26 in chapter 12). Through this activity, you will gain new confidence in your penis as a source of pleasure for yourself and your wife without demand for an erection or entry.

Poking. After a number of sexual experiences that include positive responses to paintbrushing, the poking into the vagina begins. (See Sexual Retraining Adjustment for Erectile Dysfunction, page 193, which precedes Assignment 30, Total-Body Pleasuring with Entry.) Your wife must manage these steps carefully so as not to trigger the demand of keeping the erection to have entry. In each pleasuring session, the penis is poked into the vagina just a quarter of an inch more (increments of just-noticeable difference). The first time, the wife can insert the tip of the penis into the opening of the vagina for a few moments. The next time it might be for a few moments more. The following time she can insert it a notch farther, but just briefly. Each time the penis is either left in a little longer or inserted slightly farther. Eventually you will have full entry without ever having been assigned that task.

Quiet vagina. Once entry has occurred, enjoy being together by resting without thrusting ("quiet vagina" is the term used to describe this time of resting inside the woman) and allow the erection to diminish inside the vagina. It is important that this is done intentionally to gain a sense of mastery. In other words, loss of erection does not happen to you—you allow it to happen.

Thrusting. In the next experience, mild thrusting is allowed after entry. Gradually, with each successive encounter, the thrusting can be increased. Next, you are to withdraw from the vagina and stimulate to orgasm manually. When you feel confident with the sexual activity thus far, you can decide, during the sexual experience, to allow the arousal to build to ejaculation inside the vagina.

As you build confidence by gaining, losing, and regaining an erection, continue to identify and express anxiety or monitoring of your penis. Adjust the sexual retraining process accordingly. Your wife might need a private place to vent her feelings and get support. It is important that the focus on the pleasure be as much for her as for you. When you pleasure a receptive and responsive wife, it is a great distraction from anxiety about your erection.

Because problems of arousal interrupt such a natural, ongoing physical response in your body, the sexual retraining program is designed to eliminate the negative interruptions and allow the automatic bodily responses to occur. Difficulties with erections for men tend to be experienced as more of an interruption than do problems with arousal for women. Intercourse cannot be successful without an erection, whereas an artificial vaginal lubricant can be used if there is little physical arousal for the woman, and intercourse is possible even if a woman does not *feel* aroused. Nevertheless, the woman's problems of arousal are of equal concern as the male erectile disorders. In the long term neither the man nor the woman will enjoy sexual pleasure if one of them is having difficulty allowing sexual arousal.

SEVENTEEN

Overcoming Problems of Sexual Release

M en and women tend to encounter opposite dilemmas with orgasm. Men often respond too quickly with premature ejaculation, whereas women inhibit their orgasms because they have difficulty allowing a release.

PROBLEMS OF RELEASE FOR WOMEN

Orgasmic Inhibition

Even though the reflex of orgasm is as natural as the foot jerk in response to a tap on the knee, many women have never experienced, rarely experience, do not know if they have experienced, or believe they have to work hard to experience that peak of physical release. The fact that the vaginal and uterine contractions of the orgasm are eight-tenths of a second apart in all women does not make the subjective experience of an orgasm at all the same from woman to woman or even in the same woman from one time to another.

Women who have difficulty with orgasmic release may lack knowledge about their own bodies, the sexual response cycle, or effective stimulation.

Some women have no expectation of receiving pleasure from the sexual experience, so mentally they do not recognize the buildup of the arousal response in their bodies. It is not uncommon for Christian and non-Christian women to feel they have no right to sexual pleasure. They may be unaware of the biblical concept of mutuality in the sexual relationship in marriage. For these women, sex is something they do to please their husbands. They never really grasp the idea that *their* enjoyment of sex is probably *the* most pleasing part of sex for their husbands.

Similarly, some women may see themselves as passive receptacles of the man's aggressive sexuality, so they are totally passive during all sexual experiences. They become aroused because arousal is controlled by the parasympathetic, or passive, branch of the autonomic nervous system, but their arousal stops at the end of the plateau phase right before the orgasmic response. It is as if they cannot make it over the hill. This is the point at which the involuntary control shifts from the passive (parasympathetic) branch to the active (sympathetic) branch of the nervous system. As the heart rate increases, the breathing intensifies, and the involuntary thrusting starts, the overt, active sexuality has to kick in. If the woman is passive, those responses will not happen. Women who were raised in homes that either lacked emotional expressiveness or were out of control emotionally may not know how to let go sexually or may fear the loss of control in letting go. Similarly, women who have difficulty with orgasmic release often feel embarrassed or self-conscious about the intense expression of an orgasmic response, particularly if they were raised with rigid antisexual teaching. Even their husbands' orgasms may frighten them. It is important for these women not to become orgasmic too quickly because rapid success is likely to be frightening.

Lori was a sweet young lady, rather frail and timid. She was obviously afraid of expressing herself verbally during the sessions. Her history suggested that her mother was emotionally unstable. Her stepfather was a strong, rigid, controlling man whose affection she had attempted to win. He had clear antisexual rules for her dress and behavior. When she came out in the morning dressed for school, he would often send her back to change clothes because she looked too attractive. He said that her appearance would make boys look at her for the wrong reasons.

Unfortunately and unintentionally (from our perspective and hers), Lori had her first orgasmic response too quickly in the sexual retraining process. She did not like it at all! It frightened her. It felt wrong.

The process and goals of sexual retraining had to be readjusted. She needed time to be able to understand her fear and dislike of emotional intensity and of being out of control. She also had to release the pain of her childhood. A number of months of psychotherapy were required before the sexual exercises could be resumed. During this time, we helped Lori become able to ask for trust-building affection from her husband without expectation or pressure for her to experience erotic sexuality. In turn, she was able to agree to bring him to ejaculation manually on a regular basis. Even though his orgasmic response was somewhat uncomfortable for her, it was not aversive, and she wanted to be able to give him that pleasure while he was giving her space to unravel and heal her need to be in control.

Sometimes women's inhibition of their orgasmic response is secondary to some other sexual issue. Pain during intercourse increases women's tenseness, which inhibits arousal and then blocks release. They become so guarded about preventing the pain that they cannot relax, soak in the pleasure, and allow their bodily responses to build.

The husband's premature ejaculation may also keep the woman from an orgasmic response. If the husband ejaculates quickly from any form of sexual activity, she may not have time to respond, even from manual stimulation. If she responds during intercourse and he ejaculates shortly after entry, she may not have enough time of intravaginal penile stimulation to become orgasmic. Unfortunately, many couples either lose interest in pursuing the woman's response after the husband's, or they are not creative in working out other ways for her to respond, such as using manual intravaginal stimulation. Obviously, control of ejaculation needs to be the primary focus of change, but alternative means of orgasmic response for the woman may be used in the meantime.

Relationship issues may also keep a woman from being orgasmically vulnerable with her husband. He may be her second-choice mate. She may have been engaged to be married and lost her fiancé either through his death, his or her parents' prohibition of the marriage, or his breaking the engagement. Perhaps the grief of that loss was not resolved before she quickly filled her sense of loss with her current husband. He became her second choice—perhaps not consciously, but by the fact that she was still wanting and grieving for her lost fiancé. In these cases, the attachment is never the same, and the ability to be vulnerable may be inhibited. Anger, lack of respect, or outright dislike of the husband can also be a barrier to letting go sexually. Sometimes relationship issues must be resolved (see chapter 14) and trust must be built before the couple pursues orgasmic responsiveness.

℞ Orgasmic response is not a skill to be learned, such as playing tennis, but you can learn to be sexual, and you can learn about bodily responses and how to acquire techniques for deriving sexual satisfaction. To become orgasmic, you must be able to uncover and release the potential that is already inside you. All women have a clitoris—that special apparatus designed to give and receive sexual stimulation and responsiveness. All women's bodies were designed with the ability to experience the intensity of the sexual response.

Sometimes barriers need to be removed before you can actively pursue your sexual responsiveness. You may need to give yourself permission, reduce your fears, resolve your negative feelings toward your husband, build trust with him, or address any other inhibiting factors.

Once you have addressed the underlying or interfering difficulties, you can begin the sexual retraining process described in chapter 12.

Some sexual therapists[1] recommend that women learn to be orgasmic through self-stimulation before they learn to be orgasmic with their husbands. We have not found this strategy to always be necessary or even possible. For many women in our practice, it is much more difficult to overcome the taboo of self-stimulation than it is to be able to be vulnerable orgasmically with their husbands. However, women who have difficulty being sexually free with their husbands may need to learn by themselves first.

Whether your efforts begin with self-stimulation or with your husband, we encourage you *to stop mentally focusing on the goal of orgasm and refocus on the pleasurable sensations of touch and arousal, to reduce your self-consciousness about the natural sexual response, and to take responsibility to actively go after your own sexual needs and desires.* These steps of the sexual retraining process are unique to reducing orgasmic inhibition; they should be emphasized throughout the sexual retraining process.

Redefine the goal. To stop mentally focusing on the goal of orgasm, you must redefine your goals. Look back at the goals you identified in chapter 11. You may want to rework those. Rather than the goal of trying to have an orgasm, you are encouraged to make your goal to allow longer times of arousal and more intense levels of arousal. Because the orgasm is an automatic reflex response, "trying" prevents the orgasm from happening by putting you into the evaluative role of spectatoring or watching how you are doing. The intentional, goal-oriented "trying" actually inhibits the natural response. The new goals of longer periods of arousal and more intense arousal focus on the positive sensations of the vasocongestion in the genitals, as well as pleasurable sensations of the whole body. You are encouraged to extend your enjoyment of these sensations and the level of intensity with which you allow those to be felt. Eventually the reflex of orgasm will be triggered.

Build trust by learning to give and receive pleasure. In order to refocus on pleasurable sensations, trust must be built between you and your husband so you can freely enjoy the giving and receiving of pleasure. The talking, teaching, and touching exercises of the sexual retraining process help you build trust and learn to give and receive pleasure without focusing on orgasm. Because the exercises begin nonerotically and progress gradually, the focus on pleasure feeds the newly defined goals of longer and more intense arousal.

As you learn to give and receive pleasure, you must be willing to express any spectatoring. The importance of the right-left brain shift that happens when you verbalize thoughts that interrupt the sexual response was discussed in the treatment of erectile dysfunction in chapter 16.

Another way to focus on pleasure and not on evaluating your response is by consciously listening to your body sensations while you are being touched. It also helps to become active in pursuing what feels good, as well as communicating and directing your husband in the kind of touch you enjoy.

Reduce your self-consciousness. Whether or not you feel embarrassed with the active, expressive total-body responses that occur at the end of the plateau phase (see chapter 7), you are—for some reason—inhibiting the expression of this intense buildup. Therefore, the exercises in the sexual retraining process that are designed to reduce your self-consciousness will be vital to your progress. Assignment 7, Body-Awareness/Mirror; Assignment 15, Clinical Genital Examination; and Assignment 23, Vaginal Examination and Genital Affirmation, help you reduce your self-consciousness. Assignment 22, Simulating Arousal Responses, is specifically aimed at reducing your self-conscious of the breathing, sounds, and actions of a sexual orgasm. By practicing the expression of that response, you become less self-conscious with and learn to enjoy the sounds and behaviors that accompany orgasmic release.

Once you have practiced these responses, then when you are in a sexual experience and the intensity of your arousal builds, actively choose to practice these orgasmic triggers: breathe heavily; make the noises of gasping, moaning, even screaming; point your toes to extend your feet; throw your head back. If you become aware that you are inhibiting these active responses, consciously exaggerate the breathing, sounds, grimaces, and other bodily responses. Do everything you can to exaggerate your natural bodily responses. When you feel like breathing deeply, breathe even deeper. One woman felt like arching her body when she was in the top position, but that arching would cause her to look up and she had always felt that that would look stupid. So she did not allow her body to respond in that way. When she—with her husband's encouragement—made the decision to go for it, the intensity of her arousal built with each experience until the orgasmic reflex occurred. She was delighted!

Take responsibility to get active and "go after" sexual needs and desires. What does *taking responsibility and going after* mean? It means that you give yourself permission to be sexual. You decide that you are going to actively pursue sexual feelings, expressions, and intensity. You are going to allow your body to respond and enjoy those responses. And specifically, you are going to actively help your body switch from the passive, parasympathetic nervous system to the active, sympathetic nervous system.

Instead of only being the recipient of touching, you become active in also doing the touching. You learn to delight in your husband's body and to enjoy using your body to pleasure your husband. You kiss passionately with your lips, tongue, and mouth. You use your husband's body to bring pleasure to yourself. You become an active pleasure-seeker. You begin to accept your husband's body as yours to enjoy for your pleasure. Your husband will love it!

One exercise that can be added to the sexual retraining process is *Paired Clitoral/Vaginal Stimulation*. This exercise should be added any time after the eighth day or week or after Assignment 28. The assignment is to be timed; in other words, you are *not* to continue the stimulation until orgasm (which would be sure to fail), but rather until a predesignated time period has elapsed. Use an electronic or kitchen timer to time yourselves. Enjoy total-body caressing, including your breasts and genitals in a general sense. Then set the timer. In their book *Woman's Orgasm*, Benjamin Graber and Georgia Kline-Graber suggest setting the timer for twenty minutes.[2] That may be too long at first, especially if you are a woman who places demands on yourself to be orgasmic. When there is high performance anxiety, one minute may be plenty to start. Then the amount of time can be increased in small increments when you gain greater ability to do the exercise without watching for it to "work."

The timed exercise is clitoral/vaginal stimulation. You stimulate or stroke your clitoris while your husband stimulates the PC muscle inside the vagina. If you are uncomfortable with self-stimulation, your husband could stimulate both the clitoris and your vagina. You can tighten and relax the PC muscle as your husband either strokes, taps, or in some way stimulates the PC muscle area (or the G-spot, the area just beyond the PC muscle toward the front of your body). It is important that you direct your husband to stimulate you in the way that is most enjoyable to you.

Once you have learned the clitoral/vaginal stimulation exercise, repeat it two to three times per week. Longer and longer periods of time should be allowed, up to twenty minutes. Eventually the reflex response of orgasm will happen.

It is critical to keep the balance between actively going after the stimulation so the orgasmic reflex will be triggered and yet keeping the focus on the pure enjoyment sensations of the body, rather than on the goal of the orgasm. Your focus can easily switch to evaluating your degree of success in being able to be orgasmic. Thus, it is important to constantly refocus on the goals of higher intensity of arousal, longer periods of arousal, more active participation, and less inhibition.

If you wish to work further on reducing your orgasmic inhibition, an excellent secular resource is Julia Heiman and Joseph LoPiccolo's book *Becoming Orgasmic*.[3]

Lack of Coital Orgasm

There is confusion about the importance of women having an orgasm during intercourse. More than half of all women (some studies report as many as 70 percent[4]) need clitoral stimulation to be able to respond orgasmically. Yet many husbands and wives place demands on themselves to elicit the woman's response from vaginal stimulation.

The demand for vaginally stimulated orgasms grew out of Freud's teaching about women. Freud believed that women who responded only to clitoral stimulation were immature little girls—that as little girls, they had learned to respond through self-stimulation of the clitoris and had never matured into women who could respond by receiving the man's penis into their vaginas.

Then, in the 1960s, Masters and Johnson reported there was only one source of all orgasms, the clitoris. They claimed that whether it was from manual stimulation or intercourse, an orgasm was clitorally stimulated.

Since the Masters and Johnson findings, women who experience orgasm from both direct clitoral stimulation and from intercourse have reported that there is a difference. Some prefer clitorally stimulated orgasms, some prefer vaginally stimulated orgasms, and still others delight in both. A clitoral orgasm is usually described as more intense because there is nothing in the vagina to hinder the movement of the PC muscle as it contracts. The vaginal orgasm is often described as deeper and more satisfying. The sensation that occurs with the contractions is one of bearing down, almost like the last contractions of childbirth.

All orgasmic response brings relief of the vasocongestion of sexual arousal. There is no one right or better form of stimulation to bring that about. It is not uncommon, however, for a woman to want to be able to respond orgasmically during intercourse.

℞ There are two approaches to learning to be orgasmic during intercourse. One approach is called "pairing," or "bridging." The stimulation that already works is paired with or bridged to the form of stimulation or the situation that is not working. This is very similar to the clitoral/vaginal exercise described previously in this chapter. The woman stimulates herself clitorally during intercourse and alternately tightens and relaxes her PC muscle while her husband's penis thrusts inside her vagina. Thus, clitoral stimulation that has been effective in bringing orgasmic release is combined with the vaginal stimulation of penile thrusting and PC-muscle contracting.

When the pattern of connecting intercourse with the orgasmic release from direct clitoral stimulation becomes ingrained, the manual clitoral manipulation can gradually be lessened, and eventually it can be totally withdrawn. Initially, the pairing of the two should continue until the woman's orgasm begins. Then she should stop the clitoral stimulation for a few moments before resuming it. She should practice lengthening the time when she does not stimulate herself clitorally, as long as that does not stop her orgasm. If the orgasm does stop, she should immediately resume clitoral stimulation, then stop again. Eventually she will need less time of clitoral stimulation. The clitoral stimulation during intercourse will only be necessary until the response pattern of orgasm from intravaginal stimulation is established.

The second approach to teaching women to be orgasmic during intercourse is taught in detail in *The G-Spot*, a book by A. K. Ladas, B. Whipple, and I. D. Perry.[5] The G-spot, or Graffenburg-spot, is assumed to be an area located inside the vagina beyond the inner edge of the PC muscle toward the front of the woman's body. It is an area of tissue similar to the tissue of the prostate gland in men. Information about the G-spot is comprised of clinical data that have not been confirmed by research, but the information is validated by the help it brings to many women.

Using G-spot-area stimulation to discover intravaginal responsiveness takes both clinical discovery and the pursuit of pleasure of that area. In Assignment 23, Vaginal Examination and Genital Affirmation (chapter 12), we give instructions for the discovery process. After the discovery, manual stimulation of this area can be enjoyed. During intercourse, various positions can be attempted that would put the penis at the correct angle inside the vagina to thrust against the G-spot area. This can be fun if it does not become a demand for performance.

Lack of Orgasm with Spouse

If you are able to be orgasmic by yourself through self-stimulation but have never been able to have an orgasm with your husband stimulating you manually, orally, or during intercourse, several factors could be inhibiting your orgasmic response in the presence of your husband. The difficulty may be due to lack of trust, to lack of effective stimulation, or to self-consciousness about the intense bodily responses that occur with orgasm.

℞ To learn to bring your orgasmic response into your times with your husband, plan to talk with him about the possible hindrances. If trust is the issue, you need to be clear about what you need from him to feel that trust. If effective stimulation is the issue, you can teach him how you stimulate yourself when you complete the Clinical Genital Examination (Assignment 15) and the Non-demand Teaching

(Assignment 16). If self-consciousness is interfering, Simulating Arousal Responses (Assignment 22) will be most helpful.

Once you have dealt with those issues, you can start pairing your self-stimulation results with your spouse. The shared self-stimulation assignment that follows will guide you in this next step.

SHARED SELF-STIMULATION

STEP 1: Your husband will prepare a comfortable private setting.

STEP 2: Read these instructions together. Discuss how each of you feels about this assignment.

STEP 3: Bathe or shower together.

STEP 4: Enjoy some mutual hugging and kissing without clothes on. You may proceed to some total-body pleasuring.

STEP 5: When both of you feel ready (let each other know), each of you get into the position that is most usual for you for self-stimulation.

STEP 6: Either looking at or away from each other (whichever is most comfortable for both of you), each of you begin stimulating yourself in the way that brings you the most pleasure. Continue as long as it is enjoyable. One of you will probably finish before the other. When you are finished, wait quietly without disturbing the other. Try not to feel a need to rush to finish once one of you has finished.

STEP 7: When you are both finished, talk about the experience. Write your reactions.

Repeat this exercise until you are able to be orgasmic through self-stimulation with your husband. The next step is to include your husband in the process in any way you can. Gradually increase the degree of his involvement. It might proceed like this: (1) Husband holds you while you self-stimulate. (2) Husband pleasures other parts of your body while you self-stimulate. (3) Husband's hand is over your hand while you self-stimulate. (4) Your hand guides your husband's hand while he stimulates

251

you. (5) You decrease the amount of guidance until he is stimulating you to orgasm with little or no participation from you.

Although orgasm is the apex of the sexual experience, it is not the ultimate as far as the total sexual experience is concerned. Relieving the inhibitions that prevent orgasmic release is important for a woman to experience fulfillment, but orgasm without pleasure and without emotional and spiritual connection is not totally satisfying either. The freedom to enjoy orgasm within a totally fulfilling sexual relationship is every woman's eventual hope.

PROBLEM OF RELEASE FOR MEN

Premature Ejaculation

The most common technical sexual dysfunction for men is premature ejaculation. This has been defined by Masters and Johnson as the timing of the man's ejaculation relative to the woman's response: "The Foundation considers a man a premature ejaculator if he cannot control his ejaculatory process for a sufficient length of time during intravaginal containment to satisfy his partner in at least 50 percent of their coital connections."[6] This definition was derived to counteract the definitions that refer to premature ejaculation as an inability to remain in the vagina for a designated period of time (e.g., thirty seconds or sixty seconds) without ejaculating. Still others define premature ejaculation as ejaculating prior to a certain number of thrusts (e.g., ten thrusts).

We define premature ejaculation as occurring when the man does not have control of his ejaculation—in other words, if the man ejaculates before he or his wife feel ready for him to do so. This definition grew out of our clinical practice in which we have found a great variation as to when ejaculation is desired after entry. Some couples are content with a few minutes inside the vagina. Others are frustrated with only five to ten minutes. Some men have no need to last until their wives respond because she prefers to be orgasmic before or after intercourse. Sustained intercourse may not be enjoyable for either of them. In essence, our definition is similar to Helen Singer Kaplan's:

> Premature ejaculation *(ejoculatio praecox)* is unmistakable, yet it is difficult
> to define precisely. Essentially, prematurity is a condition wherein a man
> is unable to exert voluntary control over his ejaculatory reflex, with the
> result that once he is sexually aroused, he reaches orgasm very quickly.[7]

The seriousness of premature ejaculation varies greatly. Some men experience so little control that they ejaculate before entry or even upon anticipation of entry. Even more extreme is the man who ejaculates as soon as his wife touches his penis. Others will ejaculate once entry is attempted or within a *few* seconds after entry. Probably the most common complaint is the inability to last more than a minute or two after entry.

Premature ejaculation seems to be a conditioned reflex response. The man has learned to ejaculate quickly and has not learned to attend to the warning signs that precede ejaculation.

The conditioning that causes the premature ejaculation can be both implicit and explicit. In our culture, boys at early ages begin to participate in sports. (Today this is true for many girls as well.) In sports, scoring or making goals is the reward. In sex, men even refer to "scoring" with a woman. The implicit teaching is that the faster you achieve, the better. Success in business and other male-dominated vocations similarly perpetuates this mentality: the sooner you reach your goal, the better.

More directly, the conditioning begins in early adolescence with the boy's first ejaculatory experiences. Because self-stimulation is a private discovery frequently associated with restrictive admonitions, and thus guilt, boys learn to stimulate themselves to ejaculation quickly. The focus in early masturbation is rarely on the good sensations and pleasure of the process, but rather on attaining the release. Premarital sexual stimulation to ejaculation and premarital intercourse usually continue the same pattern. These are often hurried events that take place in an unsafe setting. The male's body, again, is being taught not to heed the warnings of ejaculation as a reason to delay it, but rather to trigger the reflex as quickly as possible. The sooner the event is over (the faster he "comes"), the less danger there is of being caught. Kaplan refers to the lack of response to the warning signs as "inadequate penile sensory awareness."[8]

When men with this rushed pattern of ejaculation marry and commit themselves to a long-term relationship, they expect that the absence of hurried conditions will lead to longer loveplay and extended intercourse before ejaculation. Unfortunately, most of the time their bodies repeat their conditioned response patterns. Other men never realize that sex should be any different. They have no intention or desire to postpone ejaculation once they are married.

For men who are sensitive, aware, and concerned with more than just a sexual release, ejaculating prematurely makes them feel inadequate sexually. Lack of control of their body functioning leaves them feeling unsure of themselves. Their pleasure is often decreased by the abrupt end to the sexual experience. Eventually their preoccupation with trying to delay ejaculation will hinder their ability to fully lose themselves to sexual pleasure.

As is common to all sexual disorders, premature ejaculation affects both the man and the woman. When a man feels anxious and inadequate and ejaculates unexpectedly, the woman is probably left unsatisfied. Her frustration will increase his anxiety, which in turn will increase his lack of control. Some women reach orgasm only during intercourse, and thus they cannot be orgasmic when their husbands ejaculate prematurely. However, premature ejaculation does not have to be a negative experience for the woman. The confident man who really enjoys the pleasure of a woman's body may engage in so much sensuous body pleasuring and manual intravaginal stimulation that his wife is well satisfied before entry or ejaculation occurs. Both spouses may still desire more time together after entry, but it is not a frustration for the woman. For other women, premature ejaculation is not a problem because they are quickly and easily orgasmic from entry, so they respond before or during the husband's ejaculation.

When the wife begins to feel used and unfulfilled, her frustration affects her husband, and he becomes more and more concerned with his inability to control when he ejaculates. He usually tries to use mental games to distract himself from ejaculating. He may try to picture something sexually repulsive, imagining himself in unsexual situations, or he may start counting backward. These mental distractions may have short-term benefit, but soon they are of no avail. Both husband and wife may begin projecting their frustration outward and blame each other for the struggle. "If only you wouldn't . . ." statements begin to deflate the couple's joyful sexual anticipations. The woman begins to feel that if her husband really cared about her, he would control his ejaculation. He knows it is not a voluntary action on his part, but he feels inadequate trying to communicate this to his wife.

After a time, the couple may begin to withdraw from each other, not wanting to engage in a sexual experience that is bound to end up frustrating them both. Soon the man doubts his masculinity, and the wife has both anger toward her husband and decreasing confidence in herself as a sexual partner. If the pattern continues, the anxiety about ejaculating can lead to erectile dysfunction for the man. Even if the consequences are not this extreme, there is likely to be hostility and discouragement about their sexual relationship.

℞ The good news is that it is most possible, and not all that difficult, to *learn ejaculatory control*. Sadly, many couples never seek help and believe they have a difficulty they simply must endure. Most couples can learn ejaculatory control through the sexual retraining process and the specific directions that will follow later in this chapter. Usually professional therapeutic assistance is not necessary.

As with any sexual problem, the resolution usually requires the active involvement of both husband and wife. If a single man wants to improve his ejaculatory control, it is possible for him to begin this process by himself. The principles would be the same. The activities would be adapted to self-stimulation, rather than stimulation by the wife. This technique is taught by Alan and Donna Brauer in *ESO*,[9] by Helen Singer Kaplan in *Premature Ejaculation*,[10] and by Barry McCarthy and Michael Metz in

Coping with Premature Ejaculation: How to Overcome PE, Please Your Partner and Have Great Sex.[11]

When premature ejaculation is a sexual difficulty within marriage, it is a couple's problem, not just the man's problem. Both spouses are affected by it. Hence, we recommend that both husband and wife be actively involved in the treatment process. Certain attitudes, commitments, and communication skills are essential to effectively complete this process.

First, you must have a *working relationship*. You must be *committed to each other and to the retraining process*. If your relationship is fraught with distress and discord, marital therapy may be necessary before you work on learning ejaculatory control. If one of you is resistant to the process, this resistance must be understood and removed before beginning. You must desire control and believe it is possible for you. And you must be willing to allow your wife to help you. Similarly, she must believe that you can achieve control, and she must be willing to work toward that goal. This requires that she is able to enjoy your genitals for her pleasure. If this is not already possible for her, she can learn it in the steps of the retraining process.

Communication is also essential to the effective completion of this process. You need to begin by talking about the problem. The Communication Format in chapter 3 will guide you. In addition, each of you needs to be able to express how the premature ejaculation has affected you. Each of you needs to feel that you are being heard and understood by the other. You both must feel free to express your feelings about participating in the retraining process. Adaptations of the process may be necessary if there are personal issues that would interfere with the retraining process as prescribed.

You must be committed to following the Guidelines for Sexual Retraining (Assignment 1 in chapter 12). In addition to not engaging in sexual intercourse, you must refrain from all forms of sexual stimulation other than those prescribed, so that ejaculation is not a possibility unless it is allowed in the assigned exercise.

It is important that you realize that the more carefully the structure of the program is followed, the more rewarding the results will be. Exercises or parts of exercises must not be missed or approached carelessly. It is essential that you complete the assignments methodically and deliberately.

The steps to learning ejaculatory control were first presented to the professional community as the result of the research by Masters and Johnson. Their basic principles are now widely used by sexual therapists along with adaptations of their original "squeeze technique." Other approaches are also being used. For the most part, we continue to use our version of the squeeze technique, which we find to be very successful when followed as directed.

In her book *PE: How to Overcome Premature Ejaculation*, Helen Singer Kaplan promotes a "stop-start" method, but she refers also to the squeeze technique.[12] Whatever the method used, her emphasis is to increase full sensual awareness and thus gain ejaculatory control.

Learning to give and receive pleasure. The first goal of treatment is for you to learn to give and receive pleasure—total-body and genital pleasure. This is the first step to increase your sexual sensory awareness. The first exercises listed in the sexual retraining process through Assignment 10, Total-Body Pleasuring, Excluding Breasts and Genitals, teach the focus on total-body, *non-genital sensual awareness*. The Guidelines for Sexual Retraining and Underlying Principles for Body Caressing (Assignment 1) need to be accurately understood and practiced to begin the process of gaining sensuous awareness.

Learning ejaculatory control—the squeeze technique. The second goal in increasing your sexual sensory awareness, specifically penile sensual awareness, is for you to gain ejaculatory control.

This part of the process continues to encourage total-body sensual awareness while helping you focus specifically on your penile sensations. You gain the ability to enjoy the touching of your penis without pursuing ejaculation as you complete all assignments of the sexual retraining process *up to* Assignment 24. After Assignment 25, Sharing Love, you will start Procedure 1 of the squeeze technique to learn to control ejaculation. You will be guided through the technique with four procedures.

Procedure 1: Pleasuring and Squeezing Without Ejaculation

Step 1. Learning the squeeze technique begins with the sexual re-training plan's Assignment 24, Total-Body Pleasuring, Including Breast and Genital Stimulation. You pleasure your wife first. Then she pleasures you in the non-demand position shown on Figure 17.1 on page 259. It is important that you be able to completely relax and focus on the sensations in your body. You must be able to experience pleasure rather than hold back or feel you have to do something for your wife.

Once there is a full erection from penile stimulation, your wife applies the squeeze (Figure 17.2 on page 260). To do this, she grasps the penis with her thumb on the underside of the ridge around the head of the penis and her forefinger and middle finger above and below the coronal ridge on the upper side of the penis. The squeeze should be firm but not hard and should be held for about ten seconds. She needs to be careful not to use her fingernails in this procedure.

The emphasis in this first step is important. This is where mistakes are usually made that may keep you from gaining control of ejaculation. First, it is important that *your wife, not you,* decide when the squeeze is applied. The only time you should ask for the squeeze is if she waits too long. Second, the squeeze is applied *when there is a full erection.* Sometimes couples try to get as close as they can to ejaculation before the squeeze is applied. This decreases the effective learning and increases the risk of ejaculation before you choose to. If you think of arousal on a scale of zero to ten, zero is no erection and ten is ejaculation; the squeeze should be applied when the erection is at three or four.

You should let your wife know when you're at five or six if she has not yet applied the squeeze.

After the squeeze has been applied, some men will lose their erections; others will not. The squeeze is effective whether or not the erection diminishes. *Diminishing the intensity of arousal while enjoying the sensations of pleasure is what teaches you to control your ejaculation.* It is important that you not practice any of your habits of trying to hold back your arousal or being anxious about your ejaculation. If you find yourself repeating those habits of worrying that you will ejaculate too soon or wishing you could ejaculate, tell your wife. Verbalization is the key to interrupting those destructive thoughts and feelings. Then focus on the bodily and penile pleasure.

Figure 17.1

NON-DEMAND POSITION

Again, the squeeze technique works most effectively if it is applied once there is a full erection (at level three or four of arousal) but long before the man is approaching the point of no return (a level-eight arousal). (See Sexual Response Patterns in Figure 7.7, page 74). This may take some time for you and your wife to learn. If you are accustomed to ejaculating within seconds after a full erection, your wife will have to learn to apply the squeeze immediately when the erection is gained (level one or two).

Step 2. Whether or not the squeeze results in loss of the erection, your wife should shift away from touching your genitals to pleasuring other parts of your body. Your mental focus should move with her touch and the enjoyment of that touch so that you do not mentally continue the stimulation of your penis after the squeeze, but rather soak in the pleasure of general-body touching.

Figure 17.2

SQUEEZE TECHNIQUE

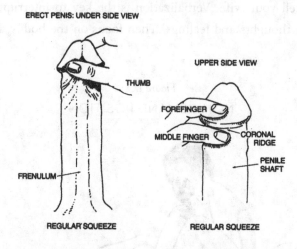

ERECT PENIS: UNDER SIDE VIEW

UPPER SIDE VIEW

THUMB

FOREFINGER

MIDDLE FINGER

CORONAL RIDGE

PENILE SHAFT

FRENULUM

REGULAR SQUEEZE

REGULAR SQUEEZE

Step 3. After a few minutes of relaxing and caressing other parts of your body, your wife moves back to penile stimulation and reapplies the squeeze when there is a full erection. You again focus on the enjoyment of that penile stimulation, allowing the squeeze to interrupt the intensity, rather than using your old methods to distract yourself from arousal. You freely enjoy the arousal without mentally or physically pursuing greater intensity.

Step 4. Repeat steps one through three of the squeeze three or four times in one sexual experience.

Step 5. After the last squeeze, rest quietly together, affirming each other, talking about your feelings, and allowing the arousal to dissipate.

Procedure 1 may be repeated for several experiences until you have a good sense of allowing arousal to build and enjoying those sensations without moving to ejaculation; that is, never taking your arousal above a level seven or eight. If an accidental ejaculation should occur, it is not a failure—only an indication that you need to be more aware of your level of arousal, and the squeeze needs to be applied a little sooner. The accidental ejaculation may have been the result of too long a time of stimulation or your reverting to your old pattern of anxiety and trying not to ejaculate rather than being fully aware of and enjoying your sexual sensations.

Procedure 2: Pleasuring, Squeezing, and Pursuing Ejaculation by Manual Stimulation

Begin this procedure by repeating steps one through four of Procedure 1, but this time use a lubricant to stimulate the penis to more closely approximate the feeling of being inside the vagina. We recommend Albolene, a facial cleanser very similar in consistency to natural vaginal lubrication, Slippery Stuff Gel, Astroglide Premium Silicone Gel, the oil-based Yes product, or Probe—all are commercial personal lubricants. You may use any suitable lubricant that keeps its slipperiness but is not sticky or irritating. (For more information on lubricants, go to pages 66–67.)

After three or four times of repeating steps one through four of Procedure 1, decide together that this time you will not apply the squeeze, but will manually stimulate to ejaculation. The decision to pursue ejaculation does not mean there will now be rapid, vigorous manual stimulation until you quickly ejaculate. It is most important that the *stimulation varies and has a playfulness* to it with a *very gradual building of the intensity* (both in vigor and in speed). This is your wife's task to control. Your task is to focus completely on the sensations of your genitals. You are to fully enjoy the building of the arousal, savoring it as you might savor your favorite ice cream—enjoying every stroke as you would enjoy every lick of the ice cream. Do not hold back the intensity or rush to finish quickly, failing to really "taste" the pleasure because you're afraid you will finish too quickly. Instead, focus on the wonderful sensations, and let yourself receive the most enjoyment from them.

After ejaculation, have a time of holding, affirming, and sharing your feelings about the experience. If your wife can delight in your ejaculation and your new control, this is an additional benefit. You encourage your wife's continued participation if you express your appreciation for her help in your gaining control.

This procedure should be repeated several times until you both feel secure that ejaculation will only happen when you both decide to pursue it. You may try lengthening the time you enjoy penile stimulation, but never beyond a level seven or eight before the squeeze is applied.

Procedure 3: Pleasuring and Squeezing with Entry but with Ejaculation Outside the Body

Step 1. Using a lubricant, repeat steps one through four of Procedure 1.

Step 2. Once your wife applies the last squeeze in step four, she moves into the top position (see Figure 17.3, page 262) and guides your penis into her vagina. If you have lost some of the fullness of your erection after the squeeze, she may have to stuff the penis in or stimulate it a little before inserting it into the vagina.

Step 3. After your wife has inserted the penis into her vagina, lie quietly together for a few moments without moving (quiet vagina). If the penis tends to fall out of the vagina because of loss of erection, additional manual stimulation or a little thrusting may be necessary to keep it erect enough to proceed. You must keep your focus on the sensation, not on how your penis is responding. That is her job. In other words, you are to focus on the touch and the sensation, not on their result. You are to thoroughly enjoy the feeling of having your penis inside your wife without ejaculating.

Figure 17.3

FEMALE SUPERIOR POSITION

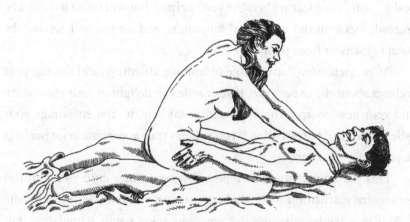

Step 4. After several minutes of lying quietly together and caressing each other's bodies, your wife may begin to gently move her pelvis in a mild thrusting manner. If you gain a full erection quickly, she is to move off of you and apply the squeeze.

Step 5. You can rest for a few moments while the intensity of arousal dissipates. If your erection has gone down much below level five, some manual stimulation may be necessary before reinsertion is possible.

Step 6. Your wife moves back on top of you and reinserts your penis into her vagina, thrusting gently until there is a full erection; then she again withdraws and applies the squeeze and you rest a short time (the length of rest time will vary greatly from one couple to another depending on how quickly the arousal lessens).

Step 7. Repeat the following cycle three or four times: entry, quiet vagina, thrust, withdraw, squeeze, and rest.

Step 8. After the third or fourth withdrawal of the penis from the vagina, the squeeze is applied. Then, instead of repeating the cycles, enjoy body caressing and penile stimulation of varied intensity until the two of you decide to go for ejaculation.

Procedure 3 should be practiced several times in different sessions. You can begin allowing longer and longer time within the vagina and increased intensity of thrusting before withdrawal and application of the squeeze.

Procedure 4: Pleasuring, Squeezing, Entry, and Ejaculation Inside the Vagina

Repeat all the steps of Procedure 3. This time, however, instead of withdrawing after the third or fourth time in the vagina, decide together to pursue ejaculation inside the vagina. Again, the mind-set should be one of savoring and enjoying the sensations while varying the thrusting, including times of resting quietly together and caressing each other without thrusting. Gradually, your wife can allow the intensity of the thrusting to build to the point of ejaculation.

Take time to delight in the ejaculation, affirming each other's participation.

If your wife has not experienced an orgasm as a result of the process, and if she desires that release, you can affirm her by delighting in pleasuring and stimulating her to orgasm.

Continue practicing Procedure 4 as your way of making love. Increasingly your experiences can become more mutual, taking turns or simultaneously pleasuring each other, hugging, and kissing. As this happens, the timing of the squeeze application will be less calculated. Your wife should apply the squeeze *randomly throughout the process*. If you notice your arousal building above a level seven or eight, ask for a squeeze and rest time. But she should not wait for you to ask.

As you gain control through interrupting the stimulation and applying the squeeze, you will learn greater and greater awareness of your body's sensations when you become aroused and approach orgasm. Eventually, you may be able to just stop the stimulation and move to other closeness or just have a time of quiet vagina during intercourse, rather than withdrawing and squeezing.

You have achieved control of ejaculation when you can flow naturally in the pleasuring, stimulating, and intercourse experience without fear that you are going to ejaculate unexpectedly. This will require that you continue to apply the squeeze or stop stimulation every now and then as part of your sexual experience. You should be able to have periods of five to ten minutes of thrusting that varies in intensity. No man is able to thrust vigorously and intensely for an extended period of time and not ejaculate unless he suffers from inhibited ejaculation. Thrusting is designed to stimulate the reflex of ejaculation.

You will gain more confidence as you have regular times together when you feel that the ejaculation is under your control. Then you are less likely to slip back into your old patterns. Once you have learned to thoroughly enjoy the sexual sensation and listen to your body's response, that ability will be with you forever. Times of anxiety or stress may cause an accidental ejaculation, but you now know how to achieve control.

SSRI antidepressants may be helpful in the process of learning control or instead of the process of learning we have suggested. One of the side effects of SSRIs is delayed orgasm, thus their use for treating PE. The most recommended is Zoloft twenty-five milligrams, taken four hours before a sexual experience. You would not take the SSRI daily, only as directed before a sexual experience. This would need to be approved and ordered by your physician.

You may now return to complete Assignments 24 through 27 of the sexual retraining process if you have not completed them before now.

Inhibited Ejaculation

Inhibited ejaculation (also called delayed ejaculation) is a man's inability to ejaculate, or to ejaculate in some way that he desires. In this situation, the ejaculatory reflex is inhibited. You may have sexual desire and be able to become aroused with a full erection; but even with (1) intense arousal, (2) felt need for release, and (3) more than sufficient stimulation, you cannot allow the reflex response of ejaculation. This inhibition is similar to what some women experience. You become highly aroused, but for some reason you hold back or do not allow yourself to let go. You enjoy the buildup of the arousal, but you inhibit the orgasmic reflex.

There are different degrees of ejaculatory inhibition. You may:

1. Have never ejaculated in any way, not even in a nocturnal emission (wet dream).
2. Have only ejaculated involuntarily—never by self-stimulation or with a woman, but only during sleep in a nocturnal emission. One man put a sock over his penis at night because of his fear of nocturnal emission. He had never ejaculated intentionally.
3. Have ejaculated by self-stimulation only—usually this occurs when you are by yourself, in secret.
4. Be able to ejaculate from oral or manual stimulation by your wife, but not during intercourse.
5. Have been able to ejaculate during intercourse, but now (with a

second wife, in an affair, or after a physical injury) you cannot; or you can ejaculate with a certain woman, but not with another because of anxiety, guilt, or feelings of being controlled. Or sometimes you can ejaculate with your wife, but at other times you cannot.

6. Have ejaculated without realizing you have. The emission phase is not impaired (the seminal fluid gathers in the duct system), but the ejaculatory phase with the eight-tenths-of-a-second contractions does not happen. Thus, the seminal fluid seeps out without contractions and the feeling of orgasmic release. Masters and Johnson believe this partial ejaculatory incompetence occurs as the result of physical causes such as diabetes, prostatic disease, or damage to the urethra.

Our experience, as confirmed by Kaplan, is that in these cases you may have conflict about allowing yourself to feel the pleasure and intensity of the ejaculatory response, hence you have a psychological or conditioned basis for ejaculation without the sensation of that response. This is similar to a woman who is aroused but does not feel aroused.

Men who struggle with ejaculatory inhibition may also suffer from erectile dysfunction or lack of desire. Again, the men's reactions are very similar to those of women who are not orgasmic. Over time they become less aroused and less interested.

Causes of inhibited ejaculation. Although physical causes for inhibited ejaculation need to be ruled out by a urological exam, the cause of ejaculatory inhibition is usually psychological. The psychodynamics that may be present include the following:

1. A dominant, controlling mother or a strong bond with an overprotective, loving mother who may have been soft and servant-like in her control.
2. Fear of being out of control with a woman, which may be related to the controlling-mother issue.
3. Fear of being abandoned by a woman.

4. A strong need to control, with difficulty in letting go in other areas. This is demonstrated by an inability to urinate in public restrooms, constipation, and difficulty with the expression of anger or other emotions.

5. A strict religious or moral upbringing connecting free expression of sexuality with guilt, anxiety, and conflict.

6. A traumatic experience—especially if sexual. This can cause the "ejaculatory response [to] become inhibited because of its association with a painful contingency."[13] Examples of this kind of traumatic experience include being beaten for masturbating, being interrupted by the police while having sex in a car, or being left by your wife through death or divorce.

7. Sexual naiveté or arrested development at the preadolescent stage associated with homosexual fantasies and fears.

Whatever the emotional or developmental causes, the ejaculatory response has become impaired, and the inhibition causing the impairment has been removed.[14]

Marty and Carrie came to us after fifteen years of marriage and two adoptions. They had been through intense physical–medical workups and had gone through sensate focus sexual retraining, which had taught them sexual pleasure without intercourse or ejaculation, with a primary focus on Carrie's pleasure. They had been counseled for about five years.

Marty had never ejaculated in any way. His history revealed the following pertinent data:

- He had suffered an illness during late elementary school that kept him home and dependent on his mother, who was very caring, loving, and protective. This illness caused him to have a seizure, which was very frightening to him.
- He had felt socially and physically inadequate throughout junior high and high school.

- He had had a rigid religious upbringing.
- He reported homosexual fantasies and worried about being homosexual. He had been preoccupied with men's bodies since puberty.

Marty and Carrie had a committed and loving relationship. Carrie was clearly the stronger partner in the relationship and in parenting the children. She was self-contained, assured, and not threatened by or affected personally by Marty's lack of ejaculation.

Marty had difficulty relaxing or letting go in all areas of life. The seizure he had had in elementary school seemed to cause him to connect letting go with pain and fear. His medical workup revealed no physical cause for inhibited ejaculation.

Gus and Judy had been married five years when they came for help. Their inability to become pregnant because Gus could not ejaculate was the frustration that led them to seek help.

Gus had only ejaculated by nocturnal emission, never intentionally, despite his and Judy's many attempts. We discovered that Gus would stop effective stimulation. He would not allow Judy to stimulate the shaft of his penis, only the tip. Judy was not assertive in encouraging him to receive more effective stimulation. Gus would also stop effective stimulation by getting headaches when his arousal intensified.

Like Marty in the previous example, Gus was troubled by homosexual fantasies, which had started in late junior high school after he had been approached by a homosexual man. He had prayed for release from the fantasies with his pastor and a few committed friends. Gus had a dominant and controlling mother. Both Gus and Judy were sexually naive.

Mark and Susan were frustrated with Mark's difficulty with ejaculating during intercourse. They had been able to conceive and have a child because of occasional ejaculations Mark had had with Susan during intercourse. He had no trouble ejaculating through self-stimulation.

Mark had been married previously and had experienced the same difficulty, but had not shared this with Susan. The reason he gave for not informing Susan of his problem was that they had become Christians so he had assumed his Christian marriage would allow him to respond freely.

Mark's description of his difficulty was much like the descriptions given by women who think they have to work hard to be orgasmic, but by doing so they actually fight their own bodies' natural responses. In these cases, the natural, involuntary reflex of orgasm occasionally wins in spite of voluntarily "trying" to be orgasmic.

Mark was raised by a dominant, controlling mother who wanted him for herself and yet physically abused him. He was also sexually abused by a man when he was ten years old.

Mark also struggled with obesity. He had had medical workups for hormonal imbalances with negative results.

℞ *Learning to allow ejaculation* involves desensitization through a gradual retraining process that reduces inhibition and allows you to risk vulnerability in small, safe increments. The response is rewarding.

The work begins with the regular sexual retraining process, starting with the Guidelines for Sexual Retraining (Assignment 1 in chapter 12). Intercourse, attempts at intercourse and ejaculation, or attempts at ejaculation are ruled out. The teaching, talking, and touching exercises of the plan, plus the specific program for unleashing the ejaculatory inhibition will be used.

Complete all the assignments in the sexual retraining process described in chapter 12. The teaching exercises help you reduce sexual naiveté. The talking exercises help you build trust and bonding with each other, which allows you to be vulnerable and let go. The touching exercises distract you from the anxiety and pressures of ejaculation and teach you to soak in pleasure for the sake of pleasure. All demands and the need to please are removed so that you can get in tune with your inner self. It is important to allow arousal to build gradually so that it is not frightening.

At the same time, follow the steps described next to reduce your ejaculatory inhibition. Alternate the assignments of the sexual retraining process with the exercises that follow. In other words, complete Sexual

Retraining Assignment 1 and then do Steps 1 and 2 of A, below. Next do Assignment 2 of the Sexual Retraining, followed by Step 3 of A, below. Then do Assignment 3, followed by Step 4, and so on.

A. Goal: Feeling comfortable in letting go with wife.

STEP 1: Urinate with wife listening.
STEP 2: Urinate with wife in room.
STEP 3: Urinate with wife watching.
STEP 4: Urinate with wife holding penis.

B. Goal: Feeling comfortable with self-stimulation to ejaculation.

STEP 5: Masturbate alone without your wife knowing. With
    each masturbatory experience, increase the intensity and
    length of your arousal. With time, this will eventually lead
    to ejaculation as you become able to focus on the good
    feelings. At the same time, you must allow yourself to be
    aware of conflicting feelings and not allow those to distract
    from your pleasure.

Reinforce yourself for any enjoyment of intensity and help yourself gain insight into your conflicts about letting go by writing about your feelings.

After you become comfortable with and have confidence in your ability to ejaculate through self-stimulation, you may move on to Step 6.

STEP 6: Masturbate with your wife knowing. You must tell
    her when you are going to masturbate. This step should
    be repeated until you are comfortable with and able to
    ejaculate through self-stimulation with your wife knowing.
STEP 7: Then masturbate with your wife outside the door.
STEP 8: Masturbate with your wife in room.
STEP 9: Masturbate with your wife watching.

STEP 10: Masturbate with your wife included in the stimulation, with her hand over yours. The first time you practice this, she may need to remove her hand so that you can bring yourself to ejaculation. Each time you practice this step, include her hand more until her hand is over yours all the way to ejaculation.

When you are able to comfortably allow yourself to ejaculate through self-stimulation in all of the above situations, you are ready to move to the next task. Wait to proceed with the next assignment in the sexual retraining process until you have successfully completed the step of the same number as the previous sexual retraining assignment.

C. Goal: Feeling comfortable with genital stimulation to orgasm by your wife. (As you work toward this goal, limit your self-stimulation to orgasm to once a week or less.)

STEP 11: This step will be combined with Assignment 14, Total-Body Pleasuring, Including Breasts and Genitals Without Purposeful Stimulation. This assignment helps you begin connecting sexual pleasure with your wife enjoying the touch of your genitals. After pleasuring each other as instructed in the assignment, put your hand over your wife's hand and guide her in bringing you to ejaculation or as close to ejaculation as possible. If you are unable to ejaculate by guiding her hand, have her put her hand on top of yours as in the previous step. *Always back up in the process until you are able to ejaculate and then move forward again.* As you repeat this step, increase the time when you guide her hand until you are able to ejaculate with you guiding her hand.

STEP 12: This exercise follows Assignment 15, Clinical Genital Examination, of the sexual retraining process. Have a time of total-body pleasuring, taking turns being the pleasurer and receiver. Include the genitals playfully. Particularly when your wife is stimulating your genitals, she should stroke, play with, and caress your genitals and then move away. She should vary the amount of time and the type of play so that you cannot anticipate her touch and become anxious. You should just be passive and enjoy, telling her if you become anxious or feel a demand to respond.

STEP 13: (Do this step after you have completed Assignment 16, Non-demand Teaching.) Repeat Step 12, increasing the amount of time of direct penile caressing. If the intensity of your arousal builds so that you desire ejaculation, leave the room to self-stimulate to ejaculation.

STEP 14: Complete Assignment 17 (which includes reading this chapter). Then repeat Step 12. When the intensity of your arousal increases from your wife's playing with and caressing your genitals, have her stay with you but look away as you self-stimulate to ejaculation.

STEP 15: Complete Assignment 19, Kissing. Then repeat Step 12. When the intensity of your arousal increases from your wife's playing with and caressing your genitals, have her actively caress your body or snuggle close to you as you self-stimulate to ejaculation.

STEP 16: Complete Assignment 20, You and Me. Then repeat Step 12. This time allow your wife to alternate body caressing with penile caressing, increasing the amount of direct penile stimulation until you build right to the urge to ejaculate. Before you lose that urge or get stuck there, you take over the stimulation yourself and have your wife move her hand on top of yours.

STEP 17: Complete Assignment 21, Creative Pleasuring. Then repeat Step 16, but this time put your hand over your wife's to guide her in bringing you to ejaculation or as close to it as possible and then take over with her hand on top of yours.

STEP 18: Complete Assignment 22, Simulating Arousal Responses. Then repeat Step 17 until you can ejaculate with you guiding your wife's hand.

STEP 19: Complete Assignment 23, Vaginal Examination and Genital Affirmation. Then repeat Step 12, but this time allow your wife to totally provide the stimulation to bring you as close to ejaculation as possible. When necessary, guide her hand.

STEP 20: Complete Assignment 25, Sharing Love. Then repeat Step 19 until the reflex of ejaculation happens without your reaching to guide her hand. You will be ejaculating by the stimulation of her hand alone.

STEP 21: This step is the same as Assignment 24, Total-Body Pleasuring, Including Breast and Genital Stimulation. You may include genital stimulation to orgasm for both of you.

D. Goal: Feeling comfortable with ejaculation from manual stimulation after intercourse. Moving to intercourse may raise your old conflicts about ejaculating with your wife. Therefore, the following steps must be honored, even though you may think this is regressing.

STEP 22: This step is the same as Assignment 26, Pleasuring, Not Using Hands (Including Using the Penis as a Paintbrush). In this exercise the penis is used like a paintbrush to pleasure the clitoris and the opening of the vagina.

STEP 23: Repeat Step 22, this time using your hands to pleasure all parts of the body and using the penis as a paintbrush. Poke the penis into the vagina, maybe a quarter of an inch. Then do other pleasuring and genital stimulation; then poke in a little farther. Stop if anxiety or loss of erection results.

STEP 24: Complete Assignment 28, Total-Body Pleasuring with Mutual Manual Stimulation, followed by Assignment 30,

Total-Body Pleasuring with Entry, but only with a time of quiet vagina so you can experience the sensation of being inside the woman without thrusting for ejaculation. After a time of quiet vagina and a little thrusting, withdraw and self-stimulate to ejaculation with your wife present and caressing or snuggling.

STEP 25: Complete Assignment 29, reviewing the principles learned, then repeat Step 24. This time when you withdraw to self-stimulate to ejaculation, have your wife's hand on top of yours. Practice this step until you feel comfortable. Then repeat this step several times with your hand on top of hers. Each time allow her more control until she is stimulating you to ejaculation manually after intercourse.

E. Goal: Feeling comfortable with ejaculation during intercourse.

STEP 26: Begin with Assignment 30, Total-Body Pleasuring with Entry, while your wife is on top. She will control the thrusting, varying it in intensity and speed to keep you off guard and not anxious about anticipating ejaculation. When she chooses, she should move off of you and manually stimulate you almost to the point of ejaculation. Even if ejaculation has just started, reinsert the penis into the vagina.

This step should be repeated in as many sessions as necessary, gradually decreasing the time between withdrawal of the penis for manual stimulation and re-entry for the ejaculation. Eventually you will ejaculate inside the vagina without withdrawing for manual stimulation.

Once you are able to stay together and ejaculate during intercourse, manual stimulation of the base of the penis may be added during intercourse.

If at any point there is ejaculatory inhibition, back up in the process until you again feel confident.

APPLICATION OF THE RETRAINING
PROCESS TO THREE CASES

Marty, the man in our first example who had never ejaculated in any way, was very eager for retraining. He had pursued medical treatment and other sexual retraining for five years, so he was coming to us as his last hope.

Because Marty and Carrie were from out of state, we initially began with telephone sessions. We did not assign the sexual retraining process because they were already practicing the pleasuring exercises. Although Marty was at first hesitant to attempt to let go with Carrie by urinating in her presence, he had no difficulty mastering those steps.

The second goal, feeling comfortable with self-stimulation to ejaculation, was more difficult for Marty. The first week he masturbated three times. The first time he had had a lot of seepage (partial ejaculatory inhibition, that is, emission without ejaculatory contractions). He reported this as being *very messy,* a situation he did not like. The second time was painful; he felt he needed to ejaculate, but could not. The third time, he had difficulty maintaining an erection, so he gave up and stopped—and then the erection came. He did self-stimulate, but without ejaculation.

We knew it was important to teach Marty that the first time he had actually ejaculated, but without the contractions. We pointed out that his aversion to the messiness of his first ejaculation inhibited the ejaculation the second time, and then the pain of that inhibition (physically needing it, but emotionally not allowing it) kept him from even approaching ejaculation the third time. It was also important for us to gather the details of how he masturbated: where, how long, what went on in his thoughts and feelings. We discovered that he was self-stimulating only thirty to ninety seconds. To get as far as he had gotten in such a short time was incredible, and we reinforced this fact to him.

Our recommendation was that the next time he self-stimulated, he set the timer for ninety seconds. Each succeeding time, he should add fifteen seconds on the timer. Instead of the regular fifty-minute sessions we usually hold with clients, Marty and Carrie's next two weekly sessions were fifteen-minute check-ins to hold Marty accountable. He had excuses for not having time to masturbate very often, and he said he had not been able to go as long as the timer. In response, we dealt with his fear of success and emphasized the need for him to attempt self-stimulation daily.

The third week proceeded with the timed self-stimulation on a daily basis. By the third day, he began ejaculating with emission—a release of seminal fluid, but no feeling of release. He said, "Something comes shooting out the end of my penis, but I don't feel anything—then my erection gradually goes down." We reinforced the fact that he was now ejaculating and that the next step was for him to allow himself to enjoy the release of those sensations.

Throughout the retraining process with us, Marty and Carrie continued the pleasuring of Carrie. She was orgasmic from manual stimulation.

At this point in the process, Marty and Carrie came to Pasadena for an intensive-therapy process. After more-thorough assessment, we decided to use our sexual retraining process, even though they had had sexual therapy previously. Many of our exercises were new to them, and they used the assignments to acquire new awareness and new skills. The two most significant assignments for them were Assignment 19, Kissing, and Assignment 22, Simulating Arousal Responses. The Penis as a Paintbrush exercise (Assignment 26) to pleasure Carrie without any demand was very arousing for Marty. In turn, Carrie became more active in pleasuring him. As a result, this was arousing for both of them.

They were able to move rather quickly to her manually stimulating him to ejaculation, but again without much intense feeling. Some regression occurred the first time he ejaculated in her presence. He lost his erection. But this was not the major barrier. His fear of letting go in a new way seemed to be more of a barrier than the problem of being with his wife. This was congruent with his fear of his childhood seizure and its connection with letting go.

They discovered that when he became excited, he tensed up; but when he was able to relax, he attained his best release. So internally he was fighting what worked best.

Moving to intercourse with poking produced another regression. He would lose his erection. Consequently, we had Carrie manually stimulate him after a little attempt at poking to practice the principles of just-noticeable difference. He got to the place of being able to enter, and then he would lose his erection. We recommended entry for only a moment, and then they were to withdraw and stimulate to ejaculation. Again, the time after entry was increased by just-noticeable differences until longer and longer times in the vagina were possible without loss of erection.

Then Marty's male fantasies became an issue as a distraction to his success. Marty resumed fantasizing that he was with men. We dealt with this issue psychodynamically and then recommended that he and Carrie create fantasies about sexual activities between them. The next inhibition we discovered was that he was not thrusting after entry. Marty and Carrie had to be verbally instructed in how to move their bodies to have the penis move in and out of the vagina.

The final steps were to have intercourse with the timer set. Each time was to be a little longer, but there were to be no attempts to ejaculate. When the desire or urge to ejaculate got high, they were to withdraw and manually stimulate to ejaculation. His first resistance was that he did not think he could recognize the warning signs.

At the same time, we had them orally or manually stimulate almost to ejaculation and then enter as he was about to ejaculate. Eventually he did ejaculate, first without feeling and then allowing more sensation, but never with full gusto—as far as we know.

Gus and Judy represented a standard inhibited ejaculation situation. We guided them through the process entirely as described in the sexual retraining process.

Gus had great success in learning to bring himself to ejaculation and was like a twelve-year-old who wanted to do it twice a day. His problem was more closely associated with his dominant mother, and thus he had more difficulty moving to ejaculation with Judy. He would sabotage her effective stimulation—actually stop her from doing what produced intense arousal—because he did not like it. Then when she was encouraged by us to continue effective stimulation even if he did not like it, he got intense headaches. We had to require him to stop his self-stimulation in order to be able to ejaculate with Judy.

During the process we also focused on Judy's hesitancies about being intensely sexual. She, too, had to be taught to be orgasmic. Today, they have children of their own and a fulfilling sexual relationship.

Treatment for Mark and Susan was simpler than that for Gus and Judy or for Marty and Carrie; yet they were not as committed to consistent involvement in the sexual retraining process.

Susan was a loving, alive, spirited woman who adored Mark and was game for anything. They worked well together. We took them through the sexual retraining process, ruling out masturbation, which was an addiction for him. We instructed him to tell her if he did masturbate. They were to have intercourse, withdraw when he got near the point of ejaculation, and manually stimulate to ejaculation. This was to be practiced every other day.

On the fifteenth day, he ejaculated inside her. On the seventeenth day, he ejaculated inside her with more intensity and feeling. On the nineteenth day, they came to our office for an appointment. Mark wanted to add the rule that he could only ejaculate inside her, not from her manual stimulation. We were hesitant, but allowed it. Immediately he was unable to ejaculate inside her, so we changed back to allowing ejaculation from her manual stimulation. We have not seen them since, but Mark telephoned and said that all was going well.

RESISTANCE TO LEARNING TO LET GO

Men who have inhibited ejaculation commonly fear success and sabotage their own progress. A typical dilemma is that the man will sabotage the stimulation that would make him ejaculate. For example, Gus would not allow Judy to effectively stimulate him. He would stop her because it gave him a headache, it did not feel good, and he did not like it. Marty tended to sabotage also, but not so obviously. Our sense was that the amount of therapy he had undergone had taught him to be more subtle in his stopping of effective stimulation. He used mental games and restricted body movement to inhibit his response. Mark sabotaged his progress with his intense trying and not being regular in keeping therapy appointments.

Lack of confidence that ejaculation is possible is also a common resistance to success. The belief that ejaculation will never be possible for you may serve as a "self-fulfilling fear." When the small steps to success outlined in this section are followed, confidence tends to build and resistance lessens.

Although sexual release is not necessary to enjoy sexual pleasure in a particular sexual event, when sexual release is inhibited, happening too soon, or in some way causing a barrier to ongoing sexual fulfillment, then the long-term effect will be a decrease in sexual pleasure.

EIGHTEEN

Overcoming Intercourse Barriers

Problems of intercourse interfere specifically with the physical act of inserting the penis into the vagina. These disorders include pain (or, more technically, dyspareunia), unconsummated marriages (or apareunia), and vaginismus, which is one of the causes of unconsummated marriages.

PAINFUL INTERCOURSE (DYSPAREUNIA)

Both men and women can experience painful intercourse (dyspareunia). However, in our practice, dyspareunia for men has been virtually nonexistent. In contrast, women frequently suffer from painful intercourse.

Men may experience pain upon gaining an erection, entering the woman's vagina, or ejaculating. Although the pain may be of psychogenic basis, it is more often caused by physical factors that are best diagnosed and treated by a urologist. For men with pelvic pain, we would highly recommend *A Headache in the Pelvis: A New Understanding and Treatment for Prostatitis and Chronic Pelvic Pain Syndromes* by David Wise, PhD, and Rodney Anderson, MD.

Painful intercourse seriously interrupts sexual fulfillment. Intercourse is supposed to be a pleasurable experience. If it hurts, it is not likely to be either eagerly anticipated or enjoyed. Thus, many times both the emotional process of lovemaking and all phases of the sexual response are interrupted by painful intercourse.

There are both emotional and physical reasons for dyspareunia. Because the source of the pain may be physical, a medical consultation is always a necessary part of diagnosing and treating painful intercourse. A pelvic-floor physical therapist is often the professional to best start the evaluation process. To find a PT who specializes in pelvic-floor issues, you may go to www. pelvicpain.org, www.icnetwork.com, or www.womenshealthapta.org. For women, a gynecologist or gynecological urologist is recommended.

Types of Pain and Their Relief

First-intercourse pain. The first experience of intercourse for a woman may be painful. In addition to the breaking of the hymen, the vaginal muscle may be tight due to eagerness and anxiety. The combination of excitement and fear of the unknown interferes with the relaxation of the body. The sympathetic nervous system overpowers the parasympathetic and prevents the physiological changes of arousal from building and preparing the body for entry. Many times, the new bride who is a virgin wants so fervently to consummate her marriage that she cannot relax enough to enjoy the pleasure that would produce the parasympathetic nervous system responses of vaginal lubrication and the opening and flattening of the labia.

If she and her husband force entry, there will be pain, which will interrupt any pleasure. That will increase her tension, which will increase her pain and prevent her from becoming aroused and responding. This can be a most disappointing first experience.

℞ Such a negative scenario can be prevented. Premarital preparation should include the following:

1. Read aloud together and work through our book for engaged and newlywed couples, *Getting Your Sex Life Off to a Great Start*. This will give

you a sound knowledge base biblically, emotionally, and physically, as well as break down barriers and help you talk openly about sex with each other.

2. Woman: Begin stretching your hymen and the opening of your vagina by using graduated dilators or inserting first one finger, then two, and then three. You may start with something as small as a slim tampon applicator and increase the size of the dilator until you are inserting a cylindrical object the size of an erect penis.

3. Woman: Practice the relaxation of your PC muscle as described in Assignment 12 of the sexual retraining process in chapter 12.

4. Woman: Have a gynecological examination, including birth-control management and testing for sexually transmitted diseases and AIDS. If the gynecologist is unable to do a vaginal examination because the opening of your vagina is too small or too tight, seek the help of a pelvic-floor physical therapist and, possibly, a sexual therapist.

In rare instances, the hymen covers too much of the opening of the vagina, and a hymenotomy may be necessary. But the need for surgical intervention should always be confirmed by a second opinion. Surgery, when it is not necessary, only leaves more scar tissue and additional pain.

5. Man: Have a routine physical examination, including testing for sexually transmitted diseases and AIDS.

6. Both: Complete the genital self-examinations (Assignment 11 in the sexual retraining process).

7. Together: Buy and use a genital lubricant for all of your sexual intercourse experiences until you unintentionally ease out of using the lubricant. As mentioned earlier, Albolene, a facial cleanser, and natural oils like coconut oil, olive oil, and others work well but should not be used with condoms or diaphragms because these oils break down the effectiveness of barrier methods of birth control. We do not recommend K-Y Jelly because its primary ingredient is glycerin, which is irritating. We recommend Astroglide Premium Silicone Gel, Astroglide Natural Liquid, Probe Silky Light, Probe Thick and Rich, Water-Based Yes and Oil-Based Yes (but not latex-condom compatible). For more details on these, refer to pages 66–67.

8. Together: Talk about your sexual pasts to alert each other to any elements that might negatively affect your first intercourse. Respond individually to the following questions and share your responses using the Communication Format, page 16:

What did you learn about sex as you were growing up?
What experiences have you had that may affect your first intercourse?
What do you think your parents' sexual life is/was like?
What would you like your own sexual life to be like?

9. Together: Talk about your fears and anticipations of your first sexual encounter.

10. Together: Plan to proceed through your first intercourse slowly. Take time to enjoy all the pleasure you have allowed before marriage and now add the total-body and genital caressing. Kissing is vital to your connecting and relaxing together.

11. Both: Place no sexual demands on yourselves or each other, but completely delight in enjoying each other's bodies.

12. Woman: Invite and guide the initial entry. Man: After entry, rest quietly together (quiet vagina) before you begin a gradual and varied pattern of rhythmic thrusting.

Pain during first-intercourse experiences can be minimized. Premarital teaching, examinations, communication, and preparation can make your first sex comfortable and satisfying for both husband and wife. That first time of consummation will be a memory that lasts forever!

Pain due to stress. All of us show tension in our own unique ways. You may tighten up your genital muscles involuntarily as an expression of your tension. You may not even be aware that the tensing is happening, yet the muscle tension is counterproductive to comfortable and fulfilling intercourse. As a result of the tension, you experience pain.

Frequently the tightening will occur immediately before entry or as entry is attempted. This can make entry very painful. Sometimes, sharp, spasmodic contractions occur after entry as your arousal intensifies near or at the point of orgasm. It is as if you are having an orgasmic response, but the tension in your body keeps that muscle from responding smoothly. The spasmodic, painful contractions reflect your stress.

℞ *Relief of pain due to stress* is aimed at reducing the stress that causes the pain or learning to relax and give and receive sexual pleasure in spite of the stress.

If the stress is due to external life issues—finances, children, moving, remodeling, job, and so on—then stress-reduction and coping techniques may be most helpful. If the stress is due to sexual conflict, psychotherapy may be required to uncover your ambivalence about being sexual. Whatever the cause of your stress, a focus on pleasuring will at least reduce the problem. Taking turns stroking and caressing each other's bodies simply for the sake of soaking in that touch can do wonders to relieve pain due to stress. Follow the sexual retraining process in chapter 12, especially focusing on the touching exercises.

Pain due to lack of release. Lack of sexual release, or orgasmic inhibition, is another source of pain for women. If you do not experience orgasm even though you become highly aroused, you may sense painful fullness in your lower abdominal and lower back areas, especially after intercourse. As you become aroused, muscle tension builds as your whole reproductive system becomes congested with blood in preparation for an orgasm. The contractions in the lower part of the vagina and in the uterus during orgasm relieve that congestion. When you have orgasm, the draining of the blood from the genitals provides a great deal of pleasure. If you do not experience orgasm, the whole pelvic area remains engorged, which may cause chronic pain. This pain is usually not intense, but it is a dull, throbbing ache deep inside your body.

℞ Obviously, the best *remedy for pain due to lack of release* is to teach yourself to experience orgasmic release. The sexual retraining process outlined in chapter 12 combined with the information on orgasmic inhibition in chapter 17 will help you let go sexually.

Physically based pain. Infection of any part of the female genitalia, internal or external, will cause pain in that part when it is touched. The inflammation, irritation, and swelling of the infected part causes that tissue to be very tender.

Any infection should be treated immediately by a physician. Sexual activity should be limited according to the physician's instructions, and it should be designed to prevent further negative painful experiences. These limitations are good opportunities for you to focus on total-body pleasuring and other, often bypassed, special pleasures.

Vaginal irritations are troublesome because there often is no specific, identifiable disease present. Yet an irritated vaginal opening or vaginal barrel can cause as much sexual distress as an infection.

The generous use of a lubricant can help reduce the irritation, even though it does not treat the cause. The lubricant is especially helpful if the irritation is due to the thinning of the vaginal walls and the reduced vaginal lubrication associated with aging. You can help slow the vaginal atrophy process with PC muscle exercises and intravaginal hormonal replacement therapy; both can be of great help in actually keeping the vaginal tissues alive and functioning longer (see Assignment 12 of the sexual retraining process in chapter 12). Uterine contractions during orgasm may be painful due to endometriosis, which would require medical intervention.

If you are a young woman suffering from vaginal irritation, have your diet, hormonal birth control, and reactions to your husband's seminal fluid evaluated. Richard Dickey's book, *Managing Contraceptive Pill Patients*,[1] is very helpful in identifying the symptoms linked to various hormonal birth control methods. You may need to work with your doctor to try a new product until you find the one that works best for your system.

To help you determine if the irritation is a reaction to your husband's seminal fluid, have him wear a lambskin condom for several sexual intercourse experiences, then compare the difference in the pain you experience with and without the condom.

Rx Our own theory, which stems from biochemical and nutritional awareness as well as a high success rate for women who have tried diet change, is that change in diet can improve the pH balance in the body and reduce or eliminate vaginal irritation. We think of adjusting the diet to affect the acid-base balance much like physicians often recommend diet changes to help women prevent susceptibility to urinary bladder irritations. We recommend that you eliminate sodas, sugar and artificial sweeteners, caffeine, processed meats and grains, citrus fruit, and any allergens in your diet. Add probiotics and cooked vegetables. Drink water before and between meals (divide your weight in half and that is the number of ounces to drink per day), use olive oil and coconut oil, eat the equivalent of a cereal bowl of steamed vegetables twice a day (juicing can be a substitute), eat small amounts of low-fat protein four to six times a day, eat no more than two servings of fruit per day and a maximum of one serving of bread or starch. Basically follow a natural, organic food plan that is high mineral, low fat, and high protein. These recommendations should be confirmed with your physician. Although nothing recommended here should be harmful, it is always best to make certain that our recommendations do not in any way interfere with your physician's diagnosis and treatment of pain.

Physically based pain can also be the result of either *tears in the opening of the vagina* or *small cuts (fissures) inside the vagina* itself. Tears in the hymen usually cause pain upon entry. Pain due to tears or fissures is usually very sharp and specific; the woman can pinpoint a specific spot inside the vagina that hurts when it is touched or thrust against. Continued sexual activity and the moist environment cause slow healing of fissures and tears. These must be treated medically.

Some women report a *sharp, stabbing pain only upon deep thrusting.* This most commonly is the result of a tipped or retroverted uterus that causes the cervix of the uterus to be thrust against during deep thrusting. The cervix is sensitive to pain, so each thrust causes a sharp, stabbing pain. You may actually cry out or react with a jarring movement.

℞ Relief can be found immediately by a slight shift in position. The pain can be prevented by putting a small pillow or folded towel under your upper buttocks if you are in the underneath position, or you can be in the top position and control the thrusting. To correct the ret-roverted uterus, seek medical consultation. In addition, two exercises can do miracles for improving uterine placement. The PC muscle exercise helps keep all the reproductive organs in place and the knee-chest exercise specifically adjusts the uterus into the desired location. The knee-to-chest exercise should be done for five minutes once or twice a day. Position your-self on the floor on your knees and then rest your chest on the floor. While in that position, separate your labia to let air rush into your vagina, and remain in that position for five minutes. VERY IMPORTANT: This posi-tion and allowing air to rush into the vagina should not be done during pregnancy.

Other *internal pathologies* such as endometriosis, ovarian cysts, pelvic inflam-matory disease, or a misplaced IUD can also cause pain upon thrusting.

Finally, physically based pain may be the outgrowth of *childbirth trauma.* One source of such pain is the sensitive scar tissue from the episi-otomy, the incision between the vagina and the rectum to assist the birth process. There may also be tears in the ligaments that hold the uterus in place, in the vaginal wall, or around the opening of the vagina. For those of you who are resuming sexual activity after childbirth, we encourage you to follow the same instructions as outlined earlier in this chapter to prevent the pain of first intercourse. If the pain continues, consult your physician or seek consultation from another physician.

℞ For reducing all types of pain, the following general guidelines will be helpful:

1. Talk with your husband about the pain. Develop a signal to let him know when you are feeling pain so you can change your activity to relieve it. *Sexual activity associated with pain should never be continued.*

2. Identify exactly *when* in your sexual experience the pain is triggered and *how long* it lasts. Note specifically *where* the pain is *located.* It is helpful if you can describe *what type of pain* you experience: stinging, burning, stabbing, dull, rubbing, sharp, and so forth.

3. Take charge of getting relief from your pain. Seek medical help and describe in detail what you have already discovered about your pain (by completing Step 2). Boldly inform your physician that the pain is interrupting your sexual pleasure and you want treatment to relieve that pain. There are excellent resources available. We will list a number of key ones in the bibliography.

4. Use your time together to discover what sexual activities are pleasurable and focus on that enjoyment.

5. After the reason for the pain is gone, you may continue to pull away or tighten up to avoid the painful sensation. You need to identify and break this conditioned response by talking about the reaction and then correcting it by purposeful distraction and relaxation.

An increasing number of women, particularly young women, are reporting pain during intercourse. Pain does not have to be tolerated. In fact, pain *cannot* be allowed to continue if you are going to enjoy sexual pleasure.

UNCONSUMMATED MARRIAGES

The ultimate problem with intercourse is the inability to have it at all. When you have not been able to have entry of the penis into the vagina, your marriage is unconsummated.

Couples may have been married three weeks or forty years and not been able to have intercourse. You may be functioning normally in every other area of life but have been unable to come together sexually, even though you know how and have been trying. The pain and the shame you carry may make it difficult for you to even seek treatment. Fortunately, the Internet has been a gift to those in this situation; you can be totally anonymous and find the help you need. We have many call or e-mail us who have not been able to find help in their vicinity, found our website, and contacted us, and we were able to connect them with the help they needed.

A number of reasons cause the inability to have intercourse:

1. You may not know how. This may be difficult to believe in our sexually enlightened age, but it is a reality. You may have had little sexual education—academic education and intelligence are not the issue. Developmental naiveté has left both of you feeling awkward sexually. You bumble. You do not seem to be able to get your bodies in the right position at the right time and at the correct angle. You do not know to separate the labia before attempting entry.

   R̶x Encouragingly, the sexually naive couple responds quickly to the sexual retraining process and sexual education. Proceeding through part 1, communication; part 2, education; and the retraining exercises of part 3 should help you become able to consummate your marriage.

2. Obesity can prevent the possibility of the penis being able to enter the vagina.

   R̶x Creative positioning can help you to be able to consummate, but weight loss is the preferred approach. A medical program for weight loss is usually recommended.

3. Physiological obstruction of the opening of the vagina due to skin growing over the opening, a rigid hymen, or any disease of the pelvic organs will prevent entry of the penis into the vagina. Medical intervention is necessary.

4. Pain at attempt at entry will prevent entry. This was discussed in detail earlier in this chapter.

   Sarah had been sexually active before her marriage to Tom, but they were unable to consummate their marriage due to extreme pain when they attempted intercourse. She had been to several physicians, and surgery had been suggested. We began treating her for vaginismus while continuing to seek a more accurate diagnosis. A gynecological urologist who specializes in pain during intercourse finally discovered that Sarah had urethritis—a highly inflamed urethra. The treatment was painful and took a long time to correct the problem. After the urethritis was corrected, Sarah and Tom still needed sexual therapy to be able to consummate their marriage because many negative patterns of sexual relating had to be reversed. The "pain effect" had had a negative impact on their entire sexual relationship.

5. Erectile dysfunction (ED) may keep you from being able to consummate your marriage. If you are not able to get or keep an erection, you will not be able to enter your wife.

   The plan for overcoming ED is discussed in chapter 16. This should be incorporated into the sexual retraining process described in chapter 12.

6. Panic attacks, probably caused by past abuse or rape, may keep you (the woman) from allowing entry. Individual psychotherapy or group therapy may be helpful. Working through the exercises of the sexual retraining process may produce enough trust and relaxation to allow entry.

7. Vaginismus is the most common reason for unconsummated marriages and is clearly a problem with intercourse.

℞ Working on your unconsummated marriage produces tangible results. There is no doubt when you have been successful. You either have been able to have intercourse or you have not. The success rate is high. We hope this news will encourage you to seek help immediately. How sad it is that some couples wait for years before they do anything about this dilemma. Some go for help but are given an ineffective treatment or inaccurate advice. Fortunately, consummation is possible.

VAGINISMUS

Vaginismus is an involuntary, spastic or rigid contracting of the muscles surrounding the vagina (the outer one-third), making penetration impossible or very painful.

Some women's vaginal muscles snap tightly shut only with attempts at intercourse. Other women's vaginal muscles tighten at penetration attempts by the finger or any other object. Yet others seem to be consistently and rigidly closed. In fact, women have been totally convinced that they do not have an opening. Their husbands report that their attempts to enter feel as though they are pushing against a wall. For some women the condition has always been there. Insertion of a tampon may have been difficult or impossible. You may have tried and become very nauseous. Or you may have incredible resistance to even trying. Other women have been able to have pain-free sexual intercourse. The spasms started after a childbirth injury, fall, rape, or other traumatic incident—physical or emotional.

Many couples with unconsummated marriages due to vaginismus have acquired great pleasuring skills because they have learned to do everything but have intercourse. For others, all the intense pleasure they enjoyed in premarital necking and petting has dissipated with the stress of not being able to have intercourse.

When a couple comes to us, they may have seen several medical doctors, counselors, psychologists, and even sexual therapists without having been offered effective treatment. A team (interdisciplinary) approach to vaginismus is most often necessary. Diagnosis is typically made by a pelvic-floor physical therapist, a gynecologist, or other pelvic-floor specialist. As sexual therapists, through the verbal assessment process, we can be fairly certain of the diagnosis, but will have that confirmed with physical examination by a PT or MD who specializes in pelvic-floor issues. Fortunately, you can, with the correct help, train your pelvic-floor muscles to relax and respond appropriately. The discouraging part for many is that it takes work. Women with vaginismus can get frustrated. When we lead therapy groups for women with unconsummated marriages due to pain, women will express their anger that they have to work at it when it just happens naturally for others. One encouragement is that often these couples learn to enjoy each other's bodies more fully, rather than just having intercourse as their means of sexual expression.

Our four-pronged approach to vaginismus is presented in the last section of this chapter.

Causes of Vaginismus

Physical injury or response. As a young girl or even later in life, a woman may have fallen on a bar, had a bad fall on her tailbone, been in a car accident when an injury to her pelvis caused the muscles in her pelvic floor to tighten, or tightened her pelvic-floor muscles in response to another frightening event. One woman with severe vaginismus had been in the car when her parents were killed in a car accident.

Misinformation. As a young girl, you may have been warned never to put anything "in there." You may have received a message of hurt or disgust at the thought of something entering your vagina. You may not have been told that the vagina is an organ of accommodation, able to receive an erect penis and even deliver a baby. In fact, the messages you got might have been quite the opposite.

Emotional inhibitions. These often come from rigid upbringing and negative conditioning to sex, based on religious orthodoxy.

Marsha was raised by her Polish grandmother and educated by the nuns at a rigid Catholic school. Her grandmother talked of men and sex with utter disgust. Marsha had never used tampons because of fear of breaking her hymen and "not being a virgin." She and Jim had enjoyed sex play before marriage but were saving intercourse for their wedding night. The wedding came and Marsha panicked. She pushed Jim away. Four months after marriage, they came for help. Because of the emotional stigma, Marsha was unable to put anything in her vagina herself, but she was soon able to allow Jim to insert his finger, then two fingers, then dilators, and finally his penis.

Traumatic sexual experiences. We find that sexual molestation or abuse is a common cause of vaginismus. The abuse may have been attempted, or actual entry may have occurred. In response, the little girl protected herself by involuntarily tightening her vaginal opening. Physical abuse can also cause a young girl to involuntarily and rigidly contract her vaginal opening. A traumatic urinary tract examination or treatment, even when performed with sensitivity, may be experienced as abuse by a young child and have the same long-term consequences. Similarly, the frequent use of enemas, a catheterization procedure, or a genital exam on a little girl may trigger vaginismus.

One woman had a ten-year unconsummated marriage. During therapy it became clear that her father had had intercourse with her before age four. She was too young to differentiate the pain of vaginal entry from urinary functioning. Therefore, she always had difficulty letting go of her urine in public restrooms. She would never urinate during a school day. This led to urological problems and procedures. She also struggled with constipation, so her mother gave her enemas and punished her for trying not to let them work. Her vaginismus was due to a combination of all her openings in the perineal area having been abused.

Excessive closeness to an overprotective mother. Fearful mothers often instill many conscious and unconscious, or nonspecific, fears of life in general that can affect the sexual arena. These mothers project their own fears of the world or of sex onto their daughters. For example, mothers who survived the painful threats of the Holocaust were left with nightmarish memories that they communicated to their daughters. Dagmar O'Connor refers to these women who have a high incidence of vaginismus as "daughters of Holocaust survivors."[2]

Jeanie was born to a single mother who had a very unhappy and painful life; Jeanie was her only source of joy and meaning. When Jeanie was twenty-eight, her mother still sewed all of Jeanie's clothes. Jeanie needed to call or visit her mother daily. She had to constantly be thinking about making her mother happy. Her mother indirectly and directly communicated to Jeanie a fear, distrust, and hatred of men, along with a contradictory dream of the white knight in shining armor coming to rescue her from her misery.

After marriage, Jeanie could enjoy all sexual activity with her husband—except intercourse. With time, Jeanie's sexual desire lessened. Psychotherapy and sexual therapy were necessary to reverse her dilemma.

Helen Singer Kaplan suggested that any adverse stimulus associated with vaginal entry may cause vaginal tightness, whether the stimulus is real or fantasized.[3] So whether the woman with vaginismus fantasizes trauma with vaginal entry because of the close protective association with her mother, the woman's emotional antisex inhibitions, or misinformation about the vaginal function, or whether she experienced physical trauma, rape, incest, or forced attempted entry, the result is the same. She experiences the rigid, conditioned restriction of the muscles controlling the vaginal inlet—vaginismus.

Getting the Right Help for Vaginismus

As we mentioned, ultimately, vaginismus must be diagnosed by physical examination. If you are located where you have access to be examined by a pelvic-floor specialist, whether an MD or a PT, you won't need these detailed instructions for the examination. But for those of you who live in areas where these specialists are not available, take care of yourself by using the details that follow.

First, the examining professional should ease your tension by talking with you. Then there should be a complete physical examination in which each body part is examined. Throughout the examination the examiner should be informing you, "Now I am going to examine your _____; to do this, I will use _____ [an instrument]. You will feel _____." Then, as each part of the examination is completed, the examiner should say, "Your _____ looks completely normal," and so on.

For the genital examination, your external genitalia should be examined first. Sometimes the involuntary tightening of the vaginal inlet is obvious from this external genital examination. In that case, insertion of a finger or a speculum should not even be attempted.

If an internal vaginal exam is necessary, the examiner should:

1. Provide support for your legs while your feet are in the stirrups.
2. Show you her gloved hand.
3. Coach you in breathing deeply.
4. Tell you exactly what she is doing and perceiving in positive terms: "I am able to _____."
5. If the examiner is able to insert a finger, the muscle will likely reflex and tighten around the finger. It may only be possible to probe with a cotton-tipped swab.

The spasm of the muscle surrounding the outer portion of the vagina is usually obvious upon vaginal examination. For some women, the tightening does not happen when examined by a physician. Your husband may be needed to describe the clamping or pinching response to his finger or penis as he attempts to enter or actually enters. When it is possible to have entry and the muscle relaxes after insertion, this is not complete vaginismus, but some degree of it. In partial vaginismus, the husband is able to insert with extreme difficulty and pain, and then relaxation occurs. The vaginal examination will confirm or rule out your suspected diagnosis of vaginismus.

If you feel unsure of the diagnosis, go for a second opinion. This is particularly important if surgery is recommended. We are very cautious about surgery as a solution for unconsummated marriages, and surgery is *not* the answer to vaginismus.

Mary had been married seven years and had had entry one or two times with extreme pain. Now entry was impossible. She was told she needed surgery for removal of an intracoital ridge. Fearful of the surgery, she sought a second opinion. The second physician expressed some doubt about surgery and recommended sexual therapy. The second physician asked Mary to have us, her sexual therapists, call to discuss her case.

After the assessment, we called the physician and explained that Mary had a history of sexual molestation by her stepfather. She also had fears that had been instilled by her mother. She fit the pattern of women who have tightened the vaginal muscle due to emotional reasons. The second physician was relieved by our information because he saw no need for surgical removal of an intracoital ridge. Surgery was not needed.

Other misdiagnoses have been given for vaginismus. However, there are conditions other than vaginismus that cause pain upon attempted entry. So another diagnosis may be accurate. When in doubt, get more than one medical opinion. This is especially important if you have a history of sexual abuse, suspected sexual abuse, or overprotective closeness with a mother who instilled fears of the world or antisex teaching or conditioning. Because these histories are clearly connected with vaginismus, any other diagnosis needs to be validated or ruled out.

The helpfulness of having the diagnosis explained was expressed so well by clients of Dr. O'Connor: "It was from the sex therapist that Larry and I finally learned that I had vaginismus, constriction of the vaginal muscles caused by fear when penetration is attempted. I was incredibly relieved to hear that my problem had a name . . . (and) that the cure rate for vaginismus was high."[4]

This woman's relief is representative of the feelings expressed by most women who seek our help for vaginismus. The women who come to us have been given tranquilizers, muscle relaxants, and stiff drinks. They have been told to "grow up," "just relax," or "fantasize some bizarre experience," or they have been urged to have surgery. When we describe their condition and its treatment, they feel great relief. The description connects with their experience. Telling the husband, "It must have felt like you were pushing against a brick wall when you tried to enter," often connects vividly with his experience. Likewise, the woman feels understood when we talk about her experience: "You have probably believed it was physically impossible to get anything in your vagina."

℞ Relaxing the tightened vaginal muscle of vaginismus requires more than just the sexual retraining process. The specific work for undoing vaginismus has four distinct tracks: (1) building trust to be able to give and receive pleasure (using the sexual retraining process); (2) embracing your sexuality and your genitals; (3a) freeing the emotional conflict and tension associated with entry into the vagina, or (3b) relieving medical/physical issues; (4) gaining control of pelvic-floor muscles and allowing penetration—entry of the penis into the vagina.

Track 1. Building trust to be able to give and receive sexual pleasure. The exercises of the sexual retraining process in chapter 12 will teach you how to give and receive sexual pleasure and help you build trust in your husband—trust that he will not violate you sexually. However, you may have developed all the skills of bodily pleasuring in your lovemaking without intercourse. You may not need this track of the process if you are able to enjoy giving and receiving pleasure to the point of orgasm, and you and your husband enjoy a mutually satisfying sexual relationship except for intercourse. Your only barrier may be the inability to have vaginal penetration.

On the other hand, if you cannot freely give and receive sexual pleasure, you desperately need to work through the sexual retraining process. It can help you learn to build trust and relax as you enjoy the giving and receiving of sexual pleasure.

Track 2. Embrace your sexuality, and accept your genitals. Women with vaginismus may have dissociated their genitals from their personhood. Your genitals may have become a source of fear, confusion, conflict, and pain. An active process of genital acceptance must ensue.

Naming and Claiming. We often refer to this process of genital acceptance and control as "naming and claiming." It begins with the Female Self-Examination (Assignment 11 of the sexual retraining process in chapter 12) and continues with the Vaginal Examination and Genital Affirmation (Assignment 23), which may not be possible to complete at first. The next step is the PC Muscle Exercise (Assignment 12). Watch the opening of your vagina as you tighten and relax the PC muscle—focus on relaxing, so you learn that you can voluntarily relax the opening of your vagina.

Patting and Affirming. Naming each other's genitals with loving names can be fun (Assignment 23). This assignment also teaches you to pat and affirm each other's genitals every night before going to sleep. This not only helps you gain genital acceptance but also continues the previous track of building trust with your husband.

Sharing. The Clinical Genital Examination (Assignment 15) and the Vaginal Examination (Assignment 23) are assigned to continue the process of not only accepting your genitals for yourself, but now being able to very openly share them with your husband for his pleasure and for your enjoyment with clarity that you can interrupt him anytime his activities become associated with violation or pain. To connect to your genitals as a part of yourself that is good, praise God for creating you as a sexual person in his image and designing your genitals for sexual pleasure, not pain.

Being able to embrace your sexuality as good and of God and to gain acceptance of your genitals is vital to your ability to pursue the steps necessary for vaginal penetration and enjoyment.

Track 3a. Freeing the emotional conflict and tension associated with entry into the vagina. Although the reason you have difficulty with entry into your vagina may not be clear to you, completing and sharing Assessment Form 2, Background History, in chapter 11 may give you a sense of what in your past could have been an injury that caused your pelvic-floor muscles to tighten or could have elicited conflict or fear about vaginal entry. Another great resource is the workbook from www.vaginismus.com. We often have women complete those forms in addition to ours.

In the assessment forms, Kathy was able to reveal the details of her rigid antisex training that had left her with extreme fear in response to anything being inserted into her vagina.

However, it was not until several sessions that she was able to tell us that when dating in high school, her boyfriend had entered her. She was naive and had not known what was happening. Being so frightened, she immediately pushed him out of her, got out of the car, and ran.

Mary was unable to tell us about the molestation by her stepfather until the third session. He was a "good Christian," she said, and her only loving father. Yet her kind, loving stepfather was the one who fondled her breasts and genitals.

Read. To help you uncover the emotional trauma that may be keeping you from allowing anything to enter your vagina, you may find it helpful to discuss with your husband the four causes of vaginismus that we listed a few pages ago. Decide which cause fits most with you. Then do a lot of reading about that particular issue. For example, if you suspect past sexual abuse, you may want to begin by reading chapter 18, "Sexual Molestation and Abuse," in our book *Sex Facts for the Family.*

Letting go of your emotional bondage and grieving your loss of healthy sexual openness may be a tedious process. Reading may stir up pain; none of us like pain, so there will likely be a tendency to want to avoid that. It may be so severe that you cannot continue with your ongoing responsibilities while you are releasing that pain. You may need to segment your life so you can deal with your underlying conflicts at separate times from your life tasks.

One woman scheduled her reading, writing, and crying about her pain (did her "grief work") from 9:00 a.m. to 2:00 p.m. Monday through Friday while her children were in school. Then she gave herself from 2:00 p.m. to 3:00 p.m. to put aside the pain and connect with her current world before her children came home.

Another woman, who had been severely beaten by her mother and who had an intense phobic reaction to any vaginal penetration, could not work on this issue while she was in graduate school. She would only work with us in confronting her pain while she was on vacation from school.

The fact is, to be healed, you cannot continue to avoid your negative feelings. You must face the pain to release its hold on your vaginal musculature.

Write. Whether you actually write in a journal, type into a document, or speak into a device that records for you, it is important to express and record your memories, feelings, reactions, dreams, thoughts, and fantasies. This helps enable you to get with the pain, rather than avoid it, because you can release it by recording the facts so that you can go back over them as needed. Some women find it extremely difficult to write about their past traumatic experiences. They feel too vulnerable: "Who knows who might read it?" Others find that writing about that painful past makes it too real. But this is exactly what needs to happen to be cured. Still others resist writing because they think these events might not really have happened. "What if I just made them up?" they ask. You can be assured that whether your painful memories are of real or fantasized events, they need to be released so that the events no longer have control over you. Instead, you will have control over their effects.

Talk. The fears you have about entry into the vagina and the history of those feelings are best released by expressing them. Talk with a caring friend, a counselor, or your husband. Being in a small group with other women who have this struggle is the most freeing. You might tell your counselor, pastor, or doctor to let you know if he or she is aware of another woman with vaginismus who would be open to talk with you.

Working with groups of women with unconsummated marriages has been most rewarding for us. They are so relieved to talk with someone else who has experienced similar thoughts and fears. Some of the common feelings they have shared are: (1) They need to be in control in life in general. For example, they prefer to drive the car rather than be a passenger. (2) Early childhood discovery of their clitoris and sexual responsiveness was associated with intense guilt. (3) They view their genitals and their husbands' penises as ugly. (4) They view sex as something the woman gives to the man. (5) They were very responsive in many forms of sexual play with their husband-to-be before marriage. (6) They approached marriage with dread (*that's when I'm going to* have to *do it*). (7) They panicked at the first attempted entry. (8) They came from homes that were rigid, lacking warmth and physical affection, with either an emotionally distant father or loss of the father through death or divorce.

If emotional pain is the reason for your vaginismus, it will be important for you to (1) recognize the reasons why you tighten up your vagina, (2) accept that your fears of vaginal penetration are irrational, (3) choose to no longer allow your mother-instilled fears, father's abuse, antisexual teaching, or whatever it is that is controlling your vagina, and (4) make a decision to stop resisting and to go after sexual pleasure and vaginal penetration. This last step occurs similarly to a conversion experience. You have been using your energies to protect yourself. Now you turn the opposite direction and use those same energies to engage. The change will require the love, care, and support of your husband.

Cheryl, whose story will be shared later, expressed this change so aptly: "Whatever they did to me, I'm not going to let them have control over me anymore. I am going to be able to have sex with my husband. Why should I allow them to keep me from that?"

Track 3b: Relieving medical/physical issues. However, if your vaginismus was triggered by a fall, injury, or pain due to infections or irritation in the genitals, your focus in Track 3 will be to seek the medical and physical therapy necessary for relief.

Track 4: Gain control of your pelvic-floor muscles, and achieve entry into the vagina through a gradual process of reduction of fear and relaxation of the vaginal opening. Although Track 3 is the most painful part of this process, Track 4 can be the most difficult to do. This is true if you have a phobic reaction to inserting anything into your vagina or you have a physical/medical barrier to entry—both take hard work. Every stage of the process may progress nicely, but the task of inserting something into your vagina may seem impossible. Even inserting a Q-tip can be overwhelmingly frightening. For those of you who have the benefit of working with a pelvic-floor physical therapist, you will not need all the details we have written here for accomplishing this task. For those who don't have access to or the ability to engage a PT, you will need support each step of the way. It would be nice to have someone in addition to your husband to be there for you—not necessarily to do the steps with you, but for the emotional encouragement.

Self or Husband Insertion. For the first assignment, you must be sure of complete privacy and no interruptions. Take a leisurely bath and pamper yourself in any way that makes you feel special and relaxed (apply lotion to your body, brush your hair, etc.). Then prop yourself up with large pillows behind your back and under your legs so that you are in a reclined sitting position against the head of a bed with your legs bent and drawn toward your body. Repeat the Female Self-Examination (Assignment 11) and the PC Muscle Exercise (Assignment 12) while watching your vagina relax. Have available a Q-tip (or some other clean object that is even thinner, if needed), a hand mirror, and a lubricant. Take a deep breathe in. Hold it. Then let go. Breathe in, tighten your PC muscle. As you exhale slowly through your mouth, relax the PC muscle and insert the lubricated Q-tip.

This may sound like a simple exercise. However, some women have spent months not being able to do this. They come back to us week after week with reasons why they could not complete the assignment. The woman who was physically abused by her mother spent forty-five minutes of shakily trying to get herself to do this exercise. This was true each time she tried. For her, we discovered it was easier for her husband to do the insertion. Some women can allow a physician or their husbands to accomplish vaginal penetration, but they cannot do it for themselves. Others are just the opposite. They need to be in control of breaking the vaginal barrier. Do you have a sense of whether it will be easier to accomplish vaginal penetration by yourself or with the assistance of your husband?

Medical Insertion. Occasionally, we refer the woman to a physician who is experienced in inserting vaginal dilators in vaginismic women. The husband's presence during the examination and insertion is helpful—it brings him into the process. In most settings, you or your husband are first told how to do the insertion; then you can ask your doctor if he or she is comfortable with assisting you and your husband in this task.

If you cannot progress beyond this task, and all the previously mentioned approaches do not allow you to insert even the thinnest object into the vagina, your phobic reaction must be dealt with, perhaps with a creative approach. A psychiatrist's evaluation and prescribed medication may be necessary. But don't give up. It *is* possible. Keep seeking help. Call us if necessary: 626-449-2525.

Visualization and Relaxation. To help you positively approach the steps to success, write a detailed description of what is to happen in the assigned vaginal-entry exercises: the actual actions, what you will feel or think, and what will happen to your vagina. You and your husband might get a tape to learn deep relaxation exercises, and then he can verbally guide you through all the steps to insert the Q-tip into your vagina. His guidance is to be warm and positive, painting the picture of the vagina as open and receptive. This visualization may need to be repeated several times. In fact, you or your husband can make a tape of this process, then you can listen to it daily. Write down the thoughts, visions, or feelings that come into your mind during the visualization.

Vaginal Dilation. Once it is possible for you, your husband, or your physician to insert something into your vagina, the gradual relaxation of the vaginal muscle begins. You can use a series of dilators, catheters, syringe covers, fingers, or any other clean, smooth objects that are graduated in size. Inserting these objects helps eliminate the involuntary spasms of the PC muscle controlling the opening of the vagina. *These dilation exercises are necessary to the successful treatment of vaginismus.* Dilators can be ordered from us or from www.vaginismus.com.

The same circumstances that brought about successful insertion of the Q-tip or a thin, rubber catheter into your vagina should be repeated as you insert each of the next-size objects. In other words, if you were able to accomplish insertion by yourself, that is how you should proceed with the progressively larger objects. If your husband was effective and you were not, your husband should insert the dilators. If your physician was the only one who was successful, transfer this ability from your physician to yourself or your husband in the physician's office with his or her direction. Transferring that ability may take some change in your home environment. The location may need to change. The bedroom might be avoided.

Continue to insert increasing sizes of dilators daily, using the same or similar setting and conditions that worked before. This is the process to follow for these dilation exercises:

1. Take a warm, relaxing bath.
2. Pamper yourself—lotion your body, brush your hair, read, listen to music, or do whatever is relaxing for you.
3. Prop yourself up with large pillows behind your back and under

your legs so that you are in a reclined sitting position against the head of a bed with your legs spread apart, bent, and drawn toward your body.

4. Using a hand mirror, examine your genitals and watch while you tighten and relax your vagina opening. (See Female Self-Examination and PC Muscle Exercises, pages 164 and 166.)

5. Have available a Q-tip (or other clean object that is even thinner), a hand mirror, and a lubricant. Take a deep abdominal breath in. As you exhale slowly through your mouth, relax the PC muscle (bear down) and insert the lubricated Q-tip or smallest dilator.

6. Leave the object in your vagina for five to twenty minutes. (You may need to start with five or less and increase gradually.)

7. While the dilator is in place, read a paraphrase of the Song of Solomon or something that is affirming of your sexuality as good and of God.

8. *Relax* the PC muscle while the dilator is in place (or follow the instructions of a pelvic-floor physical therapist—go to www. pelvicpain.org to find a pelvic-floor physical therapist).

9. Affirm your ability to allow this step of the process.

When changing to the next-size object, begin by inserting the previous size, wait for the muscle spasm to relax, remove the previous size object, and *instantly* insert the next-larger size. Use objects of increasing size until the object being inserted is the largest dilator or the circumference of your husband's erect penis. After the Q-tip or thin rubber catheter, you may use larger rubber catheters, vaginal dilators, rounded plastic tampon applicators (start with the slim size), your fingers, or other clean, smooth objects. Call our office (626-449-2525) to order dilators.

Transfer of Self-Insertion. If you have learned to relax your vaginal muscle by inserting the dilators yourself, the next step is to transfer this learning so it can occur with your husband. If your husband has not been with you during self-insertion, have him be in the room, and choose how close and involved you would like him to be. He could be stroking your leg, rubbing your feet, or just present, doing nothing—maybe not even looking until you get more comfortable with his presence. Gradually increase his involvement until you are ready to have him actually do the insertions. Then start with the smallest dilator, but this time have your husband insert it. If that is too difficult, you insert it with him watching. The next time have him put his hand over yours as you insert it. The third time you put your hand over his as he inserts it. Finally, help him insert it on his own. Then you can proceed quickly to each larger dilator.

Vaginal Dilation and Pleasuring. Once your husband is able to insert the erect-penis-size dilator without any discomfort to you, you should combine vaginal dilation with pleasuring as described in the following exercises from the sexual retraining process (chapter 12). This process will lead to insertion of the penis into the vagina:[5]

1. Total-Body Pleasuring, Including Breasts and Genitals Without Purposeful Stimulation (Assignment 14) with the largest dilator inserted in the vagina.
2. Total-Body Pleasuring, Including Breast and Genital Stimulation (Assignment 24) with the largest dilator in the vagina.
3. Pleasuring, Not Using Hands (Including Using the Penis as a Paintbrush) (Assignment 26). This is to prepare you to be able to have the penis pleasure your genitals without any demand for entry.
4. Total-Body Pleasuring (Assignment 24) with the largest dilator in the vagina. Remove the dilator, lubricate your husband's penis, use it as a paintbrush, and then, while you are in the top position, separate your labia and poke the head of the penis just barely into the opening of your vagina. Be aware of any sensations of tightening. If those occur, move the penis away and continue to enjoy each other. Practice this step as many times as needed until you notice that the vagina remains free of the spastic response to the presence of the penis.

Transition from Dilator to Penile Insertion. Now that the vagina has gotten comfortable with the penis at the entrance, there are some preparatory steps to making the transition from having the dilator inside the vagina to having the penis enter the vagina.

1. Practice getting into positions without entry, wearing undergarments or comfortable clothing. You might get a book of positions. Go through the positions and mark those you want to try. Then mark those you like or think you would like to try again at another time. Also try adapting for the two of you the position you have used when you inserted the dilators. Another position to try, if you haven't already, is with your buttocks on the edge of the bed or other surface (much like the position for a gynecological examination); with him standing or kneeling beside the bed, put your legs on his shoulders. When you are at step 3, this position will allow you to spread the labia and allow his penis easy access at a good angle.

2. In preparation, read step 3 and talk together about which position you think will work for you. We have found that most couples find the last position we described in step 1 to work best. Realize that this transition step will be very mechanical. Think of the penis as the next dilator, only it is attached to your husband. In whatever ways the two of you have been enjoying each other sexually, without entry of the penis into the vagina, pursue that enjoyment if it will help you both relax.

3. When you have decided on the position you will use, get into that position, insert a lubricated dilator the size of his erect penis. (Some prefer using a vibrator in preparation for this step—see endnote #5.) Have him lubricate his penis and stimulate it to be erect enough to enter. Have one hand on the end of the dilator and one on his erect penis. Remove the dilator and instantly (no pause in between) guide his penis into your vagina. Don't think of it as having intercourse or a pleasurable, romantic event—just the mechanical process of getting the penis into the vagina.

If this doesn't work or if the vagina tightens, reinsert the vibrator or dilator and try again, but this time just poke into the entrance as you did in step 4 of "Vaginal Dilatation and Pleasuring." Repeat this in the future, poking in just a tiny bit farther, never attempting to enter all the way. Alternate between dilator and penis until the penis has probably gone in all the way.

4. Practice this until you both are comfortable with the mechanical process of insertion, then start incorporating entry or the steps toward entry into your sexual, romantic, pleasuring times together.

Cheryl was diagnosed as having vaginismus when she went for her premarital gynecological examination. Her physician referred her for sexual therapy, which she began two months before her wedding. We had three premarital sessions and three postmarital sessions.

Cheryl came with no memory of abuse. But she clearly remembered rigid, religious, antisex training from her mother and her sister, and the promiscuity she had witnessed in her home and extended family. She had never touched her own genitals and had never been successful in inserting even a slim-size tampon. She reported being easily orgasmic with manual stimulation by her fiancé.

After the first session, when we explored the possibility of abuse, Cheryl became highly anxious, unable to sleep, and very uncomfortable around her family. At the second session, she reported she had been unable to insert the Q-tip and feared remembering "something."

By the third session: (1) She had remembered hiding in her closet every time she was home and not washing her hair for weeks so she would not have to be in the bathroom very long for fear of her father. The picture of her father's sexual abuse of her never became as vivid as her memories of her fear and avoidance of that abuse. (2) After writing about her memories, she accepted the fact that her father had sexually abused her and that she felt anger toward her mother for not protecting her. She realized that at twenty-six years of age, she was still totally under the control of her mother and father. (3) At this point, she decided that she was not going to let them control her any longer and that she was going to be able to have sex with her husband. (4) She inserted the Q-tip that evening, tried the smallest dilator the next evening, and came to her third session ready for the next-size dilators.

This rapid process has never happened in any other case. Our sense is that the timing greatly enhanced the progress. We usually do not have the opportunity to treat vaginismus until after marriage. Most women are not aware of this difficulty until they attempt to consummate their marriages.

Heidi and Mel had been married ten years when they came to us for help with their unconsummated marriage. Mel's father had sexually abused Mel's sisters, so Mel was very hesitant to push Heidi sexually. Heidi had an alcoholic father and a sexually abusive mother. Her mother would suggestively look at Heidi's body when she was undressing and pinch her nipples. At the time she came to us for therapy, her mother still insisted on being in situations with Heidi when Heidi had to undress. Heidi said she hated her own body, yet she had a very attractive body and wore seductive clothing.

Heidi and Mel had a totally fulfilling sexual relationship with intense orgasmic response for both, great passionate kissing, and total-body enjoyment except for manual breast and genital stimulation of her—and except for intercourse.

Heidi became nauseous and cried every time she tried to insert a tampon or when Mel would try to touch her genitals with his hand, tongue, or the tip of his penis. She could rub her genitals on top of the shaft of his erect penis. In fact, that is what usually triggered her orgasmic release. She was terrified of pain and visualized herself ripping apart inside if he ever entered her with his penis.

The treatment process with Heidi and Mel required twenty sessions during a year. Most sessions were with Heidi alone; Mel was included every fourth session. In the final sessions of moving toward intercourse, Mel was included in every session. Tracks 2, 3, and 4 were followed as defined. Track 1 was not necessary. Their pleasuring skills were excellent.

The turning point came for Heidi when she wrote a letter to her mother expressing her pain and anger. This letter was not to be sent; it was only for Heidi's benefit. After writing the letter, Heidi began having dreams of being about two or three years old and her father chasing her and raping her; she realized she had always felt uneasy in her father's presence. Heidi had never been able to allow Mel to be in the top position during any sexual activity. Attempts at that position caused her to have a very sick feeling. These physical symptoms indicated that the behavior that elicited the sick feeling had occurred before she was old enough to have had complete verbal skills.

Heidi's progress with this track of the therapy process fluctuated. One time she would have an easy time inserting the dilators, and the next time the insertion would become difficult. This happened several times. When she began to believe that her father had raped her when she was very young, Heidi cried intensely, as though overwhelmed by the pain of a very young child. The next session, she had made a decision similar to Cheryl's. She was so angry with her parents for having caused her such pain, she never wanted to see them again. She not only decided to stop allowing their weirdness to keep affecting her, but she was also able to say, "Yes, I am a sexual person. This is good, and I am going to enjoy a total sexual experience with Mel." From that time on, her vaginal insertions progressed rapidly.

She was able to take charge of her sexual experiences positively rather than keeping control to protect herself from feeling sick. Taking charge led her to allow herself to feel the nausea rather than avoid it, and thus, the nausea gradually lessened until it was no longer present. Penile entry into her vagina went very smoothly. There was no pain. She felt almost let down that she had resisted so long something that was so easy, even enjoyable. Their sexual experience flowed naturally from that time on.

Vaginismus is correctable! There is no need for any couple to continue in an unconsummated marriage because of vaginismus. Masters and Johnson report 100 percent success. O'Conner reports 60 to 70 percent success. Any couple who has stayed with us through the therapy process has been successful. The problem is that some women stop therapy, either because they get discouraged with the "work" or their emotional resistance is powerful enough to supersede their drive to be able to have intercourse—it just doesn't seem worth it or possible for them. This is probably the reason for the difference in reported results. Masters and Johnson's 100 percent probably refers to those who stay with therapy. O'Conner's 60 to 70 percent probably includes those who start but then stop the process. We have about a 20 percent dropout rate. This is sad for us because success is definitely possible.

NINETEEN

Controlling Sexual Addictions

One of the most perplexing and difficult of all sexual dilemmas is sexual addiction. The addiction may be evident in a number of different ways.

❤↗ Sara called to hesitantly share that she was concerned about her husband's sexual needs but felt that the problem was really her fault. She then expressed her guilt and acceptance of a major portion of the blame because she was not interested in sex. When the story came out, we discovered that her husband had been seeing prostitutes throughout their marriage and had regularly masturbated to pornography, which he watched after the rest of the family had gone to bed.

❤↗ Marie's desire began to wane the first year of their marriage because of Clarence's persistent addictive pursuit of her sexually. She had quickly become the sexual object to his anxious addictive needs, rather than the mutual participant of romantic, intimate, physical expressions of love.

❤↗ Vince claimed that he was oversexed and unable to interest his wife frequently enough. He explained that this forced him to seek sexual release through other means such as visiting topless bars or massage parlors. He presented it first as a moral problem, which it certainly was!

Bill was laden with guilt over the fact that he was the leader of the adult Sunday school at his church, and yet he regularly viewed his stepdaughters through the keyhole in the bathroom while they were changing clothes or showering. He also used every opportunity he could to have them discover him without clothes on.

We first heard about Joel's addiction from his mother's report of abuse in the family. Later on we discovered that Joel, the twenty-one-year-old son, still lived in the home and had habitually abused all of the younger siblings for the last four years. He had not gotten the necessary help needed to control his behavior.

These real-life illustrations are but a small example of the ways sexual addiction displays itself.

DEFINING SEXUAL ADDICTIONS

Simply stated, if you lack control of some sexual behavior, you are struggling with a sexual addiction. The sexual addict feels controlled by the urge in the same way an overeater is controlled by the eating disorder or an alcoholic is controlled by the urge to drink. Even as we have come to think of alcoholism as an illness, so we also should think of sexual addiction as an illness. The sexual addict has a sexual preoccupation. If the addict is married, his preoccupation interferes with his marriage; he is unable to be satisfied by an intimate sexual relationship with his spouse. (Because the great majority of those struggling with sexual addiction are male, we will refer mainly to that gender, even though women, too, can obviously become hooked on sex.)

The sexual addict may feel the urge to have sexual relations repeatedly in a short time with the same or different partners. When the sexual urge is pressing, the addict feels anxious; he is captured by the drive. But afterward he is guilty and ashamed. This pattern often takes an extensive amount of time away from the family or work as the addict pursues sexual activity or looks for the possibility of sexual activity. This secret drive escalates to become the major focus of his life. It is his way of hiding from the realities of his life that he does not want to face.

Sexual addiction is perpetuated by the mood-altering effect that comes from engaging in the experience. It can be an adrenaline addiction that is designed to give the momentary high the addict seeks. The compulsion and fulfilling that compulsion become the predominant drive in his life and the main source of his self-nurture. This is no different than a drug addict who relies on a regular daily high from cocaine or relaxation from marijuana. The sexual addict feels as though he no longer has the capacity to make choices about his activities, but is compelled to engage in them regardless of the self-loathing that follows.

Before we go too far into this chapter, we need to clarify what is *not a sexual addiction*. A great range of sexual behavior is considered normal. For example, having sex every day might be very normal for one couple. However, for certain individuals, it may be an expression of an addiction. So we cannot say that anyone who wants frequent sex is a sexual addict. For one man, visiting a prostitute may be something he does every year or two when he is out of town, but he feels no great compulsion for it. As reprehensible as this may be, it would not be an addiction. Some men may masturbate on an intermittent schedule as they experience the urge to do so, but this does not comprise an addiction. There are men and women who on occasion will view pornographic material in a magazine, movie, video, or topless bar, but they are not hooked on those activities and would not be considered sexual addicts.

The emotional factors that distinguish various behaviors as sexual addictions are the obsessive and compulsive qualities that drive the person almost against his or her own will to do them. Most sexual addicts struggle with other addictions as well. The sexual behaviors may be a symptom of underlying emotional and relational needs that have not been met; hence there is an "addictive personality" that needs help. This addict does not choose to act on his sexual urges; rather, he tends to "zone out" or "split off" from his real self and take on a life separate from his usual personality. These emotional and mental qualities are radically different from the motivations of a couple going to a topless show in Las Vegas or Atlantic City, or a couple bringing home pornography once a year. We are not implying that these are advisable or morally acceptable activities, but we *are* differentiating between a sexual addiction and choices about sexual activity.

Dr. Patrick Carnes has been the pioneer in the study and treatment of sexual addictions. Dr. Carnes first brought the subject into public awareness with his bestselling book *Out of the Shadows*.[1] Since then, he has lectured extensively throughout the country, trained many professionals in both clinical and academic settings, and further defined sexual addiction in his book *Contrary to Love: Helping the Sexual Addict*.[2] In addition, he has developed the Sexual Addiction Screening Test and many other publications on addictions. From a systematic perspective, everything we have included in this chapter is borrowed from Carnes's work.

We have come to believe very deeply in Carnes's formulations because they fit so accurately with our clinical experience. We have also come to accept his treatment approach because it is the only one we have found to work. To avoid being pedantic, we will not specifically cite Carnes as the source of every important idea presented. But it is essential for you to understand that, other than the clinical data, we are indebted to Carnes for virtually every concept that is presented here.

Addiction or Sin?

In the past, all activity that included lust or immoral behavior was simply labeled as a sin. The person was seen as having violated God's rules; the devil had control of his life, and he needed to "get right" with God by repenting, confessing his sins, experiencing forgiveness, and going on his way, cleansed.

While it is true that you are responsible for your own behavior before God, acknowledging this truth and giving over your life to him does not usually stop compulsive activities. We are not questioning the severity of the sin; neither are we focusing on the immoral quality of these "sexual sins." Rather, we will deal with their compulsive nature and certain individuals' inability to overcome them. Hence, this should not be seen as an attempt to diminish the sinful quality of the action, but rather an attempt to understand the drive and how it can be controlled.

It is Thursday night. The minister has just completed his monthly board meeting with fifteen elders, the leaders who will decide whether to recommend a new building program. The church has grown from 250 to 1,250 since the minister arrived five years ago. He is weary in every way—mentally weary from battles he has just gone through in the board meeting, physically weary from being out late every night so far this week, and emotionally weary because he knows his wife will be upset with him when he arrives home, late again. Lately she has been complaining about how little time he spends with her. When he reaches the intersection where a decision must be made, almost as if by remote control, he turns his car away from home and heads toward that section of town where prostitutes loiter near a number of motels and bars.

As he nears his destination, the board meeting, the fatigue, and the wife quickly fade as his anticipation heightens and the addictive personality takes control. A couple of women are looking for business on one street corner, but he drives on past because he only likes to deal with one at a time. Finally he spots a lone prospect coming out of a fast-food place. She smiles at him. He slows down. She comes over to the window, they negotiate, agree on a price, and then, just as she is ready to jump into his car so they can drive to her place, he changes his mind. His real self snaps back into control. He remembers something he has to do and will need to be going.

This man is not interested in having sex with prostitutes; instead, he is addicted to *negotiating* with prostitutes. His thrill, or charge (or relief from life's stresses), is obtained from reaching the point of agreement on what they will do and for how much money. Once that is accomplished, his addictive urge is over. His next step is to bail out. Is this an addiction or a sin?

Addiction or Compulsion?

Some mental-health professionals would argue that we are exercising overkill by using the term *addiction* when in fact *compulsion* would be much more accurate and less pejorative. What is the difference between a compulsion and an addiction?

When we speak of a compulsion, we are usually referring to a habit or behavior that someone finds himself engaged in that can be cured and left behind forever. When we speak of an addiction, we are referring to a habit that has an intense hold on the individual and will be a lifelong struggle.

We used to treat sexual-acting-out behavior (perversions or deviations) as compulsions, only to find—several years later—the person would be back again, going through the same dilemma with all of the accompanying turmoil and trauma. It was at that point that we began to see the addictive nature of the sexual behaviors we are discussing here.

A specific illustration comes to mind: A man in his early thirties sought help about a year after his wedding date. His wife had discovered him peering into the apartment window next door where two single, attractive young women lived. He claimed he had sought help for this problem on two separate occasions over the past five years and that each time he had felt it would never happen again. Yet here he was, two years later, again caught up in his voyeuristic activity.

His wife knew nothing about the hundreds of other times he had engaged in similar activity throughout the neighborhood. It just happened that she caught him *this* time. In the past, his voyeurism had been dealt with as a compulsion, but to no avail. The helpful way for this man to think about his struggle was to understand it as an addiction: He was hooked. He was going to be dealing with this struggle for the rest of his life, just as an alcoholic deals with alcoholism for his or her whole life.

He had repented, prayed, confessed, read his Bible regularly, and done all the spiritual disciplines recommended to him; but he still found himself back in the throes of his peeping activity. It was most difficult for him to face the reality that this would be a lifetime struggle, an addiction.

Addiction or Psychopathy?

It is not uncommon for addictive behavior to be diagnosed as psychopathic or sociopathic behavior. The main thing that distinguishes psychopathic behavior from any other behavior is that the psychopath behaves as if he does not have a conscience. He does not experience guilt. His behaviors may have an addictive, controlling quality to them, but they do not occur in the addictive cycle described later in this chapter. Ted Bundy, a convicted rapist and murderer, is an example of a psychopath who acted out addictively. Bundy attributed his severely perversive behavior to his addiction to pornography. Fathers who sexually abuse their children may be acting addictively, yet have no conscience. Frequently, the psychopathology is not as blatant as in the case of Bundy.

One father sexually abused several of his daughters—under the guise of helping them with their sex education. He wanted them to grow up sexually liberated, in contrast to their mother. This same man spoke as if he were "doing the Lord's will in his life" and seeking the "Lord's guidance." He had no sense of his culpability in the abuse of his daughters, even after it had been reported and investigated by the state authorities.

To sum up these three perspectives: Yes, virtually all sexual addictions would transgress biblical guidelines; hence they are sin. All sexual addictions involve a compulsion, but they must be treated with an addiction model rather than a neurotic-compulsion approach or the behavior will cycle back. And finally, the sexual-acting-out behavior may be psychopathic or addictive, depending on whether the violator experiences guilt.

HOW ADDICTIONS DEVELOP

While no child or adolescent starts off his or her sexual life as an addict, history taking usually reveals that there were early indications that the child was prematurely exposed to sexuality. One of the most prominent causes of this premature exposure is sexual abuse. In a high percentage of sexual addiction cases, one of the precipitating factors was childhood sexual abuse of the addict. For these victims, sexuality took on an erotic meaning long before it was age-appropriate.

In the normal developmental process, there is sexual experimentation with the same-age same-sex, same-age opposite-sex, or by oneself. This is natural. But the addict experienced something different than this innocent curiosity. In fact, his or her innocence was lost when the erotic response was first triggered by the exposure, abuse, or addictive event.

A successful attorney told about discovering the pleasure that came from dressing in his mother's undergarments while looking at explicit sexual material that he discovered in his father's desk. This was at the age of eight. His disorder developed from this early cross-dressing and enamoredness with pornographic magazines and progressed to a preoccupation with pornography, then to a large collection of vivid, explicit, erotic pictures of various girlfriends, as well as his wife. This person had progressed to the point that the pornographic material that he was now interested in included some body mutilation such as nipple and penis rings as well as "boob battles" and other physically harmful devices.

It is not uncommon for an addiction to begin between ages eight and twelve if early-childhood sexual innocence has been violated or the natural curiosities of preadolescence have been handled inappropriately. During adolescence, most young people will experiment with sexual behavior. This experimentation, too, can move from normal to abnormal. The non-addict may have had an experience with peeping, exhibiting, experimenting with the same sex or the opposite sex, or viewing pornographic materials; but he or she made a choice about that behavior, deciding the activity was not beneficial and that he or she would not repeat the destructive behavior. In contrast, the addict became hooked on the behavior(s). The feelings that were set off by the activity met some emotional or relational need, and then a ritualized pattern for acting out developed. If the sexual addict was abused in the past, the experimentation will have set off feelings of shame. He will repeat the activity to keep himself feeling shamed. He already views himself as an evil, shameful person, and the activity serves to confirm this opinion. He needs that feeling of shame.

Even in adulthood, there will be those who engage in some sexual experimentation. For most, these experimental phases are brief and temporary. Some adults have responded to their curiosity about sexually explicit materials. Others have tried nudist colonies. Many have succumbed to an affair. None of this acting out means that a person is a sexual addict. However, if the behavior becomes a compulsion with an established, secretive, ritualistic pattern, then we would identify the behavior as an addiction.

THE ADDICTIVE PATTERN

A Precipitating Event

Certain precipitating events may occur at critical times for some people, hooking them into a life of addiction. This fact is indeed frightening; we saw a clear example of it.

At age fourteen, on his way home from a basketball practice, a young man innocently walked past a window where two teenage girls were changing their clothes with the blinds up. He became highly aroused and proceeded home to masturbate for the first time. His first sexual response became paired with this event. It was as if he had been hooked, grabbed—captured. He returned many times after the first unintentional observation. In addition, he developed a whole system for discovering windows that would let him repeat the adrenaline-rush experience.

He had not been out looking for what happened on that first evening. He did not remember having looked into any windows prior to that point; but he also did not remember anything similar to the incredible rush he felt from discovering the women.

When there is this kind of precipitating event, it may be some time before the individual feels controlled by the behavior. But in reviewing the history, it appears that he is controlled by it from the moment it happens. Obviously, there were issues in his life and family that predisposed him to his response to this event. Not every fourteen-year-old boy who happened upon this sight would have reacted and become addicted. We are not always certain what causes one person to get hooked while another does not.

Frequently, precipitation of the addiction is connected with a mixture of emotional turmoil or neediness and some catalytic event. The circumstances that become fertile ground from which an addiction can grow include any type of emotional stress that causes a strong need for nurture, affirmation, comfort, or control. In adulthood, the addiction may be set off after a death, a divorce, a separation, the birth of a child, the loss of a child, the loss of a job, or added pressure at home or on the job. All of these life circumstances that provide extra stress may serve as the spark or initial nudge for acting out.

The behavior—the sexual acting out—offers the person an escape from emotional pain and problems in life. The altered mood (the "zoning out," or splitting off) that often occurs as the person moves toward the addictive behavior provides escape from the pain, loneliness, or problems. In addition, the sexual activities may be associated with fantasies of being intimate, powerful, nurtured, or whatever the need is that is not being met in the person's normal relationships. Once this habit of dealing with stress has developed, the sexually addicted person will handle periods in life when the external stresses are greater by using the addiction to resolve the problems. This, in turn, worsens his pain, and the negative vicious circle begins: the greater the stress, the more frequent the acting out; the more acting out, the greater the remorse and pain.

Paul was an aggressive businessman on his way up the corporate ladder. Yet he had a low self-esteem. This was in part due to the fact that his father had been hospitalized with tuberculosis when Paul was ten years old. Thus, Paul felt he had been abandoned by his male role model at a critical age. He had never been that attractive as an adolescent or young man, and he had always felt that he existed outside the popular circle. This was true even though he had achieved admirably in academics and was editor of the school newspaper in high school.

In college, because he was a Christian, he did not feel he could participate with the fraternities and sororities, so again he felt inadequate even though he was looked up to as student body president at the large, prestigious private college. He could not let himself enjoy all the success because the college women he really wanted to date were not a part of his Christian world.

After college, he began climbing the corporate ladder. Suddenly, he was receiving much attention—not only from the women at both the secretarial and management levels, but also from the wives of other business associates. Receiving such attention led into fifteen years of affairs with twenty or thirty different women. It finally came to a head when he was discovered by his wife at a hotel with another woman. He then sought help for the addiction that had plagued him. All his worldly success had never diminished his sense of inadequacy—even the high salary from his prestigious job with all the perks. He continued to carry a low view of himself as he went through the first twenty years of his marriage.

Carnes emphasizes that abandonment seems to be a particularly strong factor in the history of many sexual addicts, especially when they learned to bring relief to their empty, inadequate feelings through the captivating distraction of sexual acting out. But whether it is stress, abandonment, low self-esteem, or a search for fulfillment or excitement, the addictive cycle becomes established once the behavior evolves from the precipitating event into an addiction.

The Addictive Cycle

Carnes describes the four stages of the addiction cycle that follow the initial acting out: preoccupation, ritualization, sexual addictive behavior itself, and finally, the reaction of despair.

The four stages of this cycle occur in a distinct, sequential pattern. What makes an addiction an addiction is the predictability of the sequence of these stages. However, every addict is unique in the timing with which he goes through the cycle. For instance, there may be a period—days, weeks, months, or even years—in which life is lived normally and the person is not obsessed with his sexual acting out. Many even carry on a normal, fulfilling sexual life. Then some event occurs that trips off the addictive cycle. The event might be a particularly stressful time at work, inadvertently looking down a woman's blouse, driving through a certain part of town, or being criticized by his wife. Whatever the event, the cycle has begun.

Preoccupation. Once the cycle is triggered, preoccupation takes over. The individual's energy becomes focused almost totally on the sexual compulsion. The focus might be on planning how to carry out the activity, a fantasy imagining the activity, or a review of past experiences. How the obsession builds is determined by the pattern this person establishes, as well as the availability of the occasion, the material, or the people necessary to carry out the preoccupation. Some let it build slowly over days and weeks. Others begin their fantasies and feel compelled to carry them out within hours. For many, their preoccupation with the urge or plan to act distracts them from other life fulfillments.

Ralph was a middle-management executive who had grown up in a rigid, religious home. His father was always working, and his mother was cold and distant. She had been warm with him until his younger sister was born. From that point on, he never again remembered receiving a hug from her. After she died—when he was fourteen—he began dressing in her clothes for sexual gratification and comfort. He continued this activity for the first twenty-five years of his marriage without being discovered. He had a satchel full of women's undergarments, clothing, jewelry, and makeup that he kept hidden in the basement.

His addictive cycle would usually be set off by depression due to external stresses. Once the desire to cross-dress was elicited, he would wait for up to several weeks before carrying out the behavior; the preoccupation would continue until he knew that his wife and their three children would not be in the house for several hours. During these weeks of preoccupation, he would imagine what he would wear, wrestling with whether he might buy a new garment and struggling to get the time alone. The preoccupation would continue until he was able to carry out his goal of dressing in women's clothing with all the preparatory ritual and accompanying excitement and masturbation.

The ritual phase. As the cycle moves into the ritual phase, it leads in the direction of the familiar. Addictive behavior can be differentiated from occasional behavior of the same sort by determining whether the activity has been ritualized. The rituals are often simple but completely predictable for each individual; they enhance the preoccupation to act. They may include visiting a certain bar or type of entertainment, driving to certain parts of town, selecting pornographic sites or material, putting on a certain type of clothes that makes exhibiting easier, or getting ready to go for walks at night in order to fulfill the voyeuristic desires. The minister who liked to negotiate with prostitutes always drove down the same road to get there.

The ritual may also include specific behaviors that help thrust the addict in the direction of the addiction, whether that is getting into a fight with his wife or sabotaging sexual activity with his spouse to justify finding sexual gratification elsewhere. Still others engage in self-defeating behavior to make themselves believe they deserve the addictive behavior.

Melvin provides a helpful example of the latter. He had been married for three years, and his marriage was still unconsummated. Every time he attempted sexual intercourse, he would become so driven—so goal-oriented—he had no capacity to love, caress, or prepare his wife. Because she had experienced some rejection in her past, she was highly sensitive to his cold, distant, non-intimate behavior. She would fail to become aroused and eventually she had a severe case of vaginismus (see chapter 18). When she would not allow intercourse, Melvin would take this as permission to masturbate. He masturbated two or three times a day. Masturbating was his major addiction, but he also visited adult porn arcades on a regular basis, and he acted out inappropriately with other women. Until he faced the reality that he was an active participant in sabotaging the consummation of his marriage, there was no possibility that he and his wife would ever be able to have intercourse.

As the ritualistic behavior moves the person closer to the addictive behavior, the compulsion becomes more intense, blocking out all other thoughts. This is the point at which greater risks are taken in regard to being discovered, embarrassed, or arrested. By this time, the possible consequences are not even in the addict's conscious awareness. His personality shift has occurred. He has "split off" or "zoned out." This aspect of the ritualization deadens his thinking about his values, his wife, or about God. He is driven by the anticipated high from the sexual experience or the relief he will get from the anxiety or stress.

The addictive behavior. The third stage is the acting-out stage, during which the compulsive sexual behavior is carried out. There is no way to catalog all the possible addictive or compulsive behaviors that are practiced, but we certainly can refer to categories of behaviors. For both men and women, almost all sexual addictive behaviors include orgasmic release brought about by masturbation, mutual stimulation, or intercourse.

Sexual release may result from *no physical contact*. Fantasy may be the only source of stimulation. For example, arousal and release might take place in response to indecent telephone calls, the reading of sexually provocative materials, or the viewing of pornography. These addictions could be carried out in isolation without any human contact whatsoever.

Next, there is the category of *cooperative contact*, which includes visiting massage parlors, watching topless or bottomless dancers, attending peep shows where women masturbate for male clients who pay for viewing by the minute, men (or women) who have several affairs going at the same time, or the husband who wants to have sex with his wife three times a day because he is obsessed with being affirmed by her.

The final category would include *violating contact*, which could range all the way from taking inappropriate liberties on a crowded bus to voyeurism, exhibitionism, child abuse, or rape. All of these behaviors are part of the world of sexual addiction.

Despair. Once the addict has fulfilled his urge, despair is almost inevitable. The only exception is the psychopathic addict who may not allow himself to feel despair or may have so deeply seared his conscience that no despair surfaces even after he acts compulsively. For most addicts, relief is the first feeling after the peak sexual experience. It is as if whatever was controlling or driving the individual subsides. However, the relief is short-lived. Then the addict's emotions shift almost immediately to the self-loathing response that floods over him as he moves back into his normal world and out of the addictive cycle.

For the believer, this is usually the point of an intense focus on prayer, with vows to God and to himself that he will never again engage in this despicable behavior. At the same time, he floods his inner world with derogatory messages about himself. So while he feels peace from having experienced relief from his compulsion and the hope that this is indeed the last occurrence, there is also that nagging sense that this is but one more round in a never-ending cycle.

PERSONAL COMPONENTS OF SEXUAL ADDICTION

Carnes has listed four components at the foundation of the addictive system: the individual's belief system, his impaired thinking, his unmanageability, and the addictive cycle, discussed previously.

The Addict's Beliefs

In discovering the addict's beliefs, it is essential to determine his view of women and his view of himself. He probably believes that he can only find gratification in the world through sex, that no one is ever going to love him, and that he can only be gratified sexually if he goes after it for himself because there is no one who could really love him. He believes he is a shameful, despicable character.

He also may hold some of the following beliefs that are common among sexual addicts.

The shame and despair that come from the powerlessness and unmanageability help crystallize the core beliefs about sexual unworthiness that are part of the addict's addictive system.

1. I am basically a bad, unworthy person.

2. No one would ever love me as I am.

3. My needs are never going to be met if I have to depend on others.

4. Sex is my most important need.[3]

Although these core beliefs seem to be common to all men and women who struggle with mild or severe sexual addictions, the addict may not be aware of them. He may say that he comes from a very loving family, yet deeper exploration may reveal that his feeling loved depended on his being perfect or responsible or the helpful son.

Impaired Thinking

Impaired thinking shows up in a variety of ways as the addict reframes his actions to diminish the blame and avoid confronting the reality about his life, marriage, or work. It is not uncommon for *rationalization* or denial to take over as the addict's way of coping with his addictive behavior. He may justify his actions on the basis that his wife rejected him, does not like sex, is pregnant, is busy, or is preoccupied with the children. He may justify it by believing that the person he violated really wanted it, asked for it, and facilitated it, so the incident is as much the other person's doing as his. Or he may deny that it was really that bad. "Everybody" has to "get it" somehow, he rationalizes.

In addition to rationalization and denial, some use *intellectualization*, in which the addict stands back and treats the behavior as though it were some kind of experiment, helpful to the victim, or necessary for the addict. Intellectualization serves to justify his actions, diminish his despair, and reduce his shame and guilt. Whether he uses rationalization, denial, or intellectualization, the addict's faulty thinking is necessary to keep the addictive cycle going.

This was the situation for a married man who violated a younger member of his wife's family. He was able to convince himself that his action was understandable because he had not been "getting much sex" from his wife and the person was asleep when he molested her. The impaired thinking is evident.

Unmanageability

Unmanageability reveals itself as major portions of the addict's life become out of control. Life becomes unmanageable. This can affect almost any area of life: spending, sleeping, working, eating, drinking, or playing. When life is experienced as out of control and unmanageable, the addictive pattern is well established, and the addictive cycle will occur repeatedly.

HOW ADDICTIONS PROGRESS

It is important to understand that as with every other behavior, sexual addictions vary in form, expression, and intensity. Some alcoholics only drink two drinks too much two nights every weekend. Other alcoholics drink twelve drinks too much every night. They both might identify themselves as alcoholics, but there is a major difference between the amount and frequency of the alcohol use that controls them. This is also true of sexual addicts. One man who masturbates two or three times a week to pornography instead of having sex with his sexually frustrated wife might well be a sexual addict. Another man may feel the need for a new woman every day. He, too, is a sexual addict, but he is acting it out in a much more extreme manner.

Sexual addicts also vary in the development of their illness. For some, the addictive cycle is established and repeats itself somewhat predictably. Others progress to "more intensity, more frequency, more risk, more unmanageability, etc."[4] Some of these addicts reach a peak and stay at that level, where the addiction continues to control their lives and the sexual acting out is limited only by opportunity. Other addicts escalate to a peak level of being controlled by the addiction and then de-escalate, maintaining the cycle at a low-functioning level.

Levels of Addiction

One of the helpful ways Carnes has broken down the behaviors of the sexual addict is to divide them into three levels.

Level one. This includes behavior that is widely practiced in our society. This would include all addictive heterosexual relationships, from within marriage to involvement with prostitutes. It would also include such activities as masturbation in response to pornographic material, cross-dressing, and homosexual activity. This does not infer that all homosexual activity is addictive activity, just as heterosexual activity can be addictive or non-addictive. But the man who has to be with five men an evening obviously is as much a sexual addict as the man who has to be with five women an evening.

Level two. These activities are mildly illegal, usually not violent in nature but involving the risk that discovery could lead to arrest—which adds excitement. Level-two activities include such violating behavior as voyeurism, exhibitionism, indecent liberties, obscene phone calls, or fetish activities that involve stealing the objects necessary for arousal. The fear of being discovered while stealing is part of the ritual and part of what brings the high.

Level three. Behaviors that clearly violate the law and are violent in nature are classed in level three. Examples are rape, child molestation, incest, and some forms of sadomasochistic behavior.

There has been much talk about the progressive nature of sexual addictions. Our clinical experience has shown that many male sexual addicts, in fact we would say the majority, find one compulsive behavior and never progress to anything worse. So by listing three levels, we are not implying that everyone starts out at level one, progresses to level two, then moves to level three. It is not uncommon for men to make obscene phone calls year after year after year without ever engaging in any other inappropriate sexual behavior. The same is true for indecent exposure, voyeurism, and cross-dressing.

The one situation where addictive behavior does seem to be progressive is in the area of pornography. It is relatively unusual to find someone who got hooked on mild pornography and then was happy to settle for that. It is rare to find someone who is still satisfied with *Playboy* magazines after fifteen years of viewing them. They may have started there or even with the Sears catalog, but it is very likely for someone who is sexually addicted to pornography to progress to more explicit and often more violent material.

CO-ADDICTION

Common family patterns occur in most sexual addicts' histories. They were usually raised on one extreme or the other of almost any spectrum. They may have been raised in an antisex home or in a home where there were no sexual boundaries and sex was promoted almost as a means of control and communication in the family. Most addicts grew up in a shame-based system where there was a confusing mixture and overlap between what was seen as good and what was seen as bad. This brought great confusion, especially during the adolescent years when there was so much for the young person to struggle with inside himself.

The addict's current family may also be perpetuating the addictive pattern, especially if it includes someone who is in a co-addictive role. The co-addict is often the spouse who in some passive way participates with the husband in his addiction. Or a parent might be participating with a child, subtly and unconsciously facilitating the addictive behavior. The blatant co-addict, the wife for example, joins the addict in his sexual activity by "swinging," joining in on a threesome or whatever he might want. But most commonly, the co-addict is much more passive or unconscious in helping to perpetuate the system, often by not paying attention or not responding to obvious signs of inappropriate behavior. When the sexual addict finally comes to treatment, it is always necessary to work with the co-addict as well.

The addict often uses religion to perpetuate his addictive pattern. In the addict's view, God is a part of the addictive system because it is God—along with his father, mother, and society—who carries the big stick and makes him feel guilt and shame. This is true despite the fact that the great majority of the addicts we deal with in our practice come out of the conservative, evangelical community and hold to its belief system. When the addict first comes for help, God is not seen as an ally but as an adversary. Prayer is not seen as a resource but as a source of guilt. The Scriptures are not seen as a message of solace and hope but rather as one more authority telling him he is worthless. The Holy Spirit is not experienced as a comforter but as an accuser who keeps confirming, from inside the addict, that he does not measure up. Because the addict does not see his faith as an ally in the healing process, we often have to begin with restructuring and reframing his view of God as well as his grasp of his disorder. The addictive belief system must be reversed. Any person or belief that perpetuates the addiction must be assessed and eliminated.

ARE YOU A SEXUAL ADDICT?

You may need to have your behavior assessed by an expert to help you determine if you are a sexual addict. For more information in seeking help for diagnosis, you may go to www.sexhelp.com. The following tools are accessible from there:

- SAST for men (20 items)
- WSAST for women (20 items)
- SDI (detailed screening for men and women; only by certified sex-addiction therapist)
- Partner Sexual Inventory (20 items)
- Partner Trauma Sexual Inventory—Revised (20 items)

A certified sexual-addiction therapist is required for the interpretation of the above screening tools.

From reading this far in the chapter, you may already have a sense of whether you are a sexual addict.

There are so many great resources, clinics, and programs available. A very helpful book is Patrick Carnes's *A Gentle Path Through Twelve Steps* (2012). You may also benefit by reading one of Carnes's older books, *Contrary to Love*. In it he provides a list of what he calls the key steps to assessment. The key questions to ask yourself are:

- What is the extent of my sexual behavior or co-addictive behavior?
- How important to my sexual behavior are my obsessional thoughts?
- What specific rituals do I go through before I act out sexually?
- What events or environments trigger my sexual behavior?
- What is the degree of my depression?
- How do I justify my behavior?
- In what way is my behavior out of control?[5]

You may not be able to objectively answer these questions yourself. You may have to ask your wife for help, or ask a friend, or join a Sexual Addicts Anonymous group. If your sexual behavior is more than merely an isolated episode of sexual acting out, this is a clue that your problem may be addictive. If the acting out is backed up by the obsessive quality that is frequently spoken about as "sex is all I can think about," that is additional evidence. You may blame this behavior on your antisexual father, or an antisexual church, or a wife who does not want sex, but if sex is the only thing on your mind, the likelihood is that you are struggling with an addiction.

Write out the ideal sequence of the activities you would like to act out. This will reveal the pattern of your thought processes. Then identify exactly how your preoccupation (your thoughts about the sexual actions) shifts into actual acting out of the specific rituals. Describe what precipitating events occur as part of the pattern. (Carnes calls these catalytic events and environments.) Have you been in such despair over your actions that you are depressed or even suicidal? If so, your suicide risk needs to be taken seriously by getting immediate professional psychological help.

How have you made sense out of your behavior and your obsessions? How have you rationalized or distorted reality? How have you justified what you are doing? How have you played down the impact of your behavior on others? All these steps are essential in determining not only whether you are struggling with an addiction but also its extent and its shape.

The final indication that you are indeed struggling with an addiction is the fact that your out-of-control behavior is obviously bringing turmoil to your life. This is true for the female addict as well as the male.

A beautiful young woman in her late twenties presented herself to us as someone who had lost interest in sex. She had been married for three years and had been avoiding sex at all cost. As her story unfolded, we discovered that during her single years after her first marriage failed, she functioned in sexual binges. She would avoid sex for six months and then go on a rampage. She would seduce almost anyone she chose, have wild and free sex, and then go "back on the wagon," avoiding anything sexual whatsoever. These binges continued for three or four years after she became a Christian. She felt totally out of control.

Now she was married and could not let herself feel any sexual desire for fear she would act out her addiction. She controlled her behavior by shutting down all sexual awareness. But in fact she continued to be an addict who fit all the patterns except that she was no longer acting out the behavior.

Controlling Your Sexual Addiction

℞ It is crucial to understand that in addition to stopping your addictive pattern of behavior, you must shift your core beliefs that lead to the behavior and thus reduce the obsession and the cycle that follows.

Again, we are highly indebted to Carnes for defining a framework for this treatment process. Mark and Debbie Laaser have become the sexual-addiction experts in the Christian community, and they have many wonderful resources available in addition to their organization, Faithful and True Ministries (www.faithfulandtrue.com). Their resources are listed in our bibliography.

Usually, when a sexual addict presents himself or herself for help in a counselor's office, some crisis event has precipitated his or her seeking help. The addict has been caught by his wife, discovered by his children, confronted by his employer, or arrested by the police—or at least had a close call.

At this point, the addict comes for therapy with temporarily high motivation to change and to stop the addictive behavior. Because of this, change happens quickly, often leading the counselors to a false security that therapy has been helpful, even though the addict would have temporarily stopped the behavior due to the crisis even if he had not come for help. This is why it is so vital that you change the underlying impaired thoughts, feelings, and attitudes that are part of your addictive system. Just as Alcoholics Anonymous has been tremendously helpful for alcoholics, so do sexual addicts work best in groups with other sexual addicts who follow the Twelve-Step system of facing reality and coming to grips with their lives. The Twelve-Step approach is an international, lay-led, self-help program to assist all sorts of addicts overcome their obsessive thinking and compulsive behavior. Several of these groups are available.

Sexaholics Anonymous
sa.org
P.O. Box 300
Simi Valley, California 93062
866-424-8777

Sexual Addicts Anonymous
http://saa-recovery.org/Meetings

Sex and Love Addicts Anonymous
slaafws.org

Co-S.A.
cosa-recovery.org

**Celebrate Recovery is a Christ-centered
recovery program that started at Saddleback
Church in Southern California.
www.celebraterecovery.com**

**S-ANON International
Family Groups
www.sanon.org**

Changing the Addict's Belief System

Individual counseling in conjunction with a Twelve-Step group is most likely to bring about the greatest change in the sexual addict. In group settings, the addict's belief system can be challenged because he has the backup support of his individual counselor, yet he does not feel as alone as he would if he were only working individually. He is working alongside others who are struggling with the same issues. Both individual counseling sessions and the Twelve-Step group become places where he can be honest about himself and his addiction, speaking honestly about his acting-out behavior. This helps him integrate his addictive needs into a healthy self so that his needs are met rather than acted out.

Accepting the Addiction As an Illness

One of the most difficult aspects of the whole treatment process is accepting the addiction as an illness you will struggle with for the rest of your life. As is true with many alcoholics, this realization may not come until you have "bottomed out." We usually compare this scenario to that of the prodigal son who found himself in the pig sty, wishing he could eat what the pigs ate. The King James Version says, "And when he came to himself, he said . . ." (Luke 15:17). This moment of coming to oneself, of looking in the mirror, of facing the reality, of bottoming out is a vital part of acknowledging the first step in the Twelve-Step program: facing the reality that you are indeed helpless.

Reliance on God

At this point the message of grace and redemption can have its greatest impact. The Twelve-Step program talks about relying on a higher power. We certainly understand this higher being to be God, the Father of our Lord Jesus Christ, who has promised that he will be with us in whatever state we find ourselves. As we rely on him, he will give us the strength to gain control of our lives. That reliance on God and admitting our helplessness may be the beginning of a process of restructuring faith that can, indeed, bring us to a new place of joy, fulfillment, and control.

Breaking Ritualistic Patterns

As you face your addiction, realize you are helpless, and put your trust and reliance on God, the work begins. It is crucial that you thoroughly define your ritualistic patterns and take action to break them. For example, it may have been part of a traveling salesman's pattern to always stop for lunch at a certain topless bar when he was out of town. This served as a warm-up for visiting a prostitute that evening. In this case it would be vital that he not only stop visiting the prostitute but also stop the lunchtime event. To gain control he may have to stay in hotels that do not have X-rated movies available in the room. To break the ritual, it is essential that the ritualistic behaviors be defined and clearly prohibited.

Defining Celibacy

A common part of the whole recovery process and of working through the Twelve Steps will be defining celibacy. We look for abstinence in the treatment of sexual addictions, just as counselors do in the treatment of alcoholism. This may be one of the most difficult aspects of the treatment process because sex has been the central and integrating factor of the addict's life. Although not all of his sexual activity has been connected with the addiction, as treatment begins, all sexual activity is ruled out for a period of time—usually two to three months. This includes masturbation, intercourse with his wife, viewing sexual material, all possible precipitating events, and any of the addictive behaviors. This may seem rigid and excessive, but until there is a shift in the underlying beliefs, attitudes, and emotions, it is too high a risk to engage in any sexual activity at all. In milder cases, the period of abstinence and celibacy can be modified. During this time the addict learns that he can survive without sex and that he can find other ways to resolve his problems and meet his needs other than through sexual acting out.

Writing

Keeping a journal can help you abide by the abstinence rule. Write for ten minutes (or longer) right at the time you feel tempted or in the situation where the temptation is likely to surface. The writing may be in response to questions given by your therapist. These questions direct you toward healthy thinking and away from the addictive pattern.

Maintaining Sobriety

Another term that has been borrowed from Alcoholics Anonymous is *sobriety*. Sexual addicts, too, will speak of having been sober for three months, or three years, or twelve years with the same kind of pride the alcoholic expresses for such accomplishments. They know the power their addiction has held over them, so their sobriety is a valid reason for celebration.

In getting control of the addiction, you must reframe, reshape, and rethink your self-concept. This is necessary because it helps you face the aspects of your history that you were not responsible for, accept responsibility for what you did have responsibility for, discover how you are an outgrowth of your family patterns, and rethink your faith as you grow into a healthier understanding of your relationship with God. Here a Christian counselor offers an added benefit as he or she attempts to "walk" with you to a place of actually experiencing God's love. In all this, it is important to be specific in defining the exact goals you are working toward—how they will be measured, what will happen when they are accomplished, and what will happen if there is a relapse.

SLIPS OR RELAPSES

We referred earlier to Melvin, who had an unconsummated marriage, who practiced addictive masturbatory activities, and who acted out inappropriately with other women. After initial treatment and being determined not to slip back into his old acting-out patterns, follow-up treatment revealed that he was again rationalizing that because their marriage remained unconsummated, he could justify taking care of himself through masturbation and fantasy. So after four weeks of sobriety, he had slipped back into his old pattern and had masturbated three times between sessions.

His wife did not want any physical contact with him because their past contact had lacked intimacy and had been characterized by his "spacing out." This was most aversive to her. She felt like an object of his addiction. Immediately his old rationalizations and justifications were back.

℞ As is true with alcoholics, it is vital to see these slips for what they are, recognizing your impaired thinking and then enacting a new plan. Slips are not uncommon; a slip doesn't make you a despicable person.

To prevent your relapse, any co-addicts in your life must find help because your co-addicts will have established patterns that participate in your addiction. You and your co-addicts must establish new ways of living. Where you drive, eat, and sleep, who you contact, and all your life patterns should be looked at carefully. It must be determined how all these activities have participated in your addictive system and how the detrimental patterns can be changed.

IN CONTROL

As you begin to manage your life, you will be able to live without secrets, and you will sense a control where once there was chaos. Soon you will be able to maintain this control of your life without the counselor. Nevertheless, specific plans and guidelines will be needed for how to proceed if you find yourself shifting or plunging into old patterns of thinking or driving through old "neighborhoods," or if you slip. In several situations, we have continued to see a counselee every other month as a way of providing accountability. Simply knowing that the appointment is ahead on the calendar helps the addict stay on course. Accountability to a Twelve-Step group also will be ongoing. Combined with the therapy process, it should assure a lifetime system of maintaining control.

In summary, sexual addictions can be controlled. Men and women do not have to be lifelong victims to addictive patterns. The addictive tendency may be a lifelong struggle, but they do not have to succumb. Recovery is most likely when following the guidelines outlined here (and described in detail in Carnes's works). The recovery pattern has been found to be quite similar to that of alcoholics. Some addicts start the program and never look back; others go through a number of relapses. Still others make several false starts before they are able to manage long-term abstinence from the addictive behavior. And still others never recover and continue their addictive patterns. Your task is to face the true reality of your situation: that you are helpless and that you can only recover with the help of God and a daily commitment to manage your life in the way you have learned from your therapy and your group.

TWENTY

Beyond Retraining

Sexual retraining is designed to relieve your unsatisfactory sexual experiences and to teach you to communicate and behave with each other in ways that reduce demand, enhance pleasure, and facilitate the natural sexual response. By now we trust that you have successfully completed this process. We hope that your symptoms have been relieved and your goals have been achieved.

Much change can take place in a relatively short period of time. Ten to twenty days or ten to twenty weeks (depending on whether you chose intensive retraining or the weekly retraining plan) is the average amount of time needed to complete the sexual retraining process. This will depend on how faithfully you scheduled and completed your assignments, what barriers you had to break through, and the unique work you were directed to do for your specific problem. For example, overcoming inhibited ejaculation will take more time than learning ejaculatory control because there are many more steps.

Many couples have gained fulfillment and relief from difficulties through this process after years of frustration. What factors contribute to improving sexual functioning as a result of the prescribed teaching, talking, and touching exercises?

1. They alter a previously destructive sexual system. The secure ambience created by the structure provides you with an opportunity to learn to make love in freer and more enjoyable ways.
2. The sexual conflicts are resolved by gradually increasing your comfort with previously avoided sexual activities.
3. The tasks of the assignments evoke emotional issues and conflicts that then become available for resolution through caring communication with each other.

Kaplan has found that approximately 80 percent of sexually dysfunctional patients can be relieved of their symptoms by sexual retraining with a therapist.

We would like to review our observations with you by sharing the results we see in those who seek sexual therapy with us.

1. About 2 percent of the couples who come to us for sexual therapy receive the knowledge, feedback, or direction they need to relieve their symptoms from the three-hour assessment process.
2. Some couples never receive the help they were seeking because they abort the sexual therapy process.
   a. Some abort the process before they ever come for the evaluation because in the initial telephone contact (1) we may redirect them, (2) they may discover the cost is prohibitive, (3) they discover they do not want what sexual therapy is, or (4) the spouse who is calling may discover that the other partner is unwilling to participate.
   b. Some abort the process after the initial three-session evaluation process because (1) we redirect them for self-help, marital therapy, or individual psychotherapy, (2) one or both are avoiding confronting the problem, or (3) there is a break in the couple's relationship. The evaluation may bring to light the severity of the problem or some secret information.
   c. Some abort the sexual therapy process because (1) the swift

success of the process scares one or both of them. One of them may have another sexual partner on the side and have engaged in the therapy process only to prove that he or she could not be successful with the spouse. When it starts to work, he or she bolts. Or there may be a deep conflict about being sexual, which is set off by rapid success. (2) Intense emotional barriers and resistances keep the couple from being able to complete the exercises. (3) The process reveals that, rather than sex being the struggle, other issues are the problem. (4) External circumstances interfere, such as a death in the family.

3. Some couples gain minimal benefits, but the results are more difficult to measure because they never can commit to the process. They want the results, but they do not want the focus and the work. These couples come sporadically and cancel appointments frequently. Only occasionally do they complete the assignments between sessions. They seem to relieve their guilt by being able to say they are coming for help. They know that they have a problem—and this way they convince themselves that they are working on it.

   About half of these couples actually attain their goals and relieve their symptoms with this long-term, haphazard involvement with us. We have started asking these couples to keep individual journals of what happens between sessions. This has increased our success with these peripherally committed couples.

4. The sexual therapy process is sometimes used as a diagnostic process rather than to attain sexual goals and relieve sexual symptoms. When this is the case, the couple is informed and given the choice to proceed for that purpose. When diagnosis is the focus of the sexual therapy process, that process is virtually 100 percent successful. This is usually done in a ten-day intensive. There is no way a couple can be put together for ten days to do three experiences per day and see us one session a day and not have the troublesome issues surface. When the sex therapy is used in this way:

   a. Intrapersonal, emotional problems are identified that require long-term psychotherapy before the couple will be able to have a fulfilled sexual relationship.

   b. Interpersonal patterns that are destructive to the relationship or to the sexual function become clear and may be corrected.

   c. Other sexual issues such as sexual addictions, homosexuality, or adultery are identified as the real reasons the couple's sexual relationship has been stressed.

5. The large majority of our clients are couples who complete the process successfully.

Follow-up sessions are necessary to make certain the couple has grasped and applied the principles and habits they learned.

For the most part, sexual therapy is most rewarding for the client couple, as well as for us, the therapists.

Which of the above situations do you identify with? Even though you have gone through the process on your own without a therapist—that is why we refer to this process as sexual retraining rather than sexual therapy—we have given you the same assignments and directions that we would have offered had you come to our offices for therapy. The benefit you do not have is the observation and feedback from a professional therapist. That is one reason we started this book by giving you communication skills. If you have learned to hear and observe each other and nonjudgmentally reflect that input, you have been each other's therapist.

We do know, however, that your own emotions are involved, so objectivity is not easy; in fact, it may be impossible. Also, you do not have the training to interpret your observations. Therefore, if you have gotten stuck in the process, we would recommend that you seek professional help, or you may telephone us for a short session to let us help you define your barrier. Our office number is 626-449-2525. If your situation requires more time, we can set up a regular therapy session for our usual fee.

By working through the sexual retraining process and the instructions that are unique to your barrier, we hope you have found relief of your sexual barriers and your goals have been achieved. Your new challenge is to integrate these changes into your ongoing lives. How are you going to be certain you don't fall back into your previous unfulfilling or destructive patterns?

The most important guarantee is to have made a plan. In the last assignment of the sexual retraining process, Create Your Ongoing Sexual Plan (Assignment 31), you thought through, wrote down, and discussed the principles you learned that changed your sexual communication and behavior. Then you made a plan based on those principles.

Your plan should include scheduled times to be together for physical pleasure with no demand for intercourse or to have arousal or release. Decide how many scheduled times you will have per week. How will these be initiated? How will you reschedule if cancellation is necessary? We recommend that the one who cancels is the one who offers an alternative time and makes certain it happens. How are you going to decide on the setting, creativity, and so forth for your times together? How are you going to keep your experiences demand-free?

The plan should also include communication times. These can be times of sharing your feelings about each other, your dreams, or your perspectives on how the two of you are doing sexually. Books are available with exercises to guide you in this. One that we like is Harville Hendrix's book *Getting the Love You Want*.

Time should be set aside once a month to reread the principles you drew up in Assignment 29 and your plan from Assignment 31. Add any ideas you learned each month that would enhance your sexual pleasure. You might set a regular date for your sexual tune-up time. The first or last Sunday of every month often works out well.

Your plan should also include nonsexual activity times that you both enjoy. It is helpful to plan who will make those happen and how often they are expected. These can range from fifteen-minute walks to weekends away.

Finally, your plan should include any specific behaviors that are necessary to keep your particular sexual barrier from interfering with your sexual pleasure. For example, the squeeze technique may be necessary for controlling ejaculation. Verbalizing and distracting from anxiety about erections may be necessary for erectile security. Exaggerating active, involuntary bodily responses may be needed for going after intense arousal that can trigger orgasm. You will need to define in detail the specific behaviors you need.

Throughout this book we have emphasized the importance of careful attention to detail. The details of your sexual behaviors, your emotional responses, your attitudes and beliefs, and your communication are all vital ingredients that will continue to keep down the barriers and bring pleasure to your sexual relationship.

Our Formula for Intimacy, based on our clinical observations and current knowledge of sex and the brain, will help you fulfill all you have learned. Practice it faithfully.

FORMULA FOR INTIMACY

© Copyright Penner & Penner

- Fifteen minutes a day:
  - Connect emotionally: Look into each other's eyes (increases oxytocin, the "trust hormone"); share a positive thought, feeling, or affirmation of the other
  - Connect spiritually: Share an inspirational reading and prayer
  - Connect physically: Hug for twenty seconds (increases oxytocin); kiss passionately for five to thirty seconds without leading to sex (increases dopamine: the "passion hormone")
- One evening a week: Walk, date, shower, caress; no demands
- One day a quarter: Fun, play, lead, and teach enjoyable touch
- One weekend a year: Together away or at home; no distractions

May you be like the lovers of the Song of Solomon. May your love be "better than wine." May "your oils have a pleasing fragrance" and your names be "like purified oil" that you may draw to each other and "run together!" ENJOY!

Notes

Chapter 2: Sharing Your Secrets

1. Clifford Penner and Joyce Penner, *Sex Facts for the Family* (Nashville: W Publishing Group, 1992). Available at www.passionatecommitment.com.
2. Sidney M. Jourard, *The Transparent Self* (New York: B. Von Nostrand, Inc., 1972).

Chapter 5: Sex Is Good and of God

1. Louis H. Evans Jr., *Hebrews,* The Preacher's Commentary, ed. Lloyd J. Oglivie (Nashville: Thomas Nelson, 2002), 243.

Chapter 7: Sexual Response Is Automatic

1. Alan P. Brauer and Donna Brauer, *ESO (Extended Sexual Orgasm)* (Nashville: Grand Central Publishing, 2001).

Chapter 9: Mutual Respect Is Absolutely Essential

1. Dagmar O'Connor, *How to Make Love to the Same Person for the Rest of Your Life and Still Love It* (London: Black Lace, 2005).
2. Neil Warren, *Make Anger Your Ally: Harnessing One of Your Most Powerful Emotions* (Carol Stream, IL: Living Books, 1999).
3. A. K. Ladas, B. Whipple, and I. D. Perry, *The G-Spot* (New York City: Holt Paperbacks, 2004).

Chapter 10: What Is Sexual Retraining?

1. Helen Singer Kaplan, *The New Sex Therapy: Active Treatment of Sexual Dysfunctions* (London: Routledge, 1999), 187.

2. William H. Masters and Virginia E. Johnson, *Human Sexual Inadequacy* (Boston: Little, Brown, and Company, 1970), 206.

Chapter 15: Overcoming Problems of Sexual Desire

1. J. Pennebaker, J. Keicolt-Glaser, and R. Glaser, "Disclosure of Traumas and Immune Function: Health Implications for Psychotherapy," *Journal of Consulting and Clinical Psychology*, vol. 56, no. 2 (1988): 239–45.

2. Ellen Bass and Laura Davis, *The Courage to Heal: A Guide for Women Survivors of Child Sexual Abuse* (New York City: William Morrow Paperbacks, 2008).

3. Susan Forward and Craig Buck, *Betrayal of Innocence: Incest and Its Devastation* (New York: Penguin, 1988).

4. Lewis B. Smedes, *Forgive and Forget: Healing the Hurts We Don't Deserve* (San Francisco: HarperOne, 2007).

5. Erik H. Erikson, *Childhood and Society* (New York: W. W. Norton, 1993).

6. Helen Singer Kaplan, *Disorders of Sexual Desire and Other New Concepts and Techniques in Sex Therapy* (London: Routledge, 1995), 98.

7. Ibid., 203–20.

Chapter 17: Overcoming Problems of Sexual Release

1. Lonnie Barbach, *Women Discover Orgasm: A Therapist's Guide to a New Treatment Approach* (New York: The Free Press, 1980); Benjamin Graber and Georgia Kline-Graber, *Woman's Orgasm: A Guide to Sexual Satisfaction* (Las Vegas: New Falcon, 2011).

2. Graber and Kline-Graber, *Woman's Orgasm*.

3. Julia Heiman and Joseph LoPiccolo, *Becoming Orgasmic* (New York: Prentice Hall, 1988).

4. Sheri Hite, *The Hite Report: A National Study of Female Sexuality* (New York: Macmillan, 1976).

5. Ladas, Whipple, and Perry, *The G-Spot*.

6. William H. Masters and Virginia E. Johnson, *Human Sexual Inadequacy* (Boston: Little, Brown, and Company, 1970), 92.

7. Helen Singer Kaplan, *The New Sex Therapy: Active Treatment of Sexual Dysfunctions* (London: Routledge, 1999), 289–90.

8. Helen Singer Kaplan, *PE: How to Overcome Premature Ejaculation* (New York: Brunner/Mazel, 1989).

9. Brauer and Brauer, *ESO (Extended Sexual Orgasm)*.

10. Kaplan, *Premature Ejaculation*, 62–74.

11. Barry McCarthy and Michael Metz, *Coping with Premature Ejaculation: How to Overcome PE, Please Your Partner & Have Great Sex* (Oakland: New Harbinger, 2004).

12. Kaplan, *Premature Ejaculation,* 46.

13. Kaplan, *The New Sex Therapy,* 327.

14. Ibid., 327–32.

Chapter 18: Overcoming Intercourse Barriers

1. Richard Dickey, *Managing Contraceptive Pill Patients,* 15th ed. (Fort Collins, CO: EMIS Medical Publishers, 2014).

2. Dagmar O'Connor, interviewed by Hornburg in "At Last I Have a Marriage," *Ladies Home Journal,* March 1983, 27–28.

3. Kaplan, *The New Sex Therapy.*

4. O'Connor, "At Last I Have a Marriage."

5. Heather Jeffcoat, *Sex Without Pain: A Self-Treatment Guide to the Sex Life You Deserve* (Hoboken, NJ: Active Orange Publishing, 2014), 42–47.

Chapter 19: Controlling Sexual Addictions

1. Patrick Carnes, *Out of the Shadows: Understanding Sexual Addiction* (Center City, MN: Hazelden, 2001).

2. Patrick Carnes, *Contrary to Love: Helping the Sexual Addict* (Center City, MN: Hazelden, 1994).

3. Ibid., 87.

4. Ibid., 78.

5. For sexual addiction screening, go to sexhelp.com: SAST for men (20 items); WSAST for women (20 items); SDI (detailed screening for men and women; only by certified sex addiction therapist); Partner Sexual Inventory (20 items); Partner Trauma Sexual Inventory—Revised (20 items).

Resource List

Allender, Dan B. *The Wounded Heart: Hope for Adult Victims of Childhood Sexual Abuse*. Rev. ed. Colorado Springs: NavPress, 2008.

Arleque, Lillian, and Sue Goldstein. *When Sex Isn't Good: Stories and Solutions of Women with Sexual Dysfunction*. Lincoln, NE: iUniverse, Inc., 2007.

Arterburn, Stephen, and Fred Stoeker. *Every Man's Battle: Winning the War on Sexual Temptation One Victory at a Time*. With Mike Yorkey. Colorado Springs: Waterbrook Press, 2009.

Barbach, Lonnie. *For Yourself: The Fulfillment of Female Sexuality*. Rev. ed. New York: Signet Press, 2000.

———. *The Pause: Positive Approaches to Menopause*. Rev. ed. New York: Penguin, 2000.

Bass, Ellen, and Laura Davis. *The Courage to Heal: A Guide for Women Survivors of Child Sexual Abuse*. 4th ed. New York: HarperCollins, 2008.

Berman, Jennifer, and Laura Berman. *For Women Only: A Revolutionary Guide to Reclaiming Your Sex Life*. Rev. ed. New York: Henry Holt, 2005.

Billings, John J. *The Ovulation Method: Natural Family Planning*. 5th ed. N.p.: Liturgical Press, 1992.

Brauer, Alan P., and Donna J. Brauer. *ESO: How You and Your Lover Can Give Each Other Hours of Extended Sexual Orgasm*. Rev. ed. New York: Grand Central Publishing, 2001.

Brizendine, Louann. *The Female Brain*. New York: Harmony, 2007.

———. *The Male Brain*. New York: Harmony, 2011.

Buhler, Rich. *Pain and Pretending: You Can Be Set Free from the Hurts of the Past*. Nashville: Thomas Nelson, 1991.

Cane, William. *The Art of Kissing*. 3rd ed. New York: St. Martin's Griffin, 2010.

Carnes, Patrick. *Contrary to Love: Helping the Sexual Addict.* Center City, MN: Hazelden Publishing, 1994.

———. *Facing the Shadow: Starting Sexual and Relationship Recovery.* Rev. ed. Carefree, AZ: Gentle Path Press, 2015.

———. *A Gentle Path Through the Twelve Steps: The Classic Guide for All People in the Process of Recovery.* 3rd ed. Center City, MN: Hazelden Publishing, 2012.

———. *Out of the Shadows: Understanding the Sexual Addiction.* 3rd ed. Center City, MN: Hazelden, 2001.

———. "Sexual Addiction Screening Test." http://www.sexhelp.com/am-i-a-sex-addict/sex-addiction-test.

Carnes, Patrick, David Delmonico, and Elizabeth Griffin, with Joseph Moriarty. *In the Shadows of the Net: Breaking Free of Compulsive Online Sexual Behavior.* 2nd ed. Center City, MN: Hazelden Publishing, 2007.

Carnes, Patrick, with Joseph Moriarty. *Sexual Anorexia: Overcoming Sexual Self-Hatred.* Center City, MN: Hazelden Publishing, 1997.

Cattrall, Kim, and Mark Levinson. *Satisfaction: The Art of Female Orgasm.* New York: Warner Books, 2002.

Chapman, Gary. *The Five Love Languages.* Repr. ed. Chicago: Northfield Publishing, 2015.

Clarence, Ruth. *Laughing All the Way . . . to the Bedroom.* Edmonton, Alberta (Canada): Page Master, 2011.

Coady, Deborah, and Nancy Fish. *Healing Painful Sex: A Woman's Guide to Confronting, Diagnosing, and Treating Sexual Pain.* Berkeley, CA: Seal Press, 2011.

Cobb, Nancy, and Connie Grigsby. *The Best Thing I Ever Did for My Marriage: 50 Real-Life Stories.* Kindle ed. Sisters, OR: Multnomah Books, 2010.

Davies, Clair. *The Trigger Point Therapy Workbook: Your Self-Treatment Guide for Pain Relief.* Oakland, CA: New Harbinger Publications, 2013.

Decker, Kerry. *Healing for the Wounded Heart.* 3rd ed. Self-published, 2013.

Dickey, Richard P. *Managing Contraceptive Pill Patients.* 15th ed. Fort Collins, CO: EMIS, 2014.

Dillow, Joseph, Linda Dillow, Peter Pintus, and Lorraine Pintus. *Intimacy Ignited: Conversations Couple to Couple: Fire Up Your Sex Life with the Song of Solomon.* Colorado Springs: NavPress, 2004.

Dillow, Linda, and Lorraine Pintus. *Intimate Issues: 21 Questions Christian Women Ask About Sex.* Repr. ed. Colorado Springs: Waterbook, 2009.

Dobson, James C. *Love for a Lifetime: Building a Marriage That Will Go the Distance.* Colorado Springs: Multnomah Books, 2007.

———. *Solid Answers.* Carol Stream, IL: Tyndale House Publishers, 1997.

Einstein, Gillian, ed. *Sex and the Brain.* Cambridge, MA: MIT Press, 2007.

Evans, Louis H., Jr. *The Preacher's Commentary Volume 33: Hebrews.* Edited by Lloyd J. Ogilvie. Nashville: Thomas Nelson, 2003.

Ferree, Marnie C. *No Stones: Women Redeemed from Sexual Shame.* 2nd ed. Downers Grove, IL: IVP Books, 2010.

Foley, Sallie, Sally A. Kope, and Dennis P. Sugrue. *Sex Matters for Women: A Complete Guide to Taking Care of Your Sexual Self.* 2nd ed. New York: Gillford Press, 2011.

Forward, Susan, and Craig Buck. *Betrayal of Innocence: Incest and Its Devastation.* Rev. ed. New York: Penguin Books, 1988.

Foster, Richard. *Money, Sex and Power: The Challenge of the Disciplined Life.* Repr. ed. London (UK): Hodder & Stoughton, 2009.

Frank, Jan. *Door of Hope: Recognizing and Resolving the Pains of Your Past.* Nashville: Thomas Nelson, 1995.

Gilder, George. *Men and Marriage.* Gretna, LA: Pelican Publishing, 1992.

Goldstein, Andrew, Caroline Pukall, and Irwin Goldstein. *When Sex Hurts: A Woman's Guide to Banishing Sexual Pain.* Boston: De Capo Lifelong Books, 2011.

Gottman, John. *Why Marriages Succeed or Fail: And How You Can Make Yours Last.* New York: Simon & Schuster, 1995.

Gottman, John, and Nan Silver. *The Seven Principles for Making Marriage Work: A Practical Guide from the Country's Foremost Relationship Expert.* Rev. ed. New York: Harmony Publishing, 2015.

Graber, Benjamin, and Georgia Kline-Graber. *Woman's Orgasm: A Guide to Sexual Satisfaction.* Las Vegas: New Falcon Publications, 2011.

Grason, Rainee. *Facing the Sky: A True Story, a Journey to Find Healing from a Broken Past.* N.p.: Previous Grace Publications, 2013.

Gray, John. *Men Are from Mars, Women Are from Venus: The Classic Guide to Understanding the Opposite Sex.* 20th anniversary ed. New York: Harper Publishing, 2012.

Greenwood, Sadja. *Menopause, Naturally: Preparing for the Second Half of Life.* Volcano, CA: Volcano Press, 1996.

Grenz, Stanley. *Sexual Ethics: An Evangelical Perspective.* Louisville, KY: Westminster John Knox Press, 1997.

Gruber, Tom. *What the Bible "Really" Says About Sex: A New Look at Sexual Ethics from a Biblical Perspective*. Worthington, OH: Trafford Publishing, 2006.

Hancock, Maxine, and Karen Burton Mains. *Child Sexual Abuse: A Hope for Healing*. Wheaton, IL: Harold Shaw Publishers, 1997.

Hart, Archibald D., Catherine Hart Weber, and Debra L. Taylor. *Secrets of Eve: Understanding the Mystery of Female Sexuality*. Nashville: Thomas Nelson, 2004.

Heiman, Julia R., and Joseph LoPiccolo. *Becoming Orgasmic: A Sexual and Personal Growth Program for Women*. Rev. ed. London: Piatkus Books, 2009.

Hendrix, Harville. *Getting the Love You Want: A Guide for Couples*. 20th anniversary ed. New York: Henry Holt, 2010.

Herrera, Isa. *Ending Female Pain: The Ultimate Self-Help Guide for Women Suffering from Chronic Pelvic and Sexual Pain*. 2nd ed. New York: Duplex Publishing, 2014.

Hite, Sheri. *The Hite Report: A National Study of Female Sexuality*. Repr. ed. New York: Seven Stories Press, 2004.

Howard, Fred M., C. Paul Perry, James E. Carter, and Ahmed M. El-Minawi, eds. *Pelvic Pain: Diagnosis and Management*. Philadelphia: Lippincott Williams & Wilkins, 2000.

Jeffcoat, Heather. *Sex Without Pain: A Self-Treatment Guide to the Sex Life You Deserve*. Los Angeles: Active Orange Publishing, 2014.

Kalish, Daniel. *Your Guide to Healthy Hormones*. Vista, CA: Natural Path, 2005.

Kaplan, Helen Singer. *Evaluation of Sexual Disorders: Psychological and Medical Aspects*. New York: Brunner/Mazel, 1983.

———. *The Illustrated Manual of Sex Therapy*. 2nd ed. New York: Brunner-Routledge, 1988.

———. *The New Sex Therapy*. Repr. ed. New York: Brunner-Routledge, 2011.

———. *PE: How to Overcome Premature Ejaculation*. New York: Brunner/Mazel, 1989.

———. *The Sexual Desire Disorders: Dysfunction Regulation of Sexual Motivation*. New York: Routledge, 1995.

———, with Donald F. Klein. *Sexual Aversion, Sexual Phobias, and Panic Disorder*. Repr. ed. New York: Routledge, 2014.

Laaser, Debra. *Shattered Vows: Hope and Healing for Women Who Have Been Sexually Betrayed*. Grand Rapids: Zondervan, 2008.

Laaser, Mark R. *Becoming a Man of Valor*. Kansas City, MO: Beacon Hill Press, 2011.

———. *Faithful and True: Sexual Integrity in a Fallen World*. Grand Rapids: Zondervan, 1996.

———. *Healing the Wounds of Sexual Addiction*. Grand Rapids: Zondervan, 2004.

———. *A L.I.F.E. Guide for Men*. Longwood, FL: Xulon Press, 2002.

———. *The 7 Principles of Highly Accountable Men*. Kansas City, MO: Beacon Hill Press, 2011.

———. *Taking Every Thought Captive*. Kansas City, MO: Beacon Hill Press, 2011.

Laaser, Mark, and Debbie Laaser. *Seven Desires: Looking Past What Separates Us to Learn What Connects Us*. Grand Rapids: Zondervan, 2013.

Laaser, Mark, and Ralph H. Earle. *The Pornography Trap: A Resource for Ministry Leaders*. 2nd ed. Kansas City, MO: Beacon Hill Press, 2012.

Laaser, Mark, and Tim Clinton. *The Quick-Reference Guide to Sexuality and Relationship Counseling*. Grand Rapids: Baker Books, 2010.

Ladas, Alice Kahn, Beverly Whipple, and John D. Perry. *The G Spot: And Other Discoveries about Human Sexuality*. New York: Henry Holt, 2004.

Love, Patricia, and Jo Robinson. *Hot Monogamy: Essential Steps to More Passionate, Intimate Lovemaking*. N.p.: CreateSpace, 2012.

Masters, William H., and Virginia E. Johnson. *Human Sexual Response*. Repr. ed. New York: Ishi Press International, 2010.

———. *Human Sexual Inadequacy*. Repr. ed. New York: Ishi Press International, 2010.

Mayo, Mary Ann. *A Christian Guide to Sexual Counseling: Recovering the Mystery and Reality of "One Flesh."* Grand Rapids: Zondervan, 2003.

———. *Skin Deep: The Powerful Link Between Your Body Image and Self-Esteem*. Ann Arbor: Servant Publications, 1992.

Mayo, Mary Ann, and Joseph L. Mayo. *The Menopause Manager: A Safe Path for a Natural Change*. Grand Rapids: Fleming H. Revell, 2000.

McCarthy, Barry, and Emily McCarthy. *Discovering Your Couple Sexual Style: Sharing Desire, Pleasure and Satisfaction*. New York: Routledge, 2009.

———. *Female Sexual Awareness: Achieving Sexual Fulfillment*. New York: Carroll & Graf, 1989.

———. *Getting It Right the First Time: Creating a Healthy Marriage*. New York: Brunner-Routledge, 2004.

———. *Male Sexual Awareness: Increasing Sexual Satisfaction*. Rev. ed. New York: Carroll & Graf, 1998.

———. *Rekindling Desire: A Step-by-Step Program to Help Low-Sex and No-Sex Marriages*. New York: Routledge, 2003.

————. *Sexual Awareness: Your Guide to Healthy Couple Sexuality.* 5th ed. New York: Routledge, 2012.

————. *Therapy with Men after Sixty: A Challenging Life Phase.* New York: Routledge, 2015.

McCarthy, Barry W., and Michael E. Metz. *Men's Sexual Health: Fitness for Satisfying Sex.* New York: Routledge, 2008.

McIlhaney, Joe S., Jr. *1250 Health-Care Questions Women Ask.* Grand Rapids: Baker Book House, 1993.

————. *Sexuality and Sexually Transmitted Diseases: A Doctor Confronts the Myth of "Safe" Sex.* Grand Rapids: Baker Book House, 1990.

Metz, Michael E., and Barry W. McCarthy. *Coping with Erectile Dysfunction: How to Regain Confidence and Enjoy Great Sex.* Oakland, CA: New Harbinger Publications, 2004.

————. *Coping with Premature Ejaculation: How to Overcome P.E., Please Your Partner, and Have Great Sex.* Oakland, CA: New Harbinger Publications, 2004.

Michael, Robert T., John H. Gognon, Edward O. Laumann, and Gina Kolata. *Sex in America: A Definitive Study.* Boston: Little, Brown, and Company, 1994.

Moberly, Elizabeth R. *Psychogenesis: The Early Development of Gender Identity.* New York: Routledge Kegan & Paul, Inc., 1983.

————. *The Psychology of Self and Others.* New York: Routledge Kegan & Paul, Inc., 1985.

O'Connor, Dagmar. *How to Make Love to the Same Person for the Rest of Your Life, and Still Love It.* 2nd ed. Black Lace Publishing, 2005.

————. *How to Put the Love Back into Making Love.* New York: Doubleday, 1990.

Parrott, Les, and Leslie Parrott. *Making Happy: The Art and Science of a Happy Marriage.* Brentwood, TN: Worthy Publishing, 2014.

————. *Love Talk: Speak Each Other's Language Like You Never Have Before.* Grand Rapids: Zondervan, 2013.

————. *Saving Your Marriage Before It Starts: Seven Questions to Ask Before (and After) You Marry.* Rev. ed. Grand Rapids: Zondervan, 2006.

————. *The One Year Love Talk Devotional for Couples.* Carol Stream, IL: Tyndale House, 2011.

Pennebaker, James W., Janice K. Keicolt-Glaser, and Ronald Glaser. "Disclosure of Traumas and Immune Function: Health Implications for Psychotherapy." *Journal of Consulting and Clinical Psychology* 56, no. 2 (1988): 239–45.

Penner, Clifford L., and Joyce J. Penner. *52 Ways to Have Fun, Fantastic Sex: A Guidebook for Married Couples*. Nashville: Thomas Nelson, 1993.

———. *Getting Your Sex Life Off to a Great Start: A Guide for Engaged and Newlywed Couples*. Nashville: Thomas Nelson, 1994.

———. *The Gift of Sex: A Christian Guide to Sexual Fulfillment*. Nashville: W Publishing Group, 2003.

———. *Sex Facts for the Family: A Complete Resource*. 2nd ed. Nashville: W Publishing Group, 1992.

———. *Sex 101: A Guide to Intimacy for Newlywed Couples*. Nashville: W Publishing Group, 2005.

———. *The Way to Love Your Wife: Creating Greater Love and Passion in the Bedroom*. Carol Stream, IL: Tyndale House, 2007.

Penner, Joyce and Clifford. *Counseling for Sexual Disorders*. Vol. 26 of *Resources for Christian Counseling*. Nashville: Word Publishing, 1990.

Perel, Ester. *Mating in Captivity: Unlocking Erotic Intelligence*. Repr. ed. New York: Harper Perenials, 2007.

Porter, Jan. *The Sexual Abuse Survivor's Sacred Space: An Inspiring Body Mind Soul Guide for Healing of Sexual Abuse*. N.p.: CreateSpace, 2014.

Rako, Susan. *The Blessings of the Curse: No More Periods?* Author's Guild BackinPrint.com ed. Lincoln, NE: iUniverse, 2006.

———. *The Hormone of Desire: The Truth About Testosterone, Sexuality, and Menopause*. Rev. ed. New York: Three Rivers Press, 1999.

Reichman, Judith, M.D. *I'm Not in the Mood: What Every Woman Should Know About Improving Her Libido*. New York: William Morrow, 1999.

———. *Slow Your Clock Down: A Woman's Complete Guide to a Younger, Healthier You*. Repr. ed. New York: Harper Paperbacks, 2005.

Rosenau, Douglas E. *A Celebration of Sex: A Guide to Enjoying God's Gift of Sexual Intimacy*. Rev. ed. Nashville: Thomas Nelson, 2002.

Rosenau, Douglas E., Jim Childerston, and Carolyn Childerston. *A Celebration of Sex After 50*. Nashville: Thomas Nelson, 2004.

Schnarch, David M. *Constructing the Sexual Crucible: An Integration of Sexual and Marital Therapy*. New York: Norton, 1991.

———. *Intimacy & Desire: Awaken the Passion in Your Relationship*. New York: Beaufort Books, 2009.

Schwarzbein, Diana. *Menopause Power Take Charge Guide: Everything You Need to Work Effectively and Confidently with Your Doctor to Manage Menopause Correctly!* N.p.: Schwarzbein Principle Programs, 2012.

————. *The Schwarzbein Principle, the Program: Losing Weight the Healthy Way.* Deerfield Beach, FL: Health Communications, 2004.

Sears, Barry. *The Mediterranean Zone: Unleash the Power of the World's Healthiest Diet for Superior Weight Loss, Health, and Longevity.* New York: Zinc Ink, 2014.

Shippen, Eugene, and William Fryer. *The Testosterone Syndrome: The Critical Factor for Energy, Health, and Sexuality—Reversing the Male Menopause.* New York: M. Evans, 2007.

Slattery, Juli. *No More Headaches: Enjoying Sex and Intimacy in Marriage.* Carol Stream, IL: Tyndale, 2009.

Smalley, Gary, and Ted Cunningham. *The Language of Sex: Experience the Beauty of Sexual Intimacy.* Ventura, CA: Regal, 2008.

Smalley, Gary, and John Trent. *The Blessing: Giving the Gift of Unconditional Love and Acceptance.* Nashville: Thomas Nelson, 2011.

Smedes, Lewis B. *The Art of Forgiving: When You Need to Forgive and Don't Know How.* Repr. ed. New York: Ballantine Books, 1997.

————. *Forgive and Forget: Healing the Hurts We Don't Deserve.* 2nd ed. New York: HarperOne, 2007.

————. *Sex for Christians: The Limits and Liberties of Sexual Living.* Grand Rapids: William B. Eerdmans Publishing Company, 1994.

Stein, Amy. *Heal Pelvic Pain: A Proven Stretching, Strengthening, and Nutrition Program for Relieving Pain, Incontinence, IBS, and Other Symptoms.* New York: McGraw-Hill, 2008.

Ury, William. *The Power of a Positive No: Save the Deal, Save the Relationship—and Still Say No.* Repr. ed. New York: Bantam Books, 2008.

Warren, Neil Clark. *Finding the Love of Your Life: Ten Principles for Choosing the Right Marriage Partner.* Repr. ed. New York: Pocket Books, 1994.

————. *Learning to Live with the Love of Your Life and Loving It.* Carol Stream, IL: Tyndale, 1998.

————. *Make Anger Your Ally.* Carol Stream, IL: Living Books, 1999.

Weschler, Toni. *Taking Charge of Your Fertility: The Definitive Guide to Natural Birth Control, Pregnancy Achievement, and Reproductive Health.* 20th anniversary ed. New York: William Morrow Paperbacks, 2015.

Wheat, Ed and Gaye. *Intended for Pleasure: Sex Technique and Sexual Fulfillment in Christian Marriage.* 4th ed. Grand Rapids: Revell, 2010.

Williams, Warwick. *Rekindling Desire: Bringing Your Sexual Relationship Back to Life.* Oakland, CA: New Harbinger Publications, 1988.

Wise, David, and Rodney Anderson. *A Headache in the Pelvis: A New Understanding and Treatment for Chronic Pelvic Pain Syndromes*, 6th ed. Occidental, CA: National Center for Pelvic Pain Research, 2012.

Woititz, Janet Geringer. *Struggle for Intimacy*. Adult Children of Alcoholics. Deerfield Beach, FL: Health Communications, 1990.

Woititz, Lisa Sue, and Janet G. Woititz. *Unwelcome Inheritance: Break Your Family's Cycle of Addictive Behaviors*. Center City, MN: Hazelden Publishing, 2015.

Wood, Chris. *The Love, Joy and Peace of Sex*. Longwood, FL: Advantage Books, 2013.

Woodley, Julie. *A Wildflower Grows in Brooklyn: From Striving to Thriving after Sexual Abuse and Other Trauma*. Edited by Clem Boyd. Resource Publications: Eugene, OR, 2013.

Wright, H. Norman. *Discovering Who You Are and How God Sees You*. Torrence, CA: Aspire Press, 2014.

———. *Quiet Times for Couples: A Daily Devotional*. Repr. ed. Eugene, OR: Harvest House Publishers, 2011.

———. *So You're Getting Married: The Keys to Building a Strong, Lasting Relationship*. Ventura, CA: Regal Books, 1997.

Zilbergeld, Bernie. *The New Male Sexuality*. Rev. ed. New York: Bantam Books, Inc., 1999.

ONLINE RESOURCES

www.healpelvicpain.com—Guidance from a pelvic-floor physical therapist.

www.healthformyself.wordpress.com—Be encouraged and interact with other vaginismus participants using Penner's confidential vaginismus blog.

www.ioptwh.org—International Organization of Physical Therapists in Womens Health; find pelvic-floor physical therapy.

www.nva.org—National Vulvodynia Association (301-299-0775).

www.passionatecommitment.com—Penner's website for answers to FAQ, speaking schedule and much more.

www.pelvicpain.org—International Pelvic Pain Society; find pelvic-floor physical therapy.

www.sexualwholeness.com—ABCST: American Board of Christan Sex Therapists.

www.theinstituteforsexualmedicine.com—The San Diego Institute for Sexual Medicine (619-265-8865). Dr. Irwin Goldstein offers ten-minute consults by telephone.

www.thevpfoundation.org—The Vulvar Pain Foundation (336-226-0704).

www.vaginismus.com—Helping women overcome pain and penetration problems; may order kit with dilators, textbook, and workbook and enter discussion forum.

www.womenshealthapta.org—Women's section of American Physical Therapy Association; find pelvic-floor physical therapy.

About the Authors

DR. CLIFFORD AND JOYCE PENNER are sexual therapists, educators, and authors of ten books. They work together to counsel individuals and couples, lead sexual enhancement seminars for couples, teach sex education for preteens and their parents, speak with men's and women's groups, lecture at universities, and train fellow professionals throughout the world. They have taught in the United States, Canada, Mexico, Jamaica, Kenya, the Philippines, Singapore, Bali, Jakarta, Australia, Germany, Austria, Switzerland, and France.

JOYCE is a clinical nurse specialist. She has a BS in nursing from the University of Washington, and a master's degree in psychosomatic nursing and nursing education from UCLA.

CLIFF is a clinical psychologist. He received a BA from Bethel College in Saint Paul, Minnesota, earned an MA in theology at Fuller Theological Seminary, and has his PhD from Fuller's Graduate School of Psychology.

The Penners are best known for their pioneer work in encouraging people of all faiths to connect their sexuality with their belief system—helping them embrace sex as good and of God and opening the topic of sexuality within churches of many denominations.

Their group of therapists works together in Pasadena, California. You may reach them at 626-449-2525 and learn more about them and their associates through their website, www.passionatecommitment.com.

Index

Scripture Index